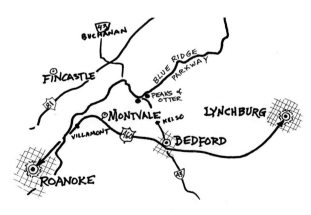

The BEALE TREASURE
NEW
HISTORY *of a* MYSTERY

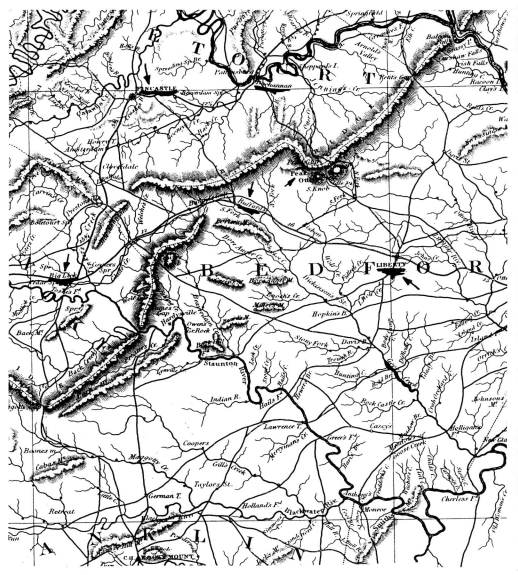

This is part of the official "Map of the State of Virginia" for 1825 corrected to 1856.
Courtesy of Virginia State Library.

The
BEALE TREASURE

NEW
HISTORY of a MYSTERY

by

Peter Viemeister

New Edition 1997

HAMILTON's • BEDFORD • VIRGINIA • 24523

To

Judge William W. Sweeney

NEW EDITION

Copyright 1997   Peter Viemeister

All rights reserved. No part of this publication may be used or reproduced in any manner, electronic, magnetic,   mechanical or optical, or transmitted or stored by any information storage and retrieval system without written publication from the publisher except in the case of brief quotations embodied in critical articles and reviews where credit is given.

First printing — October 1997

Published by:
Hamilton's
P.O. Box 932
Bedford, Virginia, 24523

ISBN : 1-883912-04-0

Library of Congress Catalog Card Number 97-94102

Printed in the United States of America

Table of Contents

Preface to New Edition 8
What is the Beale Treasure? 9

THE DIGGERS
1. Graveyard 11
2. Dynamite Big Time 14

THE PROMISE
3. "The Beale Papers" 22
4. Hope & Reason 45
5. Codesmanship 50

FETCH & BURY
6. The Spanish West 54
7. Carry to Virginia 64
8. Blue Ridge Vault 69
9. Two West or Ten East? 80

BEALE & FRIENDS
10. The Virginian 92
11. New Orleans & Burr 101
12. Lafitte & Jackson 107
13. Widow vs. Widow 112

THE RISQUE DYNASTY
14. Man of Connections 119
15. James B. Ward 128
16. Civil War 134

1885 PUBLISHERS
17. The Agent 141
18. Author Wanted 144
19. Trusted Friend 150
20. Hidden Talent 157

WHY WRITTEN
21. Fiction or Cover? 164
22. Mexican War & Confederacy 166
23. The Pirate or The Slave 174

RESOLUTION
24. Finders Keepers 181
25. Ready, Set, … 190

Some Dates for Reference 197
Acknowledgements 198
Bibliography 200
Index 205

Forward to the New Edition

Ten years have gone by since *The Beale Treasure - History of a Mystery* first appeared in print.

The mystery of the Beale Treasure is no longer just Bedford County's mystery. Now it belongs to America. Two major television programs — *Unsolved Mysteries* and Arthur Clarke's *Mysterious Universe* — TV reports, and countless magazine articles have fanned interest. Howard Woodcock keeps his *History of a Mystery* on the shelf next to Sherlock Holmes.

No one knows how many seek the treasure surreptitiously. It is no secret that hundreds of individuals have called, written or visited Bedford to share their insights or to openly search for the treasure. There are new facts and new theories that have been uncovered by Beale scholars.

Instead of a fifth printing, here is the *New History of a Mystery*, overhauled, enriched and improved. This new edition shares what I have learned during the last decade. The text has been revised and expanded. Here are new photos, new maps, new references, new leads. Several major new theories are described.

The complete answer to the mystery eludes us. Hopefully, this book will bring us closer.

Peter Viemeister
Bedford, Virginia
October 1997

What is the Beale Treasure?

Back in 1885, a green-covered booklet was offered for sale in Lynchburg, Virginia for fifty cents per copy. Entitled *The Beale Papers*, it told a story of more than two tons of gold, silver, and jewels buried in nearby Bedford County in 1819 and 1821 by a man named Thomas J. Beale.

The 23-page pamphlet describes where Beale buried it and gives the names of his associates who were to ultimately share in its wealth. But these descriptions are cipher cryptograms.

More than a hundred years have passed since that little pamphlet appeared. The hoard would now be worth about $20 million.

Some dismiss the entire matter as a very clever hoax. They see no reason for optimism and think it is fabrication, sheer fiction intended to merely entertain. Others believe the story to be true, but think that the cache has already been recovered. Yet there are intelligent, scholarly people who are trying to decode the ciphers. Some claim to have solved the ciphers and then come to Bedford to dig.

Driven by the love of challenge, or inspired by hope, believers have been heartened by the success of Mel Fisher who did find an important treasure. He, his family and his crew have salvaged about $40 million of gold, silver and jewels from the Spanish galleon *Nuestra Senora de Atocha* which sank in a September 1622 storm in 55 feet of water southeast of Key West. Fisher became intrigued by the Beale story and made an exploratory dig in Bedford in 1989.

Maybe the Beale Treasure is a hoax. If so, then the author of the pamphlet deserves an award for creating a brilliant puzzle that has captured serious minds for more than a century. But if it is indeed a true story, the payoff would justify all the effort needed to solve the mystery.

Is the treasure there? Where did it come from? Was it there, but now gone? Was it ever there?

Here is a close look at the facts and the fantasies about the legendary Beale Treasure.

And while you are reading this, the digging continues.

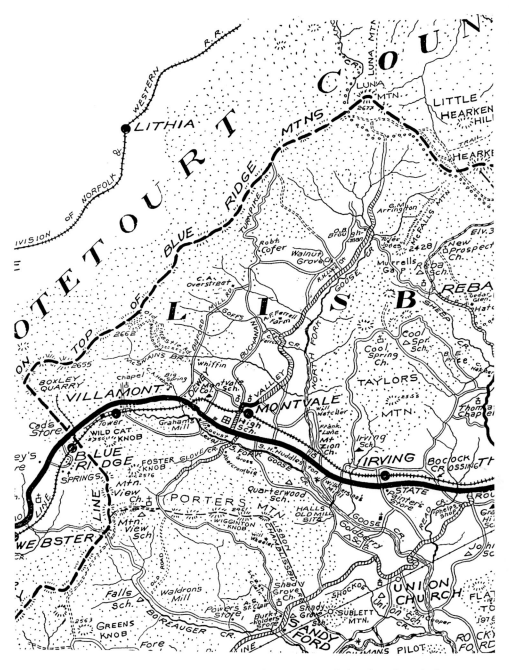

This 1931 map by surveyor S. S. Lynn shows traces of abandoned roads from Montvale to towns on the other side of the Blue Ridge Mountains.

1.
Graveyard

It was a mild day in January 1983.

A backhoe machine lumbered up the twisting mountain road, following a battered white 1967 Cadillac with Pennsylvania plates. Gray clouds of gravel dust rose behind them. Driving the car was Joseph Jancik, 31. Next to him was Marilyn Parsons, 51, and in the back was her dog, Muffin. She gestured to the driver of backhoe whom she had just hired. She was certain that they were onto something big. They were headed for the cemetery of the Mountain View Church atop Wiggington Knob of Porter's Mountain, near Montvale, in Bedford County, Virginia. They were about to dig for the legendary Beale Treasure — a hoard of gold, silver, and jewels estimated to be worth about $20 million.

They made the final, twisting turn to the right, passed the little church, and pulled in. There was a modern cemetery with handsome marble headstones a hundred yards ahead. But they stopped here, near a large, scarred maple tree. There were marker stones here and there. No names, no dates — just ordinary rocks serving as headstones.

They parked and all got out. Severe arthritis caused Mrs. Parsons to walk with a painful limp. She went to the big tree, checked her notes again, and got her bearings. She seemed so small compared to the tree and the backhoe. After some quick measuring, she pointed to a spot and asked the backhoe man to start digging.

Earlier, a neighbor had noticed a man shovelling in the cemetery. A woman seemed to be supervising. He didn't dig long. The ground was hard, he gave up, and they soon left. The neighbor then forgot about it.

But now, neighbors heard the clattering noise of the backhoe's diesel engine, and they came to look. What they saw prompted one to hurry to a phone and dial the sheriff's office: some people are digging up a grave in the cemetery!

A short while later, Sgt. D.E. Cooper and Deputy G.H. Faribault drove up in their Bedford County Sheriff cruisers. They stopped the excavating. Mrs. Parsons was polite. She said that when the hoe uncovered a piece of a coffin handle and what appeared to be part of a human bone, they put the items in the car and had the hoe operator move from that spot.

She and Jancik were arrested for damaging private property and disturbing a grave. No charges were made against the hoe operator. Then, Jancik was ordered to drive into town to the Sheriff's office, sandwich-style, preceded by one cruiser and followed by the other.

They spent the weekend in the Bedford County jail. They were unable to afford legal counsel, so the court appointed attorney J.C. McIvor to represent Mrs. Parsons and attorney Roy Thorpe to represent Jancik. In the meantime Muffin was spending time in the dog pound. There was a hearing on Tuesday. Jancik was examined by a local doctor and sent to Central State Hospital for further examination. Mrs. Parsons was released on bond and stayed at a half-way house. Muffin moved to a kennel.

Trial was set for late February. She waited.

Parsons and Jancik had arrived in Bedford from Pennsylvania on Monday, January 3rd. She had been researching the legend of the Beale Treasure for several years and had recently come up with a solution to the coded message that told where the treasure was buried. She borrowed some money, cashed her disability check, and was ready to head south. Unable to drive herself, she enlisted Jancik to bring her to Bedford.

They drove around the area and homed in on the Mountain View Church graveyard. She had hoped that the church minister might clear the way for her to dig. She went to the County County Courthouse and scanned recorded deeds to see who owned the land. It had long ago been donated for church use. The original trustees had died long ago, and no new trustees

Mountain View Church Cemetery

were on record in the courthouse. There were no names of trustees with whom she could talk. She found no way to register her claim. She found no one who would authorize her to dig. So the way seemed clear. She would just do it. That fateful Friday, the digging began.

Six weeks later, the scene shifts to the trial in the Bedford County Courthouse. Circuit Judge William Sweeney presided. Commonwealth's Attorney James Updike (who has since become a judge) was prosecuting two charges: "violation of sepulture" and "entering property with intent to damage."

Both sides presented their facts. The defense even moved to have the Beale code entered as evidence, a surprising move. The prosecution objected, arguing that it had no bearing on whether she had had criminal intent. The motion was denied. The jury finally left the courtroom. It deliberated for four hours. Foreman William L. Hodges announced the result: no verdict on the first charge, but guilty on the second. The jury fixed a $500 fine as punishment.

Aware of public sentiment surrounding the case and reluctant to go through a new trial, the prosecutor decided not to proceed further. The defendent was released. She was fined $500, plus court court costs. Jancik was fined $100, plus court costs. Mrs. Parsons accepted the verdict. She retrieved Muffin and remarked how nice everyone in Bedford had been. Unofficially, they were advised, "Don't come back."

Three years later, when interviewed by WUSA-TV (a CBS affiliate in Washington, DC), Judge Sweeney said, "She's not a crackpot," but "I'm not prepared to say if it's a hoax or not."

Marilyn Parsons is the only treasure hunter known to have dug in a Bedford County cemetery. But there have been other seekers who have dug — with landowner permission —or secretly without permission— in Bedford County. Many others.

2.
Dynamite Big Time

Dynamite and jacks were found near the Blue Ridge Parkway, not far from a favorite Bedford County treasure haunt. Apparently, some treasure hunter intended to move a big rock or two. Whoever brought the stuff has not yet been identified.

They come from Texas or Oklahoma or Massachusetts or California or overseas. Manfried A. Litz of Stutgart got interested after reading a 1985 article in the German publication *BILD am SONNTAG*. They are persistent. A man from Vancouver, Washington, was reported to have made five trips to Bedford.

Some are historical scholars. Some use meditation to get clues. Some rely on faith; some on ESP. Some are certain that their long-range detectors will pinpoint the site. Some are scientific young folks, skilled in the use of computers. All love adventure and challenge.

Bedford County citizens are used to treasure hunters on the prowl, out-of-state cars creeping along the back roads of Montvale.

In the small city of Bedford, just about everyone knows everyone else and an unfamiliar face is quickly noticed. The treasure hunter may try to be inconspicuous, but he is not as invisible as he thinks.

The seeker visits the courthouse on Main Street, to scan property maps or check for land owner names on deeds. The seeker may also visit state or federal offices to see aerial photos. He may search the files of the libraries in Bedford, Lynchburg and Roanoke.

At the Bedford City/County Museum he looks around at the exhibits and then nonchalantly asks, "Do you have any old maps? You know, showing old roads... say, about 1810 or 1820?" Now and then visitors admit that they are searching for the Beale Treasure. But more often than not, the searcher doesn't want anyone to know what he's up to.

The late Judge Minnix said that during the years he had his private law practice, perhaps as many as twenty people sought counsel as to how to get permission to dig, how to acquire rights to the treasure, or how to protect their discovery.

Attorney J.C. McIvor, in practice here since 1961, says that he averages about three inquiries a year about the Beale matters. He recalls that one person, who arrived in the area on a Friday, wanted to know where he could safely store the gold because he was sure that he would find the gold the next day, Saturday. He worried that bank vaults would be closed — so he looked into renting an armored truck.

The search has been going on for a long time. Interest may wane only to be rekindled by a magazine article or TV show. *The Beale Papers* pamphlet came out way back in 1885. Articles appeared as early as 1919 in *Colliers* magazine. An article by Pauline B. Innis in a 1964 *Argosy* magazine was a real spark. Innis and her husband, Walter, wrote the book *Gold In The Blue Ridge*, which heightened interest again in 1973. A *Smithsonian Magazine* article by Ruth Daniloff in 1981 had the effect of dignifying the subject. And a school textbook repeats the treasure story of *The Beale Papers*. Newspaper editors assign cub reporters to "find out what's new," and their reports — which primarily rehash the basic legend — keep the embers glowing.

Coverage by TV networks has kept the subject hot.

Unsolved Mysteries of 1989 left viewers with barely any doubts about the credibility of *The Beale Papers*. This segment has been shown a number of times, resulting in new believers almost every year. Arthur Clarke's *Mysterious Universe* included the Beale ciphers as part of a program on unsolved messages. Millions of people have heard of the Beale Treasure. It has become part of our modern culture.

For a fifteen-year span from 1897 to 1912, brothers Clayton and George Hart, of nearby Roanoke, pursued the treasure — on paper and in the field. They even used dynamite to dig a hole at a suspected site near the home of relatives. George gave up trying to solve the ciphers in 1912, but Clayton carried on. Later, in 1952, George wrote a summary paper about their activities.

Hiram Herbert, Jr., began his quest in 1923. He too was from Roanoke, where he was publicist for an insurance company. For more than half a century he tried to solve the ciphers. As recently as 1972, four miles from Montvale, and with permission from the landowner, he dug up their yard with a backhoe. Like many others, Herbert found no loot.

Landowners usually do not welcome the hunter. Some searchers furtively explore private property without permission. An old timer complained, "Some morning you wake up and find that somebody cut your fence and dug a trench." One cattleman feared that his animals might get hurt by falling into several deep holes that were left by midnight diggers.

The majority of hunters do respect private property and do show good manners. A steel worker from Pittsburgh not only politely asked for permission to dig, but he also gave the property owner a rattlesnake steak.

Families support — or tolerate — a relative on the quest, either out of love or because of a faint hope that they will find it. One patient Minnesota man has accompanied his wife here several times as she tried to solve the Beale mystery. One woman, who accompanied her husband here — out of love rather than conviction — says, "I think the whole thing is a hoax just to get tourists to come."

Treasure hunters do help boost the Bedford economy. Motels, restaurants, gas stations, and excavation equipment operators are the primary beneficiaries.

Not all visitors spend much money. There was a booted Texan who came into the Roanoke library — while "his wife and 5 or 6 shabby kids" waited in their bruised car. He announced that he had solved the cipher, but needed a good road map to get to the treasure. He had no money, so he borrowed a road map. Then, about two hours later he brought it back, saying that the code solution didn't quite fit. One observer remarked, "So they had to go home — all the way to Texas. It was right pitiful."

Carl Overstreet operated a helicopter charter service for many years. He doesn't recall exactly how many flights he has made over the Montvale area for treasure hunters. But one stands out. A light-haired young man from Phoenix hired Carl in 1982 to fly him up and down a creek in Goose Creek Valley while he took video footage. He said he worked with computers and had broken the code. They hovered real low to get a close look at a circular spot. The man subsequently visited the place on foot. It was a six-foot deep, dish-shaped depression. He dug there and uncovered a layer of rocks. He found no metal pots, but he did discover the skull of a razorback hog that he believes may be of an extinct boar.

Serious students of the Beale treasure formed an association in the belief that solving the puzzle would be more likely if the searchers pooled their research efforts. The Beale Cypher Association originally required that members share information and agree to split the treasure if and when it was found. This stipulation deterred many prospects from joining. The rules have since changed to delete this obligation. On average, there are about 50 members. The organization has been relatively inactive in recent years.

The Association has sponsored symposiums at which researchers present formal papers and take part in panel discussions. You might think that a BCA Symposium would be a mighty quiet conference — where everybody listens and no one tells what he knows. *LA Times-Washington Post* journalist Hank Burchard reported that one attendee said that some of the others were "ferret-faced men who use variable names and no fixed addresses." Actually, most of the attendees share considerable helpful information about their methodology and findings.

A few decades ago, Bedford's Dr. A.B. Claytor, who graduated from Washington and Lee and attended University of Pennsylvania Medical School, spent more than ten years pursuing the treasure after he retired to Bedford. Some neighborhood children thought the bachelor was solemn and haughty. Others were fond of this chunky man of medium height. He kept tools in his car for his frequent forays to Montvale. He was usually accompanied by "his colored man," Charlie Dickenson, and his bird dog, Lady. Before he died in 1948, Claytor told neighbors that he had deciphered the Beale papers and kept thinking that he really should have found the treasure.

Some attack the mystery with technology and scientific objectivity. Older metal detectors are useful for finding coins, but better sensors are needed to find heavier masses deeper in the ground.

There are even non-electronic methods. Dowsers find underground springs or buried pipes using cherry tree branches — or bent coat hangers — which dip and point. Now there is "map dowsing." It is rumored that "a man up north" does it, on your map, for a fee. Using a small weight suspended over the map, the map dowser can locate a mass within 75 feet. I've been told that "the Delaware Treasure was found that way." And some use intuition or the vision of psychics or clairvoyants.

A psychic named Roseanna gave guidance to a pleasant middle-aged couple from Oklahoma. They came as a mini-caravan: a car and a truck that carried off-road vehicles. They, too, paid Carl Overstreet to fly them over Montvale while they carefully studied terrain details below. The couple returned the following year, without the truck. They said that their psychic said that they would find it on their third trip. Overstreet suggested that next time they bring Roseanna along. They said she couldn't leave her ailing husband. There is no record as to whether they returned a third time or not.

An accountant from Cincinnati brought friends to help him dig. He claimed to have broken the code. His solution had very specific references to creeks and other landmarks that led him to a particular spot of land. They made modest excavations. He returned several times, but found nothing.

One man was tracking down the descendants of James B. Ward and visited the old family cemetery near Lynchburg. He located a great, great granddaughter of Ward and found that she still had some of his books. He photographed a number of them. Some time later, he called to say that his pictures hadn't turned out and that he would like to visit to try again. She demurred.

Later, a relative of that same searcher was shopping for a house to buy. He became interested in the old house that once belonged to renown Beale aficionado, Dr. Claytor. Before deciding not to buy, he spent considerable time in the attic, carefully examining all its nooks and crannies.

Bedford County survived a media frenzy in November 1989 when Mel Fisher came to retrieve the Beale Treasure. This confident, weathered — and now famous — man had discovered with his sons the remains of the Spanish galleon *Nuestra Senora de Atocha* off Key West, Florida. His team had salvaged nearly $40 million of gold, silver, and jewelry since 1985. That venture, financed by investors hoping to share in the findings, had been filmed by *National Geographic* and has been shown time and again on national television. The media hoped that underground Bedford would be a repeat underwater Florida.

Fisher and his agents had scouted Bedford, following a lead of a Florida woman who was sure she had solved the ciphers. His treasure museum in Key West had copies of the first edition of this book. With optimistic investors cheering him on, he came back to Bedford, ready to unearth the Beale Treasure.

Fisher, with Gordon Klemme and other key associates, stayed at the Best Western Motel in Bedford. An investor from the deep South came along to watch his money work. A New York investment banker of First Boston Corp. called to find out what was going on. The media homed in too.

Fisher made no attempt to be secretive. In fact, he seemed eager to talk with the media openly about his plans. At breakfast, he showed me the gold chain about his neck, reached in his pocket and held up a gold coin, and then showed me an emerald pendant, evidence of his prior success. During our conversation, I told him, "My wife hopes you don't find it." Taken aback, he asked why. "She says you have already found a big treasure. Now with lots of equipment and resources you want to do it again. She would rather that a deserving person, working alone, be the one to find it."

He disagreed with a chuckle. And he was ready to sign up more investors to join in the project.

2 — Dynamite Big Time

Abandoned Graham's Mill between Montvale and Villamont. Note concrete dam on left.

The dig would be made at Graham's Mill, a now abandoned water-powered grist mill once owned by Paschal Buford, located about a mile west of Buford's brick home. Rumor was that the Florida woman's cipher solution had convinced Fisher that the Beale Treasure was buried by the dam at the mill spillway.

Before the dig began, acquaintances of Fisher in California had quietly purchased the mill in the name of The Voda Family Trust, with financing by Florida investors. The seller agreed to accept a one percent share of any treasure found there.

Joe Detamore, a local excavation contractor, sent over his big, tracked hoe to the site, and cameramen and reporters swarmed in to watch as Joe Jr. began digging behind the dam by the mill. Curiosity seekers came from miles around to be present for a historical discovery. And even interstate drivers on Route 460, not tuned to local media, pulled over to see why crowds had gathered. Local radio and television reported every new development, spiced with interviews of Fisher and local citizens. Just about everyone was there, except *National Geographic*.

This was a major happening — front page news — for Bedford County.

As days wore by, the deep South investor stopped eating breakfast with the Fisher group. Instead he sat at a separate table, looking discouraged.

Even Fisher seemed to realize that the mill site would not yield up the big prize. He let it be known that he was open to alternate leads. Others, including natives who considered themselves Beale experts, approached him with their stories or their solutions to the ciphers.

Finally, the Fisher team told the media that they had found the vault, but it was empty. Had someone beaten them to it? Or was this the wrong place? The team packed up to return to Florida, and as they left, the undaunted Fisher announced that he would be back.

A great, great grandson of Paschal Buford told me that what had been found was not a vault at all, but instead merely the space between the visible concrete dam and the older rock/stone dam it had superseded. He thought his ancestor would not have interrupted his mill's operation by rerouting the creek to build a vault.

The "thrill of the mill" subsided. In 1991, the Voda Trust sold Graham's Mill to a local couple, at a reduced price. Mel Fisher and his team concentrated on treasure salvage projects off the coast of Florida.

The probability of finding the treasure is small, but the payoff could be so large as to make the effort worthwhile. It may be a story without an end. Or someone may yet uncover gold, silver, and jewels secreted inside Bedford County. So many people have dug so many holes in so many places — without finding it. Perhaps the best results will come about by accident.

As I wondered about this possibility one day in April 1997, into my book store came a man to browse for books.

After chatting a while, he noticed a copy of my book *The Beale Treasure* on the counter. He said he was a contractor and that many years ago north of Montvale he uncovered a rock with BEALE carved on it.

He had been using a rod to probe for an old septic tank and field which needed to be cleared or rebuilt when, about two or three feet down, he hit something hard. Thinking this was the septic tank, he dug down and came upon the rock, lying flat. It was rectangular, bigger than a large brick. The letters seemed to have been hand carved on the top flat. It was not the top of a septic tank. So he covered this curiosity and instead concentrated on the task he had been hired to do, probing elsewhere until he found what he was there for.

Later, he mentioned this to a wise local lady, and she opined that the rock was probably a grave marker. There had been Beales living in the County in the late 1800's. She said that heavy rain can cause the nearby Goose Creek to overflow its banks and deposit silt in the area. She thought that, over the years, silt from the nearby Goose Creek could have added a foot or two of dirt over the grave.

In recent years, when the media frenzied in Bedford around the Fisher dig, the contractor decided to remain silent. He suspected that the stone had nothing at all to do with the treasure. But most importantly, he didn't want hordes of treasure hunters or curiosity seekers to disrupt his customer's peace and quiet.

Imagine the excitement if he had spoken out! TV field crews scurrying to get pictures of the hoard and to interview the finder. Articles in magazines about "How I Found The Beale Treasure" or "America's First Bealionaire." Imagine, too, visits from agents of the State Department of Taxation and the I.R.S. But let us not get ahead of our story.

It all began with the publication of *The Beale Papers*.

3.
The Beale Papers

THE
BEALE PAPERS,

CONTAINING

AUTHENTIC STATEMENTS

REGARDING THE

TREASURE BURIED

IN

1819 AND 1821,

NEAR

BUFORDS, IN BEDFORD COUNTY, VIRGINIA,

AND

WHICH HAS NEVER BEEN RECOVERED.

PRICE FIFTY CENTS.

LYNCHBURG:
VIRGINIAN BOOK AND JOB PRINT,
1885.

Entered according to act of Congress, in the year 1885, by J. B. WARD, in the Office of the Librarian of Congress, at Washington.

The Beale Papers.

THE following details of an incident that happened many years ago, but which has lost none of its interest on that account, are now given to the public for the first time. Until now, for reasons which will be apparent to every one, all knowledge of this affair was confined to a very limited circle—to the writer's immediate family, and to one old and valued friend, upon whose discretion he could always rely; nor was it ever intended that it should travel beyond that circle; but circumstances over which he has no control, pecuniary embarrassments of a pressing character, and duty to a dependent family requiring his undivided attention, force him to abandon a task to which he has devoted the best years of his life, but which seems as far from accomplishment as at the start. He is, therefore, compelled, however unwillingly, to relinquish to others the elucidation of the Beale papers, not doubting that of the many who will give the subject attention, some one, through fortune or accident, will speedily solve their mystery and secure the prize which has eluded him.

It can be readily imagined that this course was not determined upon all at once; regardless of the entreaties of his family and the persistent advice of his friend, who were formerly as sanguine as himself, he stubbornly continued his investigations, until absolute want stared him in the face and forced him to yield to their persuasions. Having now lost all hope of benefit from this source himself, he is not unwilling that others may receive it, and only hopes that the prize may fall to some poor, but honest man, who will use his discovery not solely for the promotion of his own enjoyment, but for the welfare of others.

Until the writer lost all hope of ultimate success, he toiled faithfully at his work; unlike any other pursuit with practical and natural results, a charm attended it, independent of the ultimate benefit he expected, and the possibility of success lent an interest and excitement to the work not to be resisted. It would be difficult to portray the delight he experienced when accident revealed to him the explanation of the paper marked "2." Unmeaning, as this had hitherto been, it was now fully explained, and no difficulty was apprehended in mastering the others; but this accident, affording so much pleasure at the time, was a most unfortunate one for him, as it induced him to neglect family, friends, and all legitimate pursuits for what has proved, so far, the veriest illusion.

It will be seen by a perusal of Mr. Beale's letter to Mr. Morriss that he promised, under certain contingences, such as failure to see or communicate with him in a given time, to furnish a key by which the papers would be fully explained. As the failure to do either actually occurred, and the promised explanation has never been received, it may possibly remain in the hands of some relative or friend of Beale's, or some other person engaged in the enterprise with him. That they would attach no importance to a seemingly unintelligible writing seems quite natural; but their attention being called to them by the publication of this narrative, may result in eventually bringing to light the missing paper.

Mr. Beale, who deposited with Mr. Morriss the papers which form the subject of this history, is described as being a gentleman well educated, evidently of good family, and with popular manners. What motives could have influenced him and so many others to risk their health and their lives in such an undertaking, except the natural love of daring adventure, with its consequent excitement, we can only conjecture. We may suppose, and indeed we have his word for so doing, that they were infatuated with the dangers, and with the wild and roving character of their lives, the charms of which lured them farther and farther from civilization, until their lives were sacrificed to their temerity. This was the opinion of Mr. Morriss, and in this way only can we account for the fact that the treasure for which they sacrificed so much, constituting almost fabulous wealth, lies abandoned and unclaimed for more than half a century. Should any of my readers be more fortunate than myself in discovering its place of concealment, I shall not only rejoice with them, but feel that I have at least accomplished something in contributing to the happiness of others.

THE LATE ROBERT MORRISS.

Robert Morriss, the custodian of the Beale papers, was born in 1778, in the State of Maryland, but removed at an early age, with his family, to Loudoun county, Va., where, in 1803, he married Miss Sarah Mitchell, a fine looking and accomplished young lady of that county. In obtaining such a wife Mr. Morriss was peculiarly fortunate, as her subsequent career fully demonstrated. As a wife she was without reproach, as a generous and sympathizing woman she was without an equal; the poor will long remember her charities, and lament the friend they have lost. Shortly after his removal to Lynchburg, Mr. Morriss engaged in the mercantile business, and shortly thereafter he became a purchaser and shipper of tobacco to an extent hitherto unknown in this section. In these pursuits he was eminently successful for several years, and speedily accumulated a comfortable independence. It was during this period of his success that he erected the first brick building of which the town could boast, and which still stands on Main street, a monument to his enterprise. His private residence, the house now owned and occupied by Max Guggenheimer, Esq., at the head of Main street, I think he also built. There the most unbounded hospitality reigned, and every facility for enjoyment was furnished. The *elite* of the town assembled there more frequently than elsewhere, and there are now living some whose most pleasant recollections are associated with that period.

The happiness of Mr. Morriss, however, was of short duration, and reverses came when they were least expected. Heavy purchases of tobacco, at ruinous figures, in anticipation of an upward market, which visions were never realized, swept from him in a moment the savings of years, and left him nothing save his honor and the sincere sympathy of the community with which to begin the battle anew.

It was at this time that Mrs. Morriss exhibited the loveliest traits of her character. Seemingly unmindful of her condition, with a smiling face and cheering words, she so encouraged her husband that he become almost reconciled to his fate. Thrown thus upon his own resources, by the advice of his wife, he leased for a term of years the Washington Hotel, known now as the Arlington, on Church street, and commenced the business of hotel keeping. His kind disposition, strict probity, excellent management, and well ordered household, soon rendered him famous as a host, and his reputation extended even to other States. His was the house *par excellence* of the town, and no fashionable assemblages met at any other. Finding, in a few years, that his experiment was successful and his business remunerative, he removed to the Franklin Hotel, now the Norvell House, the largest and best arranged in the city. This house he conducted for many years, enjoying the friendship and countenance of the first men of the country. Amongst his guests and devoted personal friends Jackson, Clay, Coles, Witcher, Chief Justice Marshall, and a host of others scarcely less distinguished, might be enumerated. But it was not the wealthy and distinguished alone who appreciated Mr. Morriss; the poor and lowly had blessings for the man who sympathized with their misfortunes, and was ever ready to relieve their distress. Many poor but worthy families, whose descendants are now in our midst, can remember the fact that his table supplied their daily food, not for days and weeks only, but for months at a time; and as a farther instance of his forbearance and unparalleled generosity, there are now living those who will testify to the fact that he permitted a boarder, in no way connected with him, to remain in his house for more than twenty years, and until he died, without ever receiving the slightest renumeration, and that he was never made to feel otherwise than as a favored guest.

In manner Mr. Morriss was courteous and gentle; but when occasion demanded, could be stern and determined, too; he was emphatically the master of his house, and from his decision there was no appeal. As an "old Virginia gentleman," he was *sans peur et sans reproache*, and to a remarkable extent possessed the confidence and affection of his friends. After a chequered and eventful life of more than eighty years, passed mostly in business, which brought him in contact with all classes of people, he died, lamented by all, and leaving not an enemy behind. His death, which occurred in 1863, was just two years subsequent to that of his wife. It can be truly said that no persons ever lived in a community for such a length of time who accomplished more good during their lives, or whose death was more universally regretted.

It was the unblemished character of the man, and the universal confidence reposed in him, that induced Beale to entrust him with his secret, and in certain contingencies select him for a most important trust; that his confidence was not misplaced, every one remembering Mr. Morriss will acknowledge.

It was in 1862, the second year of the Confederate war, that Mr. Morriss first intimated the possession of a secret that was destined to make some persons wealthy. At first he was not very communicative, nor did I press him to reveal what he seemed to speak of with reluctance; in a few weeks, however, his mind seemed changed, and he voluntarily proffered his confidence. Inviting me to his room, with no one to interrupt us, he gave me an outline of the matter, which soon enlisted my interest and created an intense longing to learn more. About this time, however, affairs of importance required my presence in Richmond, and prevented further communication between us until after my return, when I found him ready to resume the interesting subject. A private interview was soon arranged, and, after several preliminaries had been complied with, the papers upon which this history is based were delivered into my possession.

The reasons which influenced him in selecting me for the trust, he gave, and were in substance as follows: First: Friendship for myself and family, whom he would benefit if he could. Second: The knowledge that I was young and in circumstances to afford leisure for the task imposed; and, finally, a confidence that I would regard his instructions, and carry out his wishes regarding his charge. These, and perhaps others, he gave during our frequent conversations upon the subject, and doubtless believed he was conferring a favor which would redound greatly to my advantage. That it has proved otherwise is a misfortune to me, but no fault of his. The conditions alluded to above were that I should devote as much time as was practicable to the papers he had given me; master, if possible, their contents, and if successful in deciphering their meaning and eventually finding the treasure, to appropriate one-half of his portion as a remuneration for my services; the other half to be distributed to certain relatives and connexions of his own, whose names he gave me; the remainder to be held by me in trust for the benefit of such claimants as might at any time appear, and be able to authenticate their claims. This latter amount, to be left intact, subject to such demands, for the space of twenty years, when, if still unclaimed, it should revert to myself or my heirs, as a legacy from himself.

As there was nothing objectionable in this, the required promise was given, and the box and contents were placed in my possession.

When the writer recalls his anxious hours, his midnight vigils, his toils, his hopes and disappointments, all consequent upon this promise, he can only conclude that the legacy of Mr. Morriss was not as he designed it—a blessing in disguise.

Having assumed the responsibilities and consented to the requirements of Mr. Morriss, I determined to devote as much time to the accomplishment of the task as could be consistently spared from other duties. With this purpose in view, I requested from Mr. Morriss a statement of every particular connected

THE BEALE PAPERS.

with the affair, or having the slightest bearing upon it, together with such views and opinions of his own as might ultimately benefit me in my researches. In reply, he gave me the following, which I reduced to writing and filed with the papers for future reference :

"It was in the month of January, 1820, while keeping the Washington Hotel, that I first saw and became acquainted with Beale. In company with two others, he came to my house seeking entertainment for himself and friends. Being assured of a comfortable provision for themselves and their horses, Beale stated his intention of remaining for the winter, should nothing occur to alter his plans, but that the gentlemen accompanying him would leave in a few days for Richmond, near which place they resided, and that they were anxious to reach their homes, from which they had long been absent. They all appeared to be gentlemen, well born, and well educated, with refined and courteous manners, and with a free and independent air, which rendered them peculiarly attractive. After remaining a week or ten days, the two left, after expressions of satisfaction with their visit. Beale, who remained, soon became a favored and popular guest ; his social disposition and friendly demeanor rendered him extremely popular with every one, particularly the ladies, and a pleasant and friendly intercourse was quickly established between them.

"In person, he was about six feet in height, with jet black eyes and hair of the same color, worn longer than was the style at that time. His form was symmetrical, and gave evidence of unusual strength and activity ; but his distinguishing feature was a dark and swarthy complexion, as if much exposure to the sun and weather had thoroughly tanned and discolored him ; this, however, did not detract from his appearance, and I thought him the handsomest man I had ever seen. Altogether, he was a model of manly beauty, favored by the ladies and envied by men. To the first he was reverentially tender and polite ; to the latter, affable and courteous, when they kept within bounds, but, if they were supercilious or presuming, the lion was aroused, and woe to the man who offended him. Instances of this character occurred more than once while he was my guest, and always resulted in his demanding and receiving an apology. His character soon became universally known, and he was no longer troubled by impertinence.

"Such a man was Thomas J. Beale, as he appeared in 1820, and in his subsequent visit to my house. He registered simply from Virginia, but I am of the impression he was from some western portion of the State. Curiously enough, he never

THE BEALE PAPERS.

adverted to his family or to his antecedents, nor did I question him concerning them, as I would have done had I dreamed of the interest that in the future would attach to his name.

"He remained with me until about the latter end of the following March, when he left, with the same friends who first accompanied him to my house, and who had returned some days before.

"After this I heard nothing from him until January, 1822, when he once more made his appearance, the same genial and popular gentleman as before, but, if possible, darker and swarthier than ever. His welcome was a genuine one, as all were delighted to see him.

"In the spring, at about the same time, he again left, but before doing so, handed me this box, which, as he said, contained papers of value and importance; and which he desired to leave in my charge until called for hereafter. Of course, I did not decline to receive them, but little imagined their importance until his letter from St. Louis was received. This letter I carefully preserved, and it will be given with these papers. The box was of iron, carefully locked, and of such weight as to render it a safe depository for articles of value. I placed it in a safe and secure place, where it could not be disturbed until such time as it should be demanded by its owner. The letter alluded to above was the last communication I ever received from Beale, and I never saw him again. I can only suppose that he was killed by Indians, afar from his home, though nothing was heard of his death. His companions, too, must all have shared his fate, as no one has ever demanded the box or claimed his effects. The box was left in my hands in the Spring of 1822, and by authority of his letter, I should have examined its contents in 1832, ten years thereafter, having heard nothing from Beale in the meantime; but it was not until 1845, some twenty-three years after it came into my possession, that I decided upon opening it. During that year I had the lock broken, and, with the exception of the two letters addressed to myself, and some old receipts, found only some unintelligible papers, covered with figures, and totally incomprehensible to me.

"According to his letter, these papers convey all the information necessary to find the treasure he has concealed, and upon you devolves the responsibility of recovering it. Should you succeed you will be amply compensated for your work, and others near and dear to me will likewise be benefitted. The end is worth all your exertions, and I have every hope that success will reward your efforts."

THE BEALE PAPERS.

Such, in substance, was the statement of Mr. Morriss in answer to the various interrogations propounded to him; and finding that I could elicit no further information, I resolved to do the best I could with the limited means at my disposal. I commenced by reading over and over again the letters to Mr. Morriss, endeavoring to impress each syllable they contained on my memory, and to extract from them, if possible, some meaning or allusion that might give, perhaps, a faint or barely preceptible hint as a guide; no such clue, however, could I find, and where or how to commence was a problem I found most difficult to solve. To systematize a plan for my work I arranged the papers in the order of their length, and numbered them, designing to commence with the first, and devote my whole attention to that until I had either unravelled its meaning or was convinced of its impossibility—afterwards to take up the others and proceed as before.

All of this I did in the course of time, but failed so completely that my hopes of solving the mystery were well nigh abandoned. My thoughts, however, were constantly upon it, and the figures contained in each paper, in their regular order, were fixed in my memory. My impression was that each figure represented a letter, but as the numbers so greatly exceeded the letters of the alphabet, that many different numbers represented the same letter. With this idea, a test was made of every book I could procure, by numbering its letters and comparing the numbers with those of the manuscript; all to no purpose, however, until the Declaration of Independence afforded the clue to one of the papers, and revived all my hopes. To enable my readers to better understand the explanation of this paper, the Declaration of Independence is given herewith, and will be of interest to those designing to follow up my investigations. When I first made this discovery, I thought I had the key to the whole, but soon ascertained that further work was necessary before my task was completed. The encouragement afforded, however, by this discovery enabled me to proceed, and I have persisted in my labors to the present time. Now, as I have already said, I am forced by circumstances to devote my time to other pursuits, and to abandon hopes which were destined never to be realized.

The following is the letter addressed to Mr. Morriss by Beale, and dated St. Lous, May, 1822, and was the latest communication ever received from him:

THE BEALE PAPERS.

ST. LOUIS, MO., May 9th, 1822.

ROBT. MORRIS, ESQ. :

My Esteemed Friend :—Ever since leaving my comfortable quarters at your house I have been journeying to this place, and only succeeded in reaching it yesterday. I have had altogether a pleasant time, the weather being fine and the atmosphere bracing. I shall remain here a week or ten days longer, then "ho" for the plains, to hunt the buffalo and encounter the savage grizzlies. How long I may be absent I cannot now determine, certainly not less than two years, perhaps longer.

With regard to the box left in your charge, I have a few words to say, and, if you will permit me, give you some instructions concerning it. It contains papers vitally affecting the fortunes of myself and many others engaged in business with me, and in the event of my death, its loss might be irreparable. You will, therefore, see the necessity of guarding it with vigilance and care to prevent so great a catastrophe. It also contains some letters addressed to yourself, and which will be necessary to enlighten you concerning the business in which we are engaged. Should none of us ever return you will please preserve carefully the box for the period of ten years from the date of this letter, and if I, or no one with authority from me, during that time demands its restoration, you will open it, which can be done by removing the lock. You will find, in addition to the papers addressed to you, other papers which will be unintelligible without the aid of a key to assist you. Such a key I have left in the hands of a friend in this place, sealed, addressed to yourself, and endorsed not to be delivered until June, 1832. By means of this you will understand fully all you will be required to do.

I know you will cheerfully comply with my request, thus adding to the many obligations under which you have already placed me. In the meantime, should death or sickness happen to you, to which all are liable, please select from among your friends some one worthy, and to him hand this letter, and to him delegate your authority. I have been thus particular in my instructions, in consequence of the somewhat perilous enterprise in which we are engaged, but trust we shall meet long ere the time expires, and so save you this trouble. Be the result what it may, however, the game is worth the candle, and we will play it to the end.

With kindest wishes for your most excellent wife, compliments to the ladies, a good word to enquiring friends, if there be any. and assurances of my highest esteem for yourself, I remain as ever,

Your sincere friend, T. J. B.

After the reception of this letter, Mr. Morriss states that he was particularly careful to see the box securely placed where it could remain in absolute safety, so long as the exigencies of the case might require ; the letter, too, he was equally careful to preserve for future use, should it be needed. Having done all that was required of him, Mr. Morriss could only await Beale's return, or some communication from him. In either case he was disappointed. He never saw Beale again, nor did a line or message ever reach him. The two years passed away during which he said he would be absent, then three, four, and so on to ten; still not a line or message to tell whether he were living or dead. Mr. Morriss felt much uneasiness about him, but had had no means of satisfying his doubts; ten years had passed; 1832 was at hand, and he was now at liberty to open the box, but he resolved to wait on, vainly hoping that something definite would reach him.

During this period rumors of Indian outrages and massacres were current, but no mention of Beale's name ever occurred. What became of him and his companions is left entirely to conjecture. Whether he was slain by Indians, or killed by the savage animals of the Rocky Mountains, or whether exposure, and perhaps privation, did its work can never be told. One thing at least is certain, that of the young and gallant band, whose buoyant spirits led them to seek such a life, and to forsake the comforts of home, with all its enjoyments, for the dangers and privations they must necessarily encounter, not a survivor remains.

Though Mr. Morriss was aware of the contents of the box in 1845, it was not until 1862, forty years after he received it, that he thought proper to mention its existence, and to myself alone did he then divulge it. He had become long since satisfied that the parties were no longer living, but his delicacy of feeling prevented his assuming as a fact a matter so pregnant with consequences. He frequently decided upon doing so, and as often delayed it for another time; and when at last he did speak of the matter it was with seeming reluctance, and as if he felt he was committing a wrong. But the story once told, he evinced up to the time of his death the greatest interest in my success, and in frequent interviews always encouraged me to proceed.

It is now more than twenty years since these papers came into my hands, and, with the exception of one of them, they are still as incomprehensible as ever. Much time was devoted to this one, and those who engage in the matter will be saved what has been consumed upon it by myself.

Before giving the papers to the public, I would say a word to those who may take an interest in them, and give them a little advice, acquired by bitter experience. It is, to devote only such time as can be spared from your legitimate business to the task, and if you can spare no time, let the matter alone. Should you disregard my advice, do not hold me responsible that the poverty you have courted is more easily found than the accomplishment of your wishes, and I would avoid the sight of another reduced to my condition. Nor is it necessary to devote the time that I did to this matter, as accident alone, without the promised key, will ever develop the mystery. If revealed by accident, a few hours devoted to the subject may accomplish results which were denied to years of patient toil. Again, never, as I have done, sacrifice your own and your family's interests to what may prove an illusion; but, as I have already said, when your day's work is done, and you are comfortably seated by your good fire, a short time devoted to the subject can injure no one, and may bring its reward.

By pursuing this policy, your interests will not suffer, your family will be cared for, and your thoughts will not be absorbed to the exclusion of other important affairs. With this admonition, I submit to my readers the papers upon which this narrative is founded.

The first in order is the letter from Beale to Mr. Morriss, which will give the reader a clearer conception of all the facts connected with the case, and enable him to understand as fully as I myself do, the present status of the affair. The letter is as follows:

LYNCHBURG, January 4th, 1822.

My Dear Friend Morriss :—You will, doubtless, be surprised when you discover, from a perusal of this letter, the importance of the trust confided to you, and the confidence reposed in your honor, by parties whom you have never seen, and whose names even you have never heard. The reasons are simple and easily told; it was imperative upon us that some one here should be selected to carry out our wishes in case of accident to ourselves, and your reputation as a man of the sternest integrity, unblemished honor, and business capacity, influenced them to select you in place of others better known, but, perhaps, not so reliable as yourself. It was with this design that I first visited your house, two years since, that I might judge by personal observation if your reputation was merited. To enable me the better to do so, I remained with you more than three months, and until I was fully satisfied as to your character. This visit was made by the request of my associates, and you can judge from their action whether my report was a favorable one.

I will now give you some idea of the enterprise in which we are engaged, and the duties which will be required of you in connection therewith; first assuring you, however, that your compensation for the trouble will be ample, as you have been unanimously made one of our association, and as such are entitled to share equally with the others.

Some five years since I, in connection with several friends, who, like myself, were fond of adventure, and if mixed with a little danger all the more acceptable, determined to visit the great Western plains and enjoy ourselves in hunting buffalo, grizzly bears, and such other game as the country would afford. This, at that time, was our sole object, and we at once proceeded to put it in execution. On account of Indians and other dangers incident to such an undertaking, we determined to raise a party of not less than thirty individuals, of good char-

THE BEALE PAPERS.

acter and standing, who would be pleasant companions, and financially able to encounter the expense. With this object in view, each one of us suggested the matter to his several friends and acquaintances, and in a few weeks the requisite number had signed the conditions, and were admitted as members of the party. Some few refused to join with us, being, doubtless, deterred by the dangers, but such men we did not want, and were glad of their refusal.

The company being formed, we forthwith commenced our preparations, and, early in April, 1817, left old Virginia for St. Louis, Mo., where we expected to purchase the necessary outfits, procure a guide and two or three servants, and obtain such information and advice as might be beneficial hereafter. All was done as intended, and we left St. Louis the 19th May, to be absent two years, our objective point being Santa Fé, which we intended to reach in the ensuing Fall, and there establish ourselves in winter quarters.

After leaving St. Louis we were advised by our guide to form a regular military organization, with a captain, to be elected by the members, to whom should be given sole authority to manage our affairs, and, in cases of necessity, ensure united action. This was agreed to, and each member of the party bound himself by a solemn obligation to obey, at all times, the orders of their captain, or, in the event of refusal, to leave the company at once. This arrangement was to remain in force for two years, or for the period of our expected absence. Tyranny, partiality, incompetency, or other improper conduct on the part of the captain, was to be punished by deposing him from his office, if a majority of the company desired his dismissal. All this being arranged, and a set of laws framed, by which the conduct of the members was to be regulated, the election was held, and resulted in choosing me as their leader.

It is not my purpose now to give you details of our wanderings, or of the pleasures or dangers we encountered. All this I will reserve until we meet again, when it will be a pleasure to recall incidents that will always be fresh in my memory.

About the first of December we reached our destination, Santa Fé, and prepared for a long and welcome rest from the fatigues of our journey. Nothing of interest occurred during the winter, and of this little Mexican town we soon became heartily tired. We longed for the advent of weather which would enable us to resume our wanderings and our exhilerating pursuits.

Early in March some of the party, to vary the monotony of their lives, determined upon a short excursion, for the purpose of hunting and examining the country around us. They expected to be only a few days absent, but days passed into weeks, and weeks into a month or more before we had any tidings of the party. We had become exceedingly uneasy, and were preparing to send out scouts to trace them, if possible, when two of the party arrived, and gave an explanation of their absence. It appears that when they left Santa Fé they pursued a northerly course for some days, being successful in finding an abundance of game, which they secured, and were on the eve of returning when they discovered on their left an immense herd of buffaloes, heading for a valley just perceptible in the distance. They determined to follow them, and secure as many as possible. Keeping well together, they followed their trail for two weeks or more, securing many and stampeding the rest.

THE BEALE PAPERS. 15

One day, while following them, the party encamped in a small ravine, some 250 or 300 miles to the north of Santa Fé, and with their horses tethered, were preparing their evening meal, when one of the men discovered in a cleft of the rocks something that had the appearance of gold. Upon showing it to the others it was pronounced to be gold, and much excitement was the natural consequence. Messengers were at once dispatched to inform me of the facts, and request my presence with the rest of the party, and with supplies for an indefinite time. All the pleasures and temptations which had lured them to the plains were now forgotten, and visions of boundless wealth and future grandeur were the only ideas entertained. Upon reaching the locality I found all as it had been represented, and the excitement intense. Every one was diligently at work with such tools and appliances as they had improvised, and quite a little pile had already accumulated. Though all were at work, there was nothing like order or method in their plans, and my first efforts were to systematize our operations, and reduce everything to order. With this object, an agreement was entered into to work in common as joint partners, the accumulations of each one to be placed in a common receptacle, and each be entitled to an equal share, whenever he chose to withdraw it—the whole to remain under my charge until some other disposition of it was agreed upon. Under this arrangement the work progressed favorably for eighteen months or more, and a great deal of gold had accumulated in my hands, as well as silver, which had likewise been found. Everything necessary for our purposes and for the prosecution of the work had been obtained from Santa Fé, and no trouble was experienced in procuring assistance from the Indians in our labors. Matters went on thus until the summer of 1819, when the question of transferring our wealth to some secure place was frequently discussed. It was not considered advisable to retain so large an amount in so wild and dangerous a locality, where its very possession might endanger our lives; and to conceal it here would avail nothing, as we might at any time be forced to reveal its place of concealment. We were in a dilemma. Some advised one plan, some another. One recommended Santa Fé as the safest place to deposit it, while others objected, and advocated its shipment at once to the States, where it was ultimately bound to go, and where alone it would be safe. The idea seemed to prevail, and it was doubtless correct, that when outside parties ascertained, as they would do, that we kept nothing on hand to tempt their cupidity, our lives would be more secure than at present. It was finally decided that it should be sent to Virginia under my charge, and securely buried in a cave near Buford's tavern, in the county of Bedford, which all of us had visited, and which was considered a perfectly safe depository. This was acceptable to all, and I at once made preparations for my departure. The whole party were to accompany me for the first five hundred miles, when all but ten would return, these latter to remain with me to the end of the journey. All was carried out as arranged, and I arrived safely with my charge.

Stopping at Buford's, where we remained for a month, under pretense of hunting, &c., we visited the cave, and found it unfit for our purpose. It was too frequently visited by the neighboring farmers, who used it as a receptacle for their sweet potatoes and other vegetables. We soon selected a better place, and to this the treasure was safely transferred.

16   THE BEALE PAPERS.

Before leaving my companions on the plains it was suggested that, in case of an accident to ourselves, the treasure so concealed would be lost to their relatives, without some provision against such a contingency. I was, therefore, instructed to select some perfectly reliable person, if such an one could be found, who should, in the event of his proving acceptable to the party, be confided in to carry out their wishes in regard to their respective shares, and upon my return report whether I had found such a person. It was in accordance with these instructions that I visited you, made your acquaintance, was satisfied that you would suit us, and so reported.

On my return I found the work still progressing favorably, and, by making large accessions to our force of laborers, I was ready to return last Fall with an increased supply of metal, which came through safely and was deposited with the other. It was at this time I handed you the box, not disclosing the nature of its contents, but asking you to keep it safely till called for. I intend writing you, however, from St. Louis, and impress upon you its importance still more forcibly.

The papers enclosed herewith will be unintelligible without the key, which will reach you in time, and will be found merely to state the contents of our depository, with its exact location, and a list of the names of our party, with their places of residence, &c. I thought, at first, to give you their names in this letter, but reflecting that some one may read the letter, and thus be enabled to impose upon you by personating some member of the party, have decided the present plan is best. You will be aware from what I have written, that we are engaged in a perilous enterprise—one which promises glorious results if successful—but dangers intervene, and of the end no one can tell. We can only hope for the best, and persevere until our work is accomplished, and the sum secured for which we are striving.

As ten years must elapse before you will see this letter, you may well conclude by that time that the worst has happened, and that none of us are to be numbered with the living. In such an event, you will please visit the place of deposit and secure its contents, which you will divide into thirty-one equal parts; one of these parts you are to retain as your own, freely given you for your services. The other shares to be distributed to the parties named in the accompanying paper. These legacies, so unexpectedly received, will at least serve to recall names that may still be cherished, though partially forgotten.

In conclusion, my dear friend, I beg that you will not allow any false or idle punctillio to prevent your receiving and appropriating the portion assigned to yourself. It is a gift not from myself alone, but from each and every member of our party, and will not be out of proportion to the services required of you.

I trust, my dear Mr. Morriss, that we may meet many times in the future, but if the Fates forbid, with my last communication I would assure you of the entire respect and confidence of

                        Your friend,   T. J. B.

THE BEALE PAPERS.

LYNCHBURG, VA., January 5th, 1822.

Dear Mr. Morriss.—You will find in one of the papers, written in cipher, the names of all my associates, who are each entitled to an equal part of our treasure, and opposite to the names of each one will be found the names and residences of the relatives and others, to whom they devise their respective portions. From this you will be enabled to carry out the wishes of all, by distributing the portion of each to the parties designated. This will not be difficult, as their residences are given, and they can easily be found.

The two letters given above were all the box contained that were intelligible; the others, consisted of papers closely covered with figures, which were, of course, unmeaning until they could be deciphered. To do this was the task to which I now devoted myself, and with but partial success.

To enable my readers to understand the paper numbered "2," the Declaration of Independence is given, by the assistance of which its hidden meaning was made plain:

DECLARATION OF INDEPENDENCE.

1 2 3 4 5 6 7 8 9 10
When, in the course of human events it becomes necessary for one people to dissolve the political bands which have (20) connected them with another, and to assume among the powers (30) of the earth, the separate and equal station to which (40) the laws of nature and of nature's God entitle them, (50) a decent respect to the opinions of mankind requires that (60) they should declare the causes which impel them to the (70) separation.

We hold these truths to be self-evident, that (80) all men are created equal; that they are endowed by (90) their Creator with certain inalienable rights; that among these are (100) life, liberty, and the pursuit of happiness; that to secure (110) their rights, governments are instituted among men, deriving their just (120) powers from the consent of the governed; that when any (130) form of government becomes destructive of these ends, it is (140) the right of the people to alter or to abolish (150) it, and to institute a new government, laying its foundation (160) on such principles and organizing its powers in such form, (170) as to them shall seem most likely to effect their (180) safety and happiness. Prudence, indeed, will dictate that governments long (190) established, should not be changed for light and transient causes; (200) and accordingly all experience hath shown that mankind are now (210) disposed to suffer, while evils are sufferable, than to right (220) themselves by abolishing the forms to which they are accustomed. (230) But, when a long train of abuses and usurpations, pursuing (240) invariably the same object, evinces a design to reduce them under (250) absolute despotism, it is their right, it is their duty, (260) to throw off such government, and to provide new guards (270) for their future security. Such has been the patient sufferance (280) of these colonies, and such is now the necessity which (290) constrains them to alter their former systems of government. The (300) history of the present King of

18   THE BEALE PAPERS.

Great Britain is a (310) history of repeated injuries and usurpations, all having in direct (320) object the establishment of an absolute tyranny over these States. (330) To prove this, let facts be submitted to a candid (340) world.

He has refused his assent to laws the most (350) wholesome and necessary for the public good. He has forbidden (360) his governors to pass laws of immediate and pressing importance, (370) unless suspended in their operation till his assent should be (380) obtained; and when so suspended he has utterly neglected to (390) attend to them.

He has refused to pass other laws (400) for the accommodation of large districts of people, unless these (410) people would relinquish their right of representation in the legislature, (420) a right inestimable to them and formidable to tyrants only. (430)

He has called together legislative bodies at places unusual, uncomfortable (440) and distant from the depositary of their public records, for (450) the sole purpose of fatiguing them into compliance with his (460) measures.

He has dissolved representative houses repeatedly for opposing with (470) manly firmness, his invasions on the rights of the people. (480)

He has refused, for a long time after such dissolutions, (480) to cause others to be elected ; whereby the legislative powers, (490) incapable of annihilation, have returned to the people at large (500) for their exercise, the State remaining, in the meantime, (510) exposed to all the danger of invasion from without, and (520) convulsions within.

He has endeavored to prevent the population of (530) these States, for that purpose, obstructing the laws of naturalization (540) of foreigners ; refusing to pass others to encourage their migration (550) hither, and raising the conditions of new appropriations of lands. (560)

He has obstructed the administration of justice by refusing his (570) assent to laws for establishing judiciary powers.

He has made (580) judges dependent on his will alone for the tenure of (590) their offices, and the amount and payment of their salaries. (600)

He has erected a multitude of new offices, and sent (610) hither swarms of officers to harass our people and eat (620) out their substance.

He has kept among us in times (630) of peace standing armies, without the consent of our legislature.

He (640) has offered to render the military independent of and superior (650) to the civil power.

He has combined with others to (660) subject us to a jurisdiction foreign to our constitution, and (670) unacknowledged by our laws, giving his assent to their acts of (680) pretended legislation.

For quartering large bodies of armed troops among (690) us ;

For protecting them, by a mock trial, from punishment, (700) for any murders which they should commit on the inhabitants (710) of these States ;

For cutting off our trade with all (720) parts of the world ;

For imposing taxes on us without (730) our consent ;

For depriving us, in many cases, of the (740) benefits of trial by jury ;

For transporting us beyond seas (750) to be tried for pretended offences ;

For abolishing the free (760) system of English laws in a neighboring province, establishing therein (770) an arbitrary government, and enlarging its boundaries so as to (780) render it, at once, an example and fit instrument for (790) introducing the same absolute rule in these colonies ;

For taking (800) away our charters, abolishing our most valuable laws and altering (810) fundamentally, (811) the (812) powers (813) of (814) our (815) governments ; (816)

For suspending our own legislatures, and declaring themselves invested with power to legislate for us in all cases, whatsoever.

He has abdicated government here, by declaring us out of his protection, and waging war against us.

He has plundered our seas, ravaged our coasts, burnt our towns, and destroyed the lives of our people.

He is, at this time, transporting large armies of foreign mercenaries to complete the works of death, desolation and tyranny, already begun, with circumstances of cruelty and perfidy, scarcely paralleled in the most barbarous ages, and totally unworthy the head of a civilized nation.

He has constrained our fellow-citizens, taken captive on the high seas, to bear arms against their country, to become the executioners of their friends and brethren, or to fall themselves by their hands.

He has excited domestic insurrections amongst us, and has endeavored to bring on the inhabitants of our frontiers, the merciless Indian savages, whose known rule of warfare is an undistinguished destruction of all ages, sexes and conditions.

In every stage of these oppressions, we have petitioned for redress in the most humble terms ; our repeated petitions have been answered only by repeated injury. A prince, whose character is thus marked by every act which may define a tyrant, is unfit to be the ruler of a free people.

Nor have we been wanting in attention to our British brethren. We have warned them, from time to time, of attempts made by their legislature to extend an unwarrantable jurisdiction over us. We have reminded them of the circumstances of our emigration and settlement here. We have appealed to their native justice and magnanimity, and we have conjured them, by the ties of our common kindred, to disavow these usurpations, which would inevitably interrupt our connection and correspondence. They, too, have been deaf to the voice of justice and consanguinity.

We must, therefore, acquiesce in the necessity, which denounces our separation, and hold them, as we hold the rest of mankind, enemies in war—in peace, friends.

We, therefore, the representatives of the United States of America, in general congress assembled, appealing to the Supreme Judge of the world for the rectitude of our intentions, do, in the name, and by the authority of the good people of these Colonies, solemnly publish and declare, that these United Colonies are, and of right, ought to be, free and independent States ; that they are absolved from all allegiance to the British crown, and that all political connection between them and the State of Great Britain is, and ought to be, totally dissolved, and that, as free and independent States, they have full power to levy war, conclude peace, contract alliances, establish commerce, and to do all other acts and things which independent States may of right do. And for the support of this declaration, with a firm reliance on the protection of Divine Providence, we mutually pledge to each other our lives, our fortunes, and our sacred honor.

The letter, or paper, so often alluded to, and marked "2," which is fully explained by the foregoing document, is as follows:

115, 73, 24, 807, 37, 52, 49, 17, 31, 62, 647, 22, 7, 15, 140, 47, 29, 107, 79, 84, 56, 239, 10, 26, 811, 5, 196, 308, 85, 52, 160, 136, 59, 211, 36, 9, 46, 316, 554, 122, 106, 95, 53, 58, 2, 42, 7, 35, 122, 53, 31, 82, 77, 250, 196, 56, 96, 118, 71, 140, 287, 28, 353, 37, 1005, 65, 147, 807, 24, 3, 8, 12, 47, 43, 59, 807, 45, 316, 101, 41, 78, 154, 1005, 122, 138, 191, 16, 77, 49, 102, 57, 72, 34, 73, 85, 35, 371, 59, 196, 81, 92, 191, 106, 273, 60, 394, 620, 270, 220, 106, 388, 287, 63, 3, 6, 191, 122, 43, 234, 400, 106, 290, 314, 47, 48, 81, 96, 26, 115, 92, 158, 191, 110, 77, 85, 197, 46, 10, 113, 140, 353, 48, 120, 106, 2, 607, 61, 420, 811, 29, 125, 14, 20, 37, 105, 28, 248, 16, 159, 7, 35, 19, 301, 125, 110, 486, 287, 98, 117, 511, 62, 51, 220, 37, 113, 140, 807, 138, 540, 8, 44, 287, 388, 117, 18, 79, 344, 34, 20, 59, 511, 548, 107, 603, 220, 7, 66, 154, 41, 20, 50, 6, 575, 122, 154, 248, 110, 61, 52, 33, 30, 5, 38, 8, 14, 84, 57, 540, 217, 115, 71, 29, 84, 63, 43, 131, 29, 138, 47, 73, 239, 540, 52, 53, 79, 118, 51, 44, 63, 196, 12, 239, 112, 3, 49, 79, 353, 105, 56, 371, 557, 211, 505, 125, 360, 133, 143, 101, 15, 284, 540, 252, 14, 205, 140, 344, 26, 811, 138, 115, 48, 73, 34, 205, 316, 607, 63, 220, 7, 52, 150, 44, 52, 16, 40, 37, 158, 807, 37, 121, 12, 95, 10, 15, 35, 12, 131, 62, 115, 102, 807, 49, 53, 135, 138, 30, 31, 62, 67, 41, 85, 63, 10, 106, 807, 138, 8, 113, 20, 32, 33, 37, 353, 287, 140, 47, 85, 50, 37, 49, 47, 64, 6, 7, 71, 33, 4, 43, 47, 63, 1, 27, 600, 208, 230, 15, 191, 246, 85, 94, 511, 2, 270, 20, 39, 7, 33, 44, 22, 40, 7, 10, 3, 811, 106, 44, 486, 230, 353, 211, 200, 31, 10, 38, 140, 297, 61, 603, 320, 302, 666, 287, 2, 44, 33, 32, 511, 548, 10, 6, 250, 557, 246, 53, 37, 52, 83, 47, 320, 38, 33, 807, 7, 44, 30, 31, 250, 10, 15, 35, 106, 160, 113, 31, 102, 406, 230, 540, 320, 29, 66, 33, 101, 807, 138, 301, 316, 353, 320, 220, 37, 52, 28, 540, 320, 33, 8, 48, 107, 50, 811, 7, 2, 113, 73, 16, 125, 11, 110, 67, 102, 807, 33, 59, 81, 158, 38, 43, 581, 138, 19, 85, 400, 38, 43, 77, 14, 27, 8, 47, 138, 63, 140, 44, 35, 22, 177, 106, 250, 314, 217, 2, 10, 7, 1005, 4, 20, 25, 44, 48, 7, 26, 46, 110, 230, 807, 191, 34, 112, 147, 44, 110, 121, 125, 96, 41, 51, 50, 140, 56, 47, 152, 540, 63, 807, 28, 42, 250, 138, 582, 98, 643, 32, 107, 140, 112, 26, 85, 138, 540, 53, 20, 125, 371, 38, 36, 10, 52, 118, 136, 102, 420, 150, 112, 71, 14, 20, 7, 24, 18, 12, 807, 37, 67, 110, 62, 33, 21, 95, 220, 511, 102, 811, 30, 83, 84, 305, 620, 15, 2, 108, 220, 106, 353, 105, 106, 60, 275, 72, 8, 50, 205, 185, 112, 125, 540, 65, 106, 807, 188, 96, 110, 16, 73, 32, 807, 150, 409, 400, 50, 154, 285, 96, 106, 316, 270, 205, 101, 811, 400, 8, 44, 37, 52, 40, 241, 34, 205, 38, 16, 46, 47, 85, 24, 44, 15, 64, 73, 138, 807, 85, 78, 110, 33, 420, 505, 53, 37, 38, 22, 31, 10, 110, 106, 101, 140, 15, 38, 3, 5, 44, 7, 98, 287, 135, 150, 96, 33, 84, 125, 807, 191, 96, 511, 118, 440, 370, 643, 466, 106, 41, 107, 603, 220, 275, 30, 150, 105, 49, 53, 287, 250, 208, 134, 7, 53, 12, 47, 85, 63, 138, 110, 21, 112, 140, 485, 486, 505, 14, 73, 84, 575, 1005, 150, 200, 16, 42, 5, 4, 25, 42, 8, 16, 811, 125, 160, 32, 205, 603, 807, 81, 96, 405, 41, 600, 136, 14, 20, 28, 26, 353, 302, 246, 8, 131, 160, 140, 84, 440, 42, 16, 811, 40, 67, 101, 102, 194, 138, 205, 51, 63, 241, 540, 122, 8, 10, 63, 140, 47, 48, 140, 288.

By comparing the foregoing numbers with the corresponding numbers of the initial letters of the consecutive words in the Declaration of Independence, the translation will be found to be as follows:

I have deposited, in the county of Bedford, about four miles from Buford's, in an excavation or vault, six feet below the surface of the ground, the following articles, belonging jointly to the parties whose names are given in number "3," herewith :.

The first deposit consisted of one thousand and fourteen pounds of gold, and three thousand eight hundred and twelve pounds of silver, deposited November, 1819. The second was made December, 1821, and consisted of nineteen hundred and seven pounds of gold, and twelve hundred and eighty-eight pounds of silver; also jewels, obtained in St. Louis in exchange for silver to save transportation, and valued at $13,000.

The above is securely packed in iron pots, with iron covers. The vault is roughly lined with stone, and the vessels rest on solid stone, and are covered with others. Paper number "1" describes the exact locality of the vault, so that no difficulty will be had in finding it.

The following is the paper which, according to Beale's statement, describes the exact locality of the vault, and is marked "1." It is to this that I have devoted most of my time, but, unfortunately, without success :

The Locality of the Vault

71, 194, 38, 1701, 89, 76, 11, 83, 1629, 48, 94, 63, 132, 16, 111, 95, 84, 341, 975, 14, 40, 64, 27, 81, 139, 213, 63, 90, 1120, 8, 15, 3, 126, 2018, 40, 74, 758, 485, 604, 230, 436, 664, 582, 150, 251, 284, 308, 231, 124, 211, 486, 225, 401, 370, 11, 101, 305, 139, 189, 17, 33, 88, 208, 193, 145, 1, 94, 73, 416, 918, 263, 28, 500, 538, 356, 117, 136, 219, 27, 176, 130, 10, 460, 25, 485, 18, 436, 65, 84, 200, 283, 118, 320, 138, 36, 416, 280, 15, 71, 224, 961, 44, 16, 401, 39, 88, 61, 304, 12, 21, 24, 283, 134, 92, 63, 246, 486, 682, 7, 219, 184, 360, 780, 18, 64, 463, 474, 131, 160, 79, 73, 440, 95, 18, 64, 581, 34, 69, 128, 367, 460, 17, 81, 12, 103, 820, 62, 110, 97, 103, 862, 70, 60, 1317, 471, 540, 208, 121, 890, 346, 36, 150, 59, 568, 614, 13, 120, 63, 219, 812, 2160, 1780, 99, 35, 18, 21, 136, 872, 15, 28, 170, 88, 4, 30, 44, 112, 18, 147, 436, 195, 320, 37, 122, 113, 6, 140, 8, 120, 305, 42, 58, 461, 44, 106, 301, 13, 408, 680, 93, 86, 116, 530, 82, 568, 9, 102, 38, 416, 89, 71, 216, 728, 965, 818, 2, 38, 121, 195, 14, 326, 148, 234, 18, 55, 131, 234, 361, 824, 5, 81, 623, 48, 961, 19, 26, 33, 10, 1101, 365, 92, 88, 181, 275, 346, 201, 206, 86, 36, 219, 324, 829, 840, 64, 326, 19, 48, 122, 85, 216, 284, 919, 861, 326, 985, 233, 64, 68, 232, 431, 960, 50, 29, 81, 216, 321, 603, 14, 612, 81, 360, 36, 51, 62, 194, 78, 60, 200, 314, 676, 112, 4, 28, 18, 61, 136, 247, 819, 921, 1060, 464, 895, 10, 6, 66, 119, 38, 41, 49, 602, 423, 962, 302, 294, 875, 78, 14, 23, 111, 109, 62, 31, 501, 823, 216, 280, 34, 24, 150, 1000, 162, 286, 19, 21, 17, 340, 19, 242, 31, 86, 234, 140, 607, 115, 33, 191, 67, 104, 86, 52, 88, 16, 80, 121, 67, 95, 122, 216, 548, 96, 11, 201, 77, 364, 218, 65, 667, 890, 236, 154, 211, 10, 98, 34, 119, 56, 216, 119, 71, 218, 1164, 1496, 1817, 51, 39, 210, 36, 3, 19, 540, 232, 22, 141, 617, 84, 290, 80, 46, 207, 411, 150, 29, 38, 46, 172, 85, 194, 39, 261, 543, 897, 624, 18, 212, 416, 127, 931, 19, 4, 63, 96, 12, 101, 418, 16, 140, 230, 460, 538, 19, 27, 88, 612, 1431, 90, 716, 275, 74, 83, 11, 426, 89, 72, 84, 1300, 1706, 814, 221, 132, 40, 102, 34, 868, 975, 1101, 84, 16, 79, 23, 16, 81, 122, 324, 403, 912, 227, 936, 447, 55, 86, 34, 43, 212, 107, 96, 314, 264, 1065, 323, 428, 601, 203, 124, 95, 216, 814, 2906, 654, 820, 2, 301, 112, 176, 213, 71, 87, 96, 202, 35, 10, 2, 41, 17, 84, 221, 736, 820, 214, 11, 60, 760.

The following paper is marked "3" in the series, and as we are informed, contains the names of Beale's associates, who are

22   THE BEALE PAPERS.

joint owners of the fund deposited, together with the names of the nearest relatives of each party, with their several places of residence.

NAMES AND RESIDENCES.

317, 8, 92, 73, 112, 89, 67, 318, 28, 96, 107, 41, 631, 78, 146, 397, 118, 98, 114, 246, 348, 116, 74, 88, 12, 65, 32, 14, 81, 19, 76, 121, 216, 85, 33, 66, 15, 108, 68, 77, 43, 24, 122, 96, 117, 36, 211, 301, 15, 44, 11, 46, 89, 18, 136, 68, 317, 28, 90, 82, 304, 71, 43, 221, 198, 176, 310, 319, 81, 99, 264, 380, 56, 37, 319, 2, 44, 53, 28, 44, 75, 98, 102, 37, 85, 107, 117, 64, 88, 136, 48, 154, 99, 175, 89, 315, 326, 78, 96, 214, 218, 311, 43, 89, 51, 90, 75, 128, 96, 33, 28, 103, 84, 65, 26, 41, 246, 84, 270, 98, 116, 32, 59, 74, 66, 69, 240, 15, 8, 121, 20, 77, 89, 31, 11, 106, 81, 191, 224, 328, 18, 75, 52, 82, 117, 201, 39, 23, 217, 27, 21, 84, 35, 54, 109, 128, 49, 77, 88, 1, 81, 217, 64, 55, 83, 116, 251, 269, 311, 96, 54, 32, 120, 18, 132, 102, 219, 211, 84, 150, 219, 275, 312, 64, 10, 106, 87, 75, 47, 21, 29, 37, 81, 44, 18, 126, 115, 132, 160, 181, 203, 76, 81, 299, 314, 337, 351, 96, 11, 28, 97, 318, 238, 106, 24, 93, 3, 19, 17, 26, 60, 73, 88, 14, 126, 138, 234, 286, 297, 321, 365, 264, 19, 22, 84, 56, 107, 98, 123, 111, 214, 136, 7, 33, 45, 40, 13, 28, 46, 42, 107, 196, 227, 344, 198, 203, 247, 116, 19, 8, 212, 230, 31, 6, 328, 65, 48, 52, 59, 41, 122, 33, 117, 11, 18, 25, 71, 36, 45, 83, 76, 89, 92, 31, 65, 70, 83, 96, 27, 33, 44, 50, 61, 24, 112, 136, 149, 176, 180, 194, 143, 171, 205, 296, 87, 12, 44, 51, 89, 98, 34, 41, 208, 173, 66, 9, 35, 16, 95, 8, 113, 175, 90, 56, 203, 19, 177, 183, 206, 157, 200, 218, 260, 291, 305, 618, 951, 320, 18, 124, 78, 65, 19, 32, 124, 48, 53, 57, 84, 96, 207, 244, 66, 82, 119, 71, 11, 86, 77, 213, 54, 82, 316, 245, 303, 86, 97, 106, 212, 18, 37, 15, 81, 89, 16, 7, 81, 39, 96, 14, 43, 216, 118, 29, 55, 109, 136, 172, 213, 64, 8, 227, 304, 611, 221, 364, 819, 375, 128, 296, 1, 18, 53, 76, 10, 15, 23, 19, 71, 84, 120, 134, 66, 73, 89, 96, 230, 48, 77, 26, 101, 127, 936, 218, 439, 178, 171, 61, 226, 313, 215, 102, 18, 167, 262, 114, 218, 66, 59, 48, 27, 19, 13, 82, 48, 162, 119, 34, 127, 139, 34, 128, 129, 74, 63, 120, 11, 54, 61, 73, 92, 180, 66, 75, 101, 124, 265, 89, 96, 126, 274, 896, 917, 434, 461, 235, 890, 312, 413, 328, 381, 96, 105, 217, 66, 118, 22, 77, 64, 42, 12, 7, 55, 24, 83, 67, 97, 109, 121, 135, 181, 203, 219, 228, 256, 21, 34, 77, 319, 374, 382, 675, 684, 717, 864, 203, 4, 18, 92, 16, 63, 82, 22, 46, 55, 69, 74, 112, 134, 186, 175, 119, 213, 416, 312, 343, 264, 119, 186, 218, 343, 417, 845, 951, 124, 209, 49, 617, 856, 924, 936, 72, 19, 28, 11, 35, 42, 40, 66, 85, 94, 112, 65, 82, 115, 119, 233, 244, 186, 172, 112, 85, 6, 56, 38, 44, 85, 72, 32, 47, 63, 96, 124, 217, 314, 319, 221, 644, 817, 821, 934, 922, 416, 975, 10, 22, 18, 46, 137, 181, 101, 39, 86, 103, 116, 138, 164, 212, 218, 296, 815, 380, 412, 460, 495, 675, 820, 952.

The papers given above were all that were contained in the box, except two or three of an unimportant character, and having no connection whatever with the subject in hand. They were carefully copied, and as carefully compared with the originals, and no error is believed to exist.

Complete in themselves, they are respectfully submitted to the public, with the hope that all that is dark in them may receive light, and that the treasure, amounting to more than three-quarters of a million, which has rested so long unproductive of good, in the hands of a proper person, may eventually accomplish its mission.

In conclusion it may not be inappropriate to say a few words regarding myself: In consequence of the time lost in the above investigation, I have been reduced from comparative affluence to absolute penury, entailing suffering upon those it was my duty to protect, and this, too, in spite of their remonstrances. My eyes were at last opened to their condition, and I resolved to sever at once, and forever, all connection with the affair, and retrieve, if possible, my errors. To do this, as the best means of placing temptation beyond my reach, I determined to make public the whole matter, and shift from my shoulders my responsibility to Mr. Morriss.

I anticipate for these papers a large circulation, and, to avoid the multitude of letters with which I should be assailed from all sections of the Union, propounding all sorts of questions, and requiring answers which, if attended to, would absorb my entire time, and only change the character of my work, I have decided upon withdrawing my name from the publication, after assuring all interested that I have given all that I know of the matter, and that I cannot add one word to the statements herein contained.

The gentleman whom I have selected as my agent, to publish and circulate these papers, was well-known to Mr. Morriss; it was at his house that Mrs. Morriss died, and he would have been one of the beneficiaries in the event of my success. Like every one else, he was ignorant of this episode in Mr. Morriss' career, until the manuscript was placed in his hands. Trusting that he will be benefited by the arrangement, which, I know, would have met the approval of Mr. Morriss, I have left the whole subject to his sole management and charge. All business communications should be addressed to him. It is needless to say that I shall await with much anxiety the development of the mystery.

**Thus ends the pamphlet,
copyright 1885 by J.B. Ward.**

4.
Hope & Reason

The Beale Papers is quite a story. Should we believe it, or not?

Is this all just a fantasy or hoax? Is there in Bedford a pot of gold at the end of the rainbow? Is it possible that a group of people could bury a treasure without someone coming back for it? Could they keep the story from leaking out? Could a large party of men go forth and back and not be noticed, leave no record, and keep their secret?

In 1934, Dr. Clarence Williams, a researcher at the Library of Congress, didn't believe it. "To me, the pamphlet story has all the earmarks of a fake," he wrote, noting there was "no evidence save the word of the unknown author of the pamphlet that he ever had the papers."

Some modern investigators don't believe it either. After careful research they may start to have gnawing doubts, then find contradictions, and finally abandon the subject. Richard H. Greaves worked the problem for more than four years, conducted three excavations, and then concluded, "There is no treasure; there never was any treasure. The pamphlet is fictional narrative." He saw it as "a dream without possibility for success." Greaves was so certain that he even paid for a large ad in the Sunday edition of the *Lynchburg News* to proclaim his conclusion.

David Kahn, in his 1967 book, *The Code Breakers*, said that it is a clever, elaborate, and thoroughgoing hoax. Then, in 1974, amateur cryptologist A.B. Chandler claimed that he had decoded the ciphers and found one part that said "end of my joke." In a copyrighted article by James Berry in the *Richmond Times-Dispatch*, Chandler said it is all a practical joke, and that he suspected that Robert Morriss was the hoaxer.

In spite of these and other denunciations, other serious treasure hunters do careful research and conclude that the story is indeed plausible. They, too, may find contradictions, but these are offset by facts that seem to be beyond the ability of a hoaxer to know or to create.

Still others believe it because they want to believe it and because they see that others believe it. They reason that if others make great effort to solve the ciphers or find the treasure, then it must be true.

Research concentrates on unraveling the ciphers. Less effort goes to determining if the story is true.

This author is fascinated by the phenomena of the Beale Treasure. What is the truth about it? If it is true, what happened to it? If it is not true, the creator of the story deserves credit for a job well done. Local historical researcher Charles T. Burton doubts if there ever was a treasure but, because the pamphlet is so plausible, believes that "the man who made up this stuff was a remarkable mental giant." If there was a treasure, is it still there, waiting to be found? The Beale story has been widely publicized. Millions have heard about it and dreamed about it. Many hundreds have combed the Bedford area searching for it. Did they find it?

Bedford area residents have differing views about the subject. An informal poll of residents showed that less than half think it is not true. Real estate magnate Lawrence Dick is one who doubts the tale. "People search for it because it's a fun outing. It's sort of like going to Las Vegas. Most people know that they won't really win, but they go for the fun of it."

More than half of those polled do believe that the story is indeed true. However, slightly more than half of those believers think that the treasure has already been found.

The treasure could have been retrieved by members or relatives of Beale's party. Secrets about hidden wealth don't stay secret between loved ones. Maybe some of the men sneaked back and got it. Another theory has it that Beale then killed his own men, only to be later killed himself by Indians.

Or perhaps a Bedford resident found it. The finder may have quietly disposed of the gold, silver, and jewels in distant cities, selling just a bit at a time, always being careful not to display sudden wealth that would raise questions. The local finder might already have been wealthy and therefore escaped suspicion.

Or the local finder may have moved away, taking the new wealth along to start a new life some place where there would be few questions.

Or some out-of-towner found it. A local Beale aficionado had a revelation during meditation. The picture was that two people from New York did find it, back in the 1930's. It was near a big tree, on a knoll. There were pots in a wooden box that had now rotted away. One of the two men was a scientist, and the other was a doctor. The doctor is still alive — though very elderly — and living in South America. He is unhappy.

There was a magazine article in 1982 saying that the treasure was found near Taylor's Mountain. But people living near the alleged discovery site doubt that.

The late S.S. Lynn, a land surveyor who walked Bedford County for more than fifty years said, "I have not lately been apprised of its discovery."

Elton Hite, a furniture company vice-president who has lived most of his life just a few miles from Montvale, says, "Thousands of people have spent years and years and years and haven't found it. I find it hard to believe that anything is there." He pauses and then adds, "Another thought. Maybe they've been looking in the wrong place. I've got a feeling that instead of looking in the mountains south of US 460, they should be looking in the range north of US 460."

Montvale resident Frank Smith suspects the story to be true and that the treasure has already been found. Col. J.J. Holland, who sought the solution for many years, told Ruth Daniloff that "the treasure has been removed, probably by Beale himself."

About one of four Bedford residents feel that the treasure is still out there. The late Judge Ray Minnix observed that many knowledgeable people have put so much effort into it that "there's got to be something to it."

A local teacher thinks she knows where it is: on family property near Goose Creek. She has not dug for it because, she says, "I'm afraid I couldn't stop." She may also be reluctant to risk the shattering of her lifelong dream.

There are inconsistencies in the treasure story. The pamphlet has contradictions in it, and some people contradict themselves.

At least two Bedford residents are certain that they know exactly where the treasure is. But neither one takes any action to go get it. They think about it. They do not dig. Perhaps they suspect that if they dug, they might find nothing, and their hopes would be shattered. They fear being wrong and would rather enjoy the process — hoping the hopes.

Gold north of Santa Fe? How could the Beale group mine thousands of pounds of gold in 1818, and then have almost forty years elapse before the general public learned that there was gold in the area?

Some hunters say that the gold did not come from the Santa Fe area, but they do believe that Beale did bury a treasure. If one part of Beale's letters in *The Beale Papers* is untrue, why should the rest of the story be true?

The pamphlet reports that Morriss said he met Beale in 1820 "while keeping" the Franklin Hotel. Morriss did not manage that hotel until several years later. Critics cite this as evidence that the story is untrue. Is this discrepancy because the story is fiction, or is it because the author's memory was flawed, or because the memory of octogenarian Morriss was imperfect?

Morriss told the story to the pamphlet author twenty years before the author wrote it down. The author had to paraphrase much of what Morriss said. Remember, too, that Morriss was recalling events that had happened forty years before he talked with the author. We should expect errors in the recalling of dates, dialog, and details.

The author says he solved the second cipher using the Declaration of Independence quite by chance. Of all the keys in the world, this somehow came into the mind of the author as he toiled at the ciphers. Col. George Fabyan wrote in 1925 that stumbling upon the Declaration of Independence as the key is "rather beyond the range of possibility."

Beale wrote to Morriss that he left the key to the ciphers, sealed, with a friend in St. Louis, addressed to Morriss and to be delivered in 1832. The package may never have existed at all, except in the fertile mind of a hoaxer. Obviously, Morriss never received it. If he had, he would have unraveled the mystery and retrieved the treasure. That key may still be somewhere.

It seems odd that Thomas Beale would ask a stranger, Robert Morriss, to hold the information about the treasure, instead of his wife, his parents, or his children. We will later see that there may have been very good reasons.

The titling of the three cryptograms raises doubts in some minds. The author says that "to systematize a plan for my work I arranged the papers in order of their length, and numbered them...." Then, much later in the pamphlet, the decoded message of No. 2 says, "Paper number 1 describes the exact locality of the vault...." Does this mean that the pamphlet author created the ciphers, or does it mean that the author and Beale used the same logic for numbering the sheets?

Cryptogram No. 3 is supposed to give the names and addresses of Beale's associates. It is a short cryptogram. Some critics argue that there are not enough digits to provide for 29 names and addresses. But believers counter by pointing out that Beale said all had visited Bedford, and many may well have been from Bedford. Many may have shared the same address, or have had the address of an organization, such as a Lodge. The surnames could be short ones.

The decoded cipher No. 2 doesn't check out. In the pamphlet, the solution to cipher No. 2 includes the words "four miles ....." That solution depends upon the 95th word of the Declaration of Independence to begin with a "u." However, the Declaration shown in the pamphlet has as its 95th word "inalienable," which begins with an "i."

Critics use this example to refute the veracity of the story. However, the original Declaration of Independence did use the word "unalienable." Later in the 1800's the usage shifted to "inalienable." Beale and the author were referring to the early wording of the Declaration. Perhaps the printer, working in the 1880's, instinctively used the then current wording, and the author failed to proofread the pamphlet.

A language analyst noted that one of the Beale letters used the word "stampeding." The analyst found no published usage of the word "stampede" earlier than 1844, which is more than two decades after Beale wrote his letters. Defenders of the Beale story suggest that the analyst cannot be certain that there was no earlier printed use of the word and neither can the analyst disprove that the word may have been in general use in the west for decades.

A 1982 article in *Virginia Magazine* by Joe Nicklell reasoned that "one must reasonably conclude that both Thomas Jefferson Beale and his fabulous treasure were fictitious and that James B. Ward was the author of the fraudulent Beale Papers." Ward himself wrote that he was "agent for the author," and there is no compelling reason to question Ward's veracity.

We might wonder, too — how it could be that the location of such a valuable stash could be kept secret for so long? Men have killed for less. Any one of the thirty men, or any one of the group of ten men who brought the treasure to Virginia, could have turned on the leader and then taken it all.

Most past students of the Beale controversy had never seen nor read the words of *The Beale Papers* pamphlet as they were actually printed. They have based their analyses — and their conclusions — upon secondary sources. The sources are sincere, but often contain errors that have been repeated unknowingly. One example is the hero's name. Most popular articles refer to him as Thomas Jefferson Beale. Careful reading of the pamphlet shows that Beale has only a middle initial, and no middle name at all.

You may find some other inconsistencies in the pamphlet, or in the analyses of it. The following chapters look at the people who shaped the Beale Treasure story. This history of a mystery may help you decide what is true and what is not true.

5.
Codesmanship

Computers have not solved the Beale mystery. The type of cipher used in *The Beale Papers* is a substitution cipher. The solution requires reference to a code "key" or "book." Without the key, solution is nearly impossible. Here's why.

The cryptographer had some message he wanted to protect. He encrypted it into a cipher or cryptogram so that only people who had or knew the code key would be able to decipher the message.

The cryptographer chose the text of a popular book or famous document to be his key. He serially numbered the words in that text. This gave him a supply of letters: the first letter of each word was represented by the number of that word. A letter may appear many times in the key, each time with a new number, so deciphering one number gives no clue to the meaning of another number. Now, he replaced the letters of his message with numbers he picked from his supply. The multiple substitution book cipher of *The Beale Papers* is classic and is perhaps the most widely discussed cryptogram of this type.

The identity of the key or code book is essential to solving such puzzles. Usually, the creator picks as his key some publication that he knows his ally has or can get. As you can imagine, if you don't know which book it is, you have a real challenge trying to make a selection from the hundreds of thousands of documents or books that have been printed.

One-time Vice President Aaron Burr and U.S. Army General Wilkinson communicated in code. Each had a copy of the key: a pocket-sized *Entick's Dictionary*. A communication would use "page and entry" numbers to represent words.

The Declaration of Independence was the key to Beale cipher Number 2. Some suggest that since Thomas Jefferson was the primary author of the Declaration, then the key for the other two ciphers may also be something written by Jefferson. These might include his speech dedicating the University of Virginia or the Statute on Religious Freedom.

In the pamphlet there are problems with the Declaration of Independence printed there. As we have noted, the word "inalienable" suggests that the Declaration shown is a newer version. But more perplexing is the numbering of the words in the Declaration. Words are numbered serially. But, the word numbered 250 is actually the 251st word. Another discrepancy: after No. 480, ten words go by and the number 480 appears again. There are others.

The Declaration printed in *The Beale Papers* must be a different version than the one used for the ciphers. The numbering errors may have been the fault of the typesetter. There may be typographical errors as well. Clearly, the printed Declaration and its numbering was not proofread carefully. If there are errors in this, could there also be errors in ciphers No. 1 and No. 3? Any errors make it even more difficult to solve the ciphers.

One man wrote that the only reason for publishing the pamphlet was to flush out the key book. Robert Hohmann, a communications specialist, theorized in 1973 that though Ward had the key to Cipher No. 2, he did not have the key to either No. 1 or No. 3, so he published *The Beale Papers* as a device to find the missing keys. Ward hoped, Hohmann suggested, that the pamphlet would get the attention of those who might possess the key documents. He points out that the pamphlet itself reveals this notion: "by publication of this narrative... bringing to light the missing papers."

He speculated that Ward doctored the ciphers just enough so that if someone did have the keys, they could not get the treasure without seeking Ward's help in untangling the scramble.

Rational people with keen minds analyze the Beale ciphers — discuss them — write about them — and come up with different solutions.

Professionals who have wrestled with the Beale ciphers include: Dr. Carl Hammer, retired from Univac and described in *Computer News* as "one of the most distinguished computer experts in the country"; the late Carl Nelson, Jr., a retired intelligence officer; and Dr. Stephen Matyas, who is with I.B.M.'s Cryptography Competency Center and co-author of the John Wiley & Sons reference book *Cryptography*. It was the Beale ciphers that inspired Matyas to do his doctoral thesis on "A Computer Oriented Cryptanalytic Solution for Multiple Substitution Enciphering Systems" and then pursue a career in cryptography at I.B.M.

He studied the Beale story in his spare time for two decades. He is suspicious that *The Beale Papers* could be a hoax. But he believes that the unsolved ciphers can be decoded, if the key book or document can be found. This last possibility has kept many hopes alive.

Fletcher Pratt's book *Secret and Urgent* says that an 1819 issue of the popular *Ree's Encyclopedia* stimulated public interest in cryptology. The

Encyclopedia described a number of substitution cipher systems which would enable an intelligent person to set up or use such concepts. Matyas found that some *Encyclopedia* subscribers lived in Lynchburg and one, John Watt, in Bedford County. Perhaps a *Ree's* reader was inspired to concoct or be part author of *The Beale Papers*.

The U.S. diplomatic service relied on a book cipher. Fletcher Pratt wrote that the book "… contained nearly 1600 numbers, with representations for every possible English syllable, numerous valued for each letter, and considerable numbers of word signs." Similar code books were developed for Benjamin Franklin and others.

An article by Matyas and Albert C. Leighton concludes that the Beale ciphers are "excellent proof that sometimes book ciphers are very secure indeed." (Leighton, while a history professor at State University of New York at Oswego, decoded a Papal cipher that had been unsolved since 1576.)

It may not be a matter of simply making substitutions with a key. The solution could involve multiple choice substitutions or even multi-stage layering. A problem with multiple choice methods is the tendency to "force" the process to produce a solution which has been subconsciously predetermined by your own desires.

Big, "numbers-crunching" computers offer hope that "the key" may be unnecessary. Bigger, faster computers might try every imaginable combination of numbers into letters into words, guided by a program which would continuously eliminate obvious non-use letter pairs and triples. This approach remains untried. More clever programs and better computers may be on the way.

Chess champion Kasparov showed that the human mind is a respectable challenger for even the most specialized computer in his competition with "Deep Blue." And there are Beale seekers who ignore searching for a key. Instead, they try to solve the ciphers in much the same way they would try to decode a newspaper's daily cryptogram. They make assumptions, test the assumptions, reiterate, make further assumptions … until it all makes sense. A Canadian gentleman used this procedure and came up with the names of the beneficiaries of No. 2 — in alphabetical order.

Some doubt that the ciphers have a solution as all. Lt. Col. William F. Friedman, a widely acclaimed expert in the field of cryptology, studied the papers a number of decades ago. Friedman is credited with having broken the diplomatic code of Japan in World War II. After Friedman died in 1969 at age 76, his wife reported that her husband had decided that the Beale cryptographic system is of "diabolical ingenuity specifically designed to lure the unwary reader … in fruitless research … or searching for a key book."

Attendees at the 1986 Beale Cypher Association were polled as to what they thought the prospects were. Most endorse Dr. Hammer's conclusion of 1970: the unsolved ciphers are not random gibberish — but actually do contain real messages. Most recognize that the Beale treasure story may be a hoax and that there is only a very small probability that the ciphers can be decoded and that the solution may or may not lead to a treasure. But because the potential payoff is so large, the quest has some merit.

Others throw up their hands. They don't even try to solve the ciphers. They seek the treasure using a different approach. They try to "psyche out" Beale and deduce what Beale would have done. How would he have decided where to stash the treasure? What would have been the logical thing for him to do?

Let us analyze the possibilities. We will take a closer look at the people involved and examine some of the issues. Each subject or character leads to another, maybe at a different time or place. There will be some overlap. The reader is asked to have forbearance as the trail winds circuitously through history. Let us see where it goes.

6.
Spanish West

The treasure is said to have come from near what is now Santa Fe, New Mexico. Was there really gold and silver to be found there? Could a group of Easterners have come in, gotten it, and then taken it back East? Perhaps there is something somewhere that verifies the Beale pamphlet.

Most history we know is based upon the written word. If it's not written down, then it's hard to believe. History does not confirm that Thomas Beale was in Santa Fe in 1817, 1818 or 1820. Nor is there written evidence that he and his companions went 250 to 300 miles northward from Santa Fe and there found gold and silver. But the written history doesn't disprove it either. Most hunters, trappers, adventurers, and wheeler-dealers are usually too involved in action to take time to write down their experiences. They may or may not leave traces.

A look at the history of New Mexico and Santa Fe can help evaluate the Beale story. The town — located in a generally dry and mostly sunny region about 7,000 feet above sea level — is still a special place on the North American continent. It was under Spanish or Mexican influence for three centuries. New Mexico became a State of the Union only recently, in 1912.

Santuario de Guadelupe mission church, built at the end of the 1790's at Santa Fe, the government center of New Spain and the Spanish Southwest.

6 — Spanish West

The southwestern part of the United States was initially inhabited by primitive peoples, perhaps 20,000 years ago. When the white man first came here, they met up with long-established native American Indians. The first Europeans to claim and take possession were Spanish. Explorer Coronado traveled into the area and claimed the region for Spain. Franciscan de Niza explored the area in 1539 looking for gold. Part of Coronado's route became part of the Santa Fe Trail. Santa Fe was selected in 1610 to be the seat of government for New Spain, which included most of what we consider the far west.

The region was long coveted by early Americans. Settlers kept moving westward from the eastern colonies, infiltrating regions west of the Mississippi claimed by Britain, France, and Spain. The borders were neither marked nor enforced.

By the end of the eighteenth century, half the population of Spanish Louisiana was American. Spain couldn't control that area. They ceded it to France in 1800, while retaining their jurisdiction over the far west. Spain also kept Spanish Florida — which extended to the Mississippi River and included Baton Rouge.

France didn't keep Louisiana very long. Napoleon realized that France would be unable to keep the settlers out. He also badly needed money to finance his European campaigns.

So, in 1803 France was happy to sell this vast Louisiana territory to the United States for $15 million. Thomas Jefferson, president of a nation of just six million people, found himself presiding over a nation whose area virtually doubled in size because of just one deal.

Spain was not happy with the transaction. The Spanish has hoped that France would provide a buffer between the spreading Americans and New Spain. In contrast, Americans were excited by the prospects of expansion. They eyed Texas. They dreamed of reaching the Pacific Ocean. The Spanish of New Spain were leery. They didn't want to share the area with anyone. They feared America's territorial ambitions, and justifiably so. Powerful men in the U.S. were even then conspiring to take over the Southwest and create an entirely new, separate republic.

Spain and the United States disagreed as to where the border was between the New Spain and the land just purchased from France. The border of America's new territory was disturbingly close to Santa Fe. The ruling Spaniards were determined to keep Americans out, even if it meant imprisoning, or even killing, the trespassers.

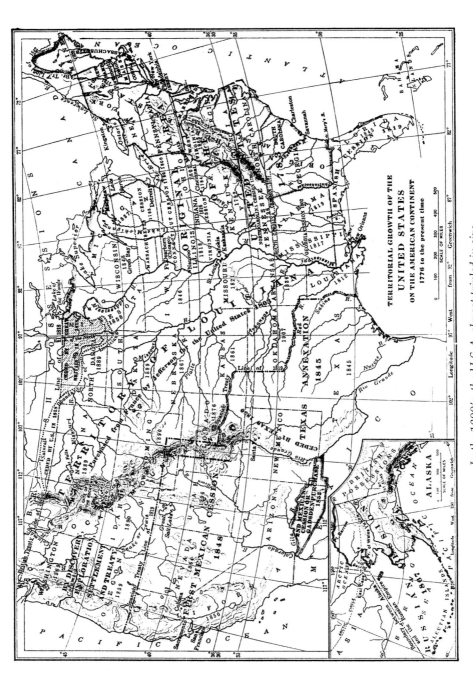

In the 1800's, the U.S.A. almost tripled in size.

6 — Spanish West

The Comanches (to the north) and the Apaches (to the south) were equally hostile to white men coming in. Travel from Missouri was terribly risky. The word was out that if the Spanish didn't get you, the Indians would.

But American and French trappers quested for furs. Traders looked for new markets. Adventurers hungered for excitement. They were all risk-takers. They headed West in spite of the hazards. Some men made it there and back, and some didn't

In 1804, trader Baptiste Lalande went up the Platte River, through Nebraska and on to Colorado. He stayed north, clear of the Spanish territory. His sponsor was Illinois merchant William Morrison, who provided the trading goods and supplies. Lalande liked the area. He sold the trading goods and then stayed there, keeping Morrison's money for himself.

According to an 1824 newspaper story, James Purcell (or Pursley) said he had been in Santa Fe in 1805, and he spoke of gold near there, and even showed off small nuggets. Such stories — true or not — whetted the appetites of adventurers.

Jefferson approved the sending of an expedition to explore the northerly area of the Louisiana territory, from St. Louis to the Pacific and back. Two young army officers, Lewis and Clark, led a party on this venture, leaving St. Louis in 1804. They stayed away from potential encounters with the Spanish. They weren't looking for gold. Their purpose was to map the territory.

Before Lewis and Clark had finished their mission, the new governor of the Upper Louisiana Territory, Army General James Wilkinson, sent out a different team to head west. Wilkinson, based near St. Louis, was bold, hard drinking, and greedy. He may have liked gold, but he lusted after power more. He wanted to find a good route for possible conquest of the Spanish. Without any approval from Washington, he dispatched U.S. Army Lieutenant Zebulan Montgomery Pike and fifteen men across the prairies towards the Rockies, taking a more southerly route than Lewis and Clark.

Pike and his party rode into southeastern Colorado. It was too cold for them to climb the mountain they found, now known as Pike's Peak. Pike then probed southwest towards the Rio Grande, into Spanish territory. He didn't come across any gold, but he found the Spanish — or they found him. Spanish troops captured Pike and his crew and held them for a time in Santa Fe before dispatching them home.

In October 1806, Wilkinson double-crossed his scheming partner when he alerted President Jefferson that former Vice-President Aaron Burr was scheming to seize the Southwest. The general further double-dealed by sending an envoy to Mexico City to warn the Spanish Viceroy and then asking for $121,000 for his services of informing them. There was no attack on the Spanish.

Demand for furs prompted more trappers to go west. By 1808, Manuel Lisa's Missouri Fur Company was working with 250 hunters of the wilderness. Americans kept trickling towards Santa Fe, long before Beale. Three Missourians wandered into Spanish territory in 1809 and were captured and held for three years.

In 1810, Pike published the journal of his expedition. He wrote glowingly about the area's resources and potential. The book was widely circulated. It reinforced American aspirations for trade and settlement. It reported huge herds of buffalo. Perhaps Beale heard these alluring tales as well as Purcell's allusions to gold.

Meanwhile, down in Mexico, Father Hidalgo was calling for reforms and stirring the minds of the peasants. Some 80,000 responded and clamored for changes. But royal troops easily squelched the mobs. Hidalgo withdrew. Thousands of refugees fled into Texas. Hidalgo was seized and executed in 1811. But scattered news of this apparent revolt led to the assumption that the spirit of change was spreading north into New Spain as well. Optimistic adventurers thought that the Spanish would not mind them coming in. Some decided to sneak in.

James Baird and Robert McKnight ventured across the prairies and into New Mexico in the spring of 1812. But they discovered that Americans were still unwelcome. They were captured and imprisoned — to be without their freedom for years. At least one man claimed that neither the Spanish nor the Indians were a problem. Ezekial Williams said that he travelled 400 miles alone down the Arkansas River and had no trouble that same year. Not everyone believed him.

Elsewhere, in the Atlantic Ocean and in the Gulf of Mexico, the British had been harassing American ships. The United States declared war on Britain in 1812.

Wilkinson showed his patriotism. He flaunted the Spaniards and seized their fort at Mobile. Napoleon's forces in Europe were faltering, so the British could divert more attention to America. The British beat American forces in many land battles in the East. They aspired to capture New Orleans. But General Andrew Jackson led a combined force of army regulars and civilian militia men to a decisive victory in January 1815, beating back the English invaders. The British conceded.

6 — Spanish West

Now Britain was out. France was out. The only players left were the Americans, the Spanish, and the Indians.

In the spring of 1816, Congress enacted a law requiring permits for any non-citizen travelling into Indian territory of the United States. Military posts checked people passing through. Missouri developed as the departure area for all of the West. St. Louis, near the intersection of the Missouri and Mississippi Rivers, was optimistic about its future. In contrast, the rest of the American economy was shaky. Confidence in banks weakened.

Trapper Jules de Mun headed to Santa Fe to seek formal permission to trap on the headwaters of the Rio Grande. A new Spanish governor had taken office, so he expected approval. He was met with the same policies as the men before. De Mun was arrested in 1817 and held in chains for almost two months. He was released with instructions to warn other Americans to stay out.

Only the bravest and most adventurous Americans risked going into Spanish lands. Beale said that he and his associates arrived in Santa Fe in December 1817.

I asked Dr. Myra Ellen Jenkins, the premier historian of New Mexico, if there was any evidence or record of a group of 20 or 30 Virginians having visited Santa Fe in December 1817, who then went North. She replied, "None whatever. Obviously I place no credence in the Beale story, but your account (*Beale Treasure — History of a Mystery*) is the best I have ever read and is objective."

On the other hand, there are tantalizing references to what could have been a Beale party in the area in 1817-1818 and at the end of 1821. Consider the information in travel reports.

Very few Americans risked going into Spanish lands as relations between the U.S. and the Spanish continued to deteriorate. President Adams demanded in 1818 that Spain cede Florida to the United States. General Jackson led a force into Florida. Spain did concede, the next year.

In February 1819, the U.S. and Mexico did agree on boundaries between New Spain and U.S. Louisiana Territory. America dropped any claim to Texas. Promoters speculated about land and business opportunities in the West. The Second Bank of the United States failed. There was a bank panic; people lost their faith in banks and paper money and wanted only gold and silver coins.

Next, history recorded that David Meriwether dared to travel into New Mexico in 1819. He too was captured and imprisoned by the Spaniards.

Though he had made friends with some Pawnees, who accompanied him, he was nevertheless overpowered by Spanish troops led by Col. Vizcarra. He was later released near Taos by Governor Melgares.

Finally, a new revolution in Mexico, led by Iturbide, succeeded in 1821. Mexico gained its independence from Spain by a formal treaty. New policies emerged. Baird and McKnight were released at last. Trade on the Santa Fe Trail became legal.

With the news that traders could come to Santa Fe, William Becknell organized a group of traders. Written history says that this was the first such group. It was certainly the earliest for which good records exist. They left Franklin, Missouri on September 1st. Until then, goods were said to have been transported by pack mules. Historians say that Becknell was the first to use wagons. They arrived in Santa Fe on November 16, 1821 with their load of goods after traveling two and a half months. They did their trading and headed for home in December.

One diary alludes to a group that could have been Beale's. *The Journal of Jacob Fowler*, edited with notes by Elliot Coues and published by the University of Nebraska, presents the narrative by Jacob Fowler about his early travel and exploration of the Southwest in 1821-22.

Fowler wrote that "… the Pawnee Cheef then Said that some four or five years back [1817-1818] He Had Seen Some English men and french men together … tho the Ware nearly as Black as pall — but at all Events the Ware Blacker than the Indeans them Selves." Fowler could not fur-

The Beale party did not escape notice.

ther identify or describe this group. We are left to guess if they were heavily sunburned white men or black slaves.

In November 1821 Fowler reported that "... the Indeans Inform us that there are White men near the great [Pike's] Peak of the mountain...." Then at Santa Fe, January 1, 1822, Fowler wrote the story of Colonel Glenn: "... the Crowes Say the left the White People on the Platt about 10 nights ago.... the speake on the most friendly terms of the White men and Say the are about 35 in number...." These 1821-1822 sightings appear to relate to Becknell or a Beale group without Beale, because *The Beale Papers* contain a letter from Beale to Morriss dated January 4, 1822.

Becknell's travel time was quicker than that of Beale. Becknell went from eastern Missouri to Santa Fe in 2 1/2 months. Beale took 7 1/2 months.

If the Crowe report date is correct, and if it referred to Becknell, then he really hustled on the way home. Because history record that Becknell's group arrived back in Franklin on January 29, 1822, after traveling just one month. Perhaps the Crowes had seen a different group in December. Becknell's group displayed bags of Spanish silver dollars gotten for their wares. This show of wealth attracted more traders to enter into the Santa Fe trade. Becknell made another trip, this time with 30 men.

Writer Vic Thayer reports that Pawnee Rock in Kansas Territory has this carved on it: "Thomas Jefferson Beale, William Buford, James Bird, July 17, 1822." Did these men carve their own names or did some hoaxer? The rock has always interested tourists, and a monument was put up there in 1912. No one knows if the three names were there before the monument was dedicated, or were added after the treasure story became known. Perhaps Bird was Baird and Baird was Bird.

The people of New Mexico clamored for more products from the East — cloth, hardware, and medicines. For exchange, they paid with mules and Spanish coins. As a result, far more mules travelled the Santa Fe Trail eastward than westward.

James Baird returned to Santa Fe to trade, unconcerned about being arrested. Now his only worry was Indians. The experiences of others justified that fear. Andrew Henry went upriver on the Missouri, and four of his men were killed by Indians.

And in 1826 two Frenchmen near the Platte River told General Ashley a story about how Indians had earlier robbed and killed 15 or 20 men from St. Louis. Was that the Beale party, returning west after completing its second haul to Bedford?

We can wonder about the hostility of the Indians and the Spanish. It would not have been easy for Beale to get in and out of Santa Fe. It is possible that he did, but there is no proof.

Tantalizing facts were uncovered by Carl Nelson, Jr. The *Missouri Gazette* of October 4th and October 18th, 1817 listed mail being held by the postmaster for "S.T. Beall." There was no mail being held for Beall in later issues. Nelson also found a similar item in the *Franklin* (Missouri) *Intelligenser* of April 1, 1820. The postmaster's list of held mail included an item for "Thomas Beall." This is evidence that one Thomas B. was expected in St. Louis. Is this our Thomas Beale, going to and from Santa Fe? We can hope that the April first date does not imply that the Franklin report is itself a hoax.

There had to be a reason why Beale was tolerated there in the Spanish West. Perhaps there was some political consideration. A psychic in Blackstone, Virginia, theorized that Beale did indeed bring back gold and silver from Santa Fe, but that it was not something he dug out of the ground. She suggests that he made a deal with Spanish authorities. They gave him coins and bars, and he agreed to represent their cause with powerful politicians in the United States. She says that the U.S. government was weak and stumbling and that people had lost faith in banks. Spain hoped to capitalize in Washington's uncertainties by buying influence to protect Spanish interests. Beale was to be their agent to buy the men needed to buy off the right politicians. He would park the treasure where he could access it when dealing with the power players in Richmond and Washington.

Let us assume that Beale did get to Santa Fe as he said. Could he have discovered silver and gold there? Silver is not rare in New Mexico and Colorado. Even the earliest explorers found some. Indians had long used it for jewelry and ornamentation. Gold is a different story.

It wasn't until 1858 that word spread that gold has been found in Colorado, north of Santa Fe. To get to that gold ore area from Santa Fe, prospectors travelled on the west side of the Sangre de Cristo Mountains, north to Taos. They rode northward and then headed northeast, through the Sangre de Cristo Pass and on towards Pueblo, Colorado. Fountain Creek then leads northward to the eastern slope of Pike's Peak. Twenty miles further northwest is Fairplay. Overall, by land, the route is a bit more than 250 miles. That's just about the distance that Beale's letter talks about. It is a slow, tough trek in winter snow.

In Beale's time, travelers could head back to Virginia from Colorado without passing through New Mexico and without encountering Spaniards. Then they could follow or float on the Arkansas River eastward into Kansas and ride on to Independence, Missouri. The Missouri River flows to St. Louis and joins the Mississippi River, which leads down past the western border of Kentucky and Tennessee. From there they could ride over land home to Virginia.

Yes, it is conceivable that gold and silver could have been found north of Santa Fe, and then brought to Virginia. But the pamphlet may have lied about "Indian" mines.

A Cheyenne legend, passed along to Joseph Durand by his grandfather, coincided with the Beale story. It told of Spanish gold and silver taken from the West and buried in Eastern mountains.

There are some theories, however, that say that the Santa Fe mining tale is just a cover story. Attendees at the 1986 Beale Cypher Association were polled on this. The responses showed that although 73% think that there is or was a treasure, only 16% think that it came from the West.

Some say Beale never went to Santa Fe at all. Maybe he got the treasure somewhere else. One theory is that the real source of the treasure was pirate Jean Laffite.

Still another notion is that Beale made up the Santa Fe story to cover the fact that he had stolen the gold from his three brothers. This story says that the brothers owned 17,000 acres of land in Virginia, including a gold mine. John Wood's 1821 map of Botetourt County shows that Beale owned land near the junction of Craig Creek and James River.

The Beale Papers say the treasure came out of the ground north of Santa Fe. Other stories suggest that it was pirate loot, bribe coins, stolen, or a portion of the Confederate treasury. Wherever it came from, it is a heavy treasure.

7.
Carry to Virginia

Tom Martin, retired Bedford realtor and auctioneer, has said that the problems of moving a treasure of this magnitude renders the tale unlikely. He points out that there would have been such a sizeable mule train that secrecy would be almost impossible.

The treasure was of substantial weight. It would take several pickup trucks to carry it all. How could it have been transported? How big a hole or "vault" would have been needed to contain it? What kind of place are we looking for? The size of a house, a breadbox, a shoe box, or what? It is possible to calculate an answer.

The pamphlet defines the weight of gold and silver brought in each of the two trips. It also says that it was placed in iron pots, with covers, before burial.

Whether carried in wagons or on the backs of pack mules, the treasure and its caravan involved at least eleven men (he said he returned with ten men) and no less than a dozen animals.

	First trip	Second trip	Total
Gold - pounds	1040	1907	2947
Silver - pounds	3811	1288	5099
Total pounds	4851	3195	8046

The first trip involved the greatest weight. On the second trip some precious metals had been exchanged for jewels to reduce the load burden.

It was a big group that came to Virginia that first trip. If the trail was adequately passable for wagons — and this is uncertain — the load could have been carried in a single wagon that carried the metal, the supplies, and perhaps two men, with the wagon being pulled by two horses. The remaining nine men — including leader Beale — would have been on horses. Total animals: 11.

The trails of 1819 were really rough. Beale probably had to get by without a wagon. Each man would have had a horse, and the metals could have been in bags carried by pack mules. If each mule carried about 300 pounds, there would have been about 18 mules, including those carrying supplies. Total animals: 29.

7 — Carry to Virginia

Confusion between monetary and weight terms could distort this analysis. Back in the early 1800's there was little standard money. There were nondescript banknotes. Foreign coins were commonly used. The Spanish dollar was widely used as legal tender in the U.S. until 1857. There were few U.S. coins in circulation. Virginians were transacting business in terms of British currency: shillings and pounds.

If Beale had been referring to "pounds" in the sense of British monetary Pound Sterling units, his load would have been much lighter. One Pound Sterling did then weigh exactly one pound, which is equal to 12 Troy ounces. On the other hand, gold was so precious one quarter ounce of the stuff was equal in value to a pound of silver. The total load of the two trips would have been almost 3,000 pounds lighter. If this were so, then the first Beale party would have had 23 animals instead of 29.

In any case — 11 animals and a wagon, or 29 animals, or 23 animals — the Beale party was big. Imagine the noise of creaking leather, snorting horses, and thudding hooves. Imagine, too, the dust. A party that size would have attracted attention. To obscure his real mission, Beale probably carried decoy burdens. He could have posed as a dealer in buffalo skins. A few skins could hide almost anything underneath.

If Beale and his party went directly to Buford's tavern, they could not easily have slipped away and buried the treasure. Not many people lived in the area, yet some would have been curious enough to see what the group was doing. Instead, Beale stopped a few miles from Buford's at his chosen spot, where no one would see them. Just Beale and a couple others went to the tavern.

Bedford County natives might later find telltale hoofprints or crushed weeds or broken branches to follow. Beale chose to divert his group from established trails and leave no traces crossing a rocky area or the bed of a stony stream. Once off that public trail, Beale's party would have left no detectable tracks. The Montvale area of Bedford County does have some rock-faced surfaces and many streams and creeks.

The creek route would be consistent with another part of Ward's deciphered story. Beale supposedly put the pots on solid rock and lined the "vault" and covered it with rocks. Bedford terrain is generally not littered with rocks. But creek beds are. If you wanted to dig a hole and line it with rocks, you could do this readily if you were close to a creek.

How big would the hole have been? We can calculate the volume for each metal. We can estimate the size of the iron pots and the number of them. Then we can calculate how big a hole would be needed to put it all in. Before we calculate, we must make assumptions about the nature of the gold and silver. Was it ore? Was it pure metal? Prospectors and miners do find gold nuggets. More common is placer gold : dust mixed in the soil. It can be separated out by careful washing. But silver ore usually needs some smelting. The following analysis presumes that the silver has been reasonably refined before transporting.

Pure (24 carat) gold weighs a bit more than 1200 pounds per cubic foot, and pure silver weighs almost 650 pounds per cubic foot. The Beale crew probably used bags that could have been handled easily by one man. The pots mentioned may have been employed only for the actual burial. If the material travelled in the pots, or was inside pots carried by mules, then the pots would have to have been relatively small.

A pot holding about 200 pounds or so could strain one man, but two could handle it. If the 200 pounds were gold, it would fit nicely into a two-gallon pot, with room to spare. If the 200 pounds were silver, it would need close to a three-gallon pot. The first load could have fit inside 20 three-gallon pots. The second load could have fit in 10 three-gallon pots. These calculations presume that the metals had some extraneous rock or ore mixed in, so we'll assume some wasted space.

If only large pots were used, the volume needs would be slightly different. Three twenty-gallon pots could hold the first load, and two twenty-gallon pots would be big enough for the second load.

Miss Jean Hamilton told the 1981 Beale Cypher Symposium that her analysis finds that there was a total of seven iron pots.

The hole dug would have to have been oversized in order to accom-

7 — Carry to Virginia

modate the lining of rocks described in the Ward decipher solution. The pots were put on existing rock. Suppose that an eight-inch layer of rocks were used on all sides and then on top of the pots; the hole still would not be very large. For the first load, a hole of about 30 to 40 cubic feet would do. Exact proportions would depend upon what size pots were used and how they were arranged. But even allowing for gaps between pots, we can calculate a hole just about the size of a typical refrigerator.

A rectangular hole might be 2x3x6 feet or a round hole about 3 or 4 feet in diameter and 4 feet deep. The "vault" need not have been a great big room. Beale must have had mixed emotions when he put the treasure in, took a last look, and then covered it up. He carefully noted nearby landmarks and estimated that he was about four miles from Buford's.

If, on his second Buford visit, Beale saw that no one had disturbed the first treasure, he probably would have used the same site again.

How could you dig a hole and not leave evidence? Cover the hole with leaves? Cover it with rocks? You could move existing rocks, dig the hole, throw most of the dirt in a stream, line the hole with small rocks, put the pots in, cover them with rocks, and then put back some dirt and cover the work by putting back the original rocks. Maybe Beale found a cave, filled it, and then covered it with a big rock.

Or you could remove something like a casket, bury everything under the casket, and then replace the casket, knowing that it would be unlikely for someone to tamper with the dead.

Digging a suitable hole would have been hard work. Much of Bedford County soil is somewhat like firm clay. A cave would have been easier. Beale indicated that he and his associates were familiar with the area. There is one cave that he said he had considered but dismissed because it was too well known. There are other natural cavities that he may have used and then covered up.

The first load alone might have involved 20 small iron pots. If Beale had no wagon, it would have been awkward for mules to carry big pots that would be noticeably gone after the burial. Either way, there would be no sense in bringing iron pots from the West to the East. But buying them in Buford's would have raised eyebrows. They could have been acquired just a few days earlier, in Fincastle or Buchanan.

Beale need to be sure that those ten confederates of his first trip would not come back and dig up the loot or ultimately tell someone else. The story might leak out eventually. There must have been important incentives for the twenty other men to have been willing to stay behind in

Santa Fe? Did they figure that there was so much more in the ground that they were glad to see Beale and the ten men depart so that they could keep the mines to themselves?

Legendary pirate captains kept their secrets intact by implementing the slogan "dead men tell no tales." But Beale would have had trouble eliminating ten men. One or two, perhaps. But ten? Surely if he started picking them off, some would have seen the trend and done him in instead. Maybe he paid them off so generously that the buried loot seemed superfluous. Or were they so dedicated to him or some cause that they did whatever he asked them to.

When Beale returned in late 1821, he would have needed precise landmarks to guide him to the burial site. Trees do get blown over. Streams wander. But there are several ways he could have made a navigational fix. He could have used the intersection where a major trail or road crossed a creek or river. He could have relied on obvious sight lines, such as the alignment of the peaks of two prominent mountains or distinctive hills or knolls and the intersection of two such sight lines.

The Beale Papers leads to Goose Creek Valley in Bedford County. The decoded cipher No. 2 says that the treasure is buried about four miles from Buford's, which is today called Montvale. This area does have distinctive topography. The famous Peaks of Otter mountains are nearby. Other mountains contain the valley. There are streams and creeks.

One man believes that the treasure lies at the point of the shadow of Sharp Top Mountain. That shadow falls at a different spot at different times of day and on different days of the year. He hasn't figured out the precise moment to consider yet. He hopes that when he does it will not be a cloudy day.

A traveler passing along US 460 through Bedford County might well fail to see the great natural beauty of Goose Creek Valley. He may get the impression that Montvale is just an oil tank depot. But for treasure hunters, Montvale is a magnet.

8.
Blue Ridge Vault

Montvale is not what it used to be. Since Beale's visit of 1819, roads have been improved and some have been deleted. The center of "town" has moved, and even the name has changed. Churches spring up, disappear or endure and grow. Industry changes. Only the geography is the same.

Montvale is in a beautiful bowl-like valley, bisected by US 460. On the south are Wiggington Knob and Porter's Mountain. To the east are Taylor's and McFall's Mountains. On the west and north are the Blue Ridge Mountains, atop which runs the Blue Ridge Parkway, built just before World War II. The valley walls drain down into streams that, in turn, join to form Goose Creek, which then meanders eastward.

Entering Montvale from the cities of Lynchburg or Bedford from the east is relatively easy: there is just rolling terrain. Coming from Roanoke and the southwest is also reasonably easy, with level passage through Buford's Gap. But travel from Fincastle, to the west, or Buchanan, to the north, is more of a challenge: you must climb up and over the Blue Ridge.

This area was long known as Buford's. It changed its name to Bufordville in 1876, and finally in 1890 to Montvale. Informal names were Buford's

Tourists get a broad view of Goose Creek Valley from the Blue Ridge Parkway.

Depot or Buford's Station. Goose Creek itself was once called Tiber. Most of the area was granted by King George III to the four Buford brothers: Thomas, William, James, and Henry. William moved to Kentucky fairly early on, and James moved there later. Thomas died from wounds at the battle of Point Pleasant in 1774. Henry stayed in Bedford County and became a prominent citizen. Some kinfolk settled in Botetourt County.

Henry was appointed High Sheriff by the governor. He also operated a tavern and inn that was the convenient stopping place for travelers. He could not have known that the site of his family business would be the center of an enduring treasure hunt.

And in 1822, when Henry died, his son Paschal took over the business and built a new brick home. Behind it is an old chimney; legend says it is the last remnant of the Buford's tavern where Beale is said to have stayed.

Paschal was an enterprising man who traded in real estate, operated at least two water-powered mills, established a stage coach line, built and operated a turnpike to Buchanan in 1851, had a US Mail contract, donated land for the railroad right-of-way, and was a Justice of the Peace. Because of his influence, and the prominence of other family members who continued to hold land, it is not surprising that the area was commonly called "Buford's."

There was traffic between Buford's and the town of Fincastle, which was the county seat of Botetourt County about twenty miles westward and was a gateway to the West. Travelers from Liberty (now city of Bedford) enroute to Fincastle could also visit Buford's tavern before riding up and over the mountain into Botetourt County.

Other traffic directly westward went from Buford's, through Buford's Gap, then to Big Lick, and to the frontier. This was the main route even in the earliest times. The Indians were the first to realize that, although the route was longer, it was much easier than climbing up and over the Blue Ridge. This old path was widened and became a segment of the Lynchburg-Salem Turnpike; today it is the four-lane US 460. Big Lick is now known as Roanoke.

In the 1700's and early 1800's, activity centered around Buford's tavern. This was true until the railroad came. The Virginia and Tennessee RR (which ultimately became part of the Norfolk and Western Railway) laid down tracks in 1851. The first train came through in 1852. The railroad station was located almost a mile northeast of Buford's tavern.

The railway depot then became the center of action. A bank was built across the way. Next to that was the Montrose Hotel. Nearby was the

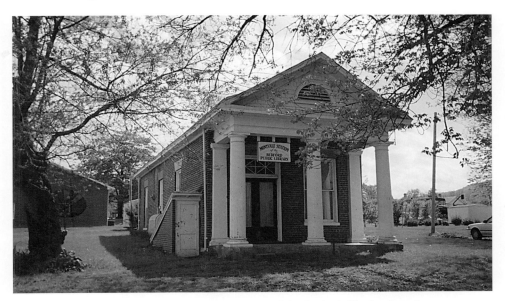

The bank building is a lonely remnant of the Bufordville Station plaza.

general store. Today the station is gone, the hotel is gone, and the bank was last used as a branch of the Bedford Public Library. On maps the center still appears to be the station area, but motorists on US 460 miss this area completely.

Also on Buford land, just east of the tavern, was a small airport. Aviator James Buford was the last family member to operate it. Profound changes came in 1963 when a pipeline was laid down through the area near the airport and a petroleum depot sprang up in the lowland of the valley. Major oil companies bought more than 500 acres and erected tanks for storing oil and gasoline. No more runways. (The old hangar, now painted bright green, is used as a truck maintenance facility.) The "tank farms" and the attendant pumping equipment represent a major investment of capital, but the number of employees required for the operation is few.

The decoded cipher No. 2 says that the treasure is "deposited in the county of Bedford, about four miles from Buford's, in an excavation or vault, six feet below the surface...."

Some treasure seekers limit their search to within four miles of Buford's and interpret the "Buford's" starting point to mean Paschal Buford's brick house (on Route 460) or the old Bufordville/Montvale railroad depot (now gone). But others who believe they have solved the ciphers allow themselves to search beyond those four miles.

The tip of Sharp Top Mountain can be seen from Montvale. This view from Sharp Top Mountain looks back towards Taylor's Mountain (left foreground), Montvale petroleum tanks (right), and Wiggington Knob (deep right).

There are treasure hunters who believe that Beale's party would have deposited the valuable cargo where a route crosses the crest, such as the Black Horse Gap, or at Bobblet's Gap, or at Bearwallow Gap, where the road to Buchanan crosses.

A favorite suspected site is up the mountain, towards Fincastle. Some theories focus on a Black Horse Tavern of long ago. There is confusion as to where the Tavern was. Some believe it was three miles from Buford's, high near the crest of the Blue Ridge. Once part of the original land grant to the Henry Buford, the site is now a part of federal land.

This rumored location of the old Black Horse Tavern is a favorite site for Beale prospectors. It is just 0.6 miles south of — and downhill from — the Blue Ridge Parkway's Black Horse Gap, on the east side of what was once the "Sweet Springs" stagecoach road. There, with a spring across the road, is a flat spot of several acres, covered over with periwinkle. The site would be suitable for a cabin or house. However, the only ruins there give no evidence of ever being part of substantial structure.

The gap in the mountain ridge was a gateway for one of the shortest routes between Liberty and Fincastle and was one of the early paths for travelers. Here, weary horses could be rested before heading down again.

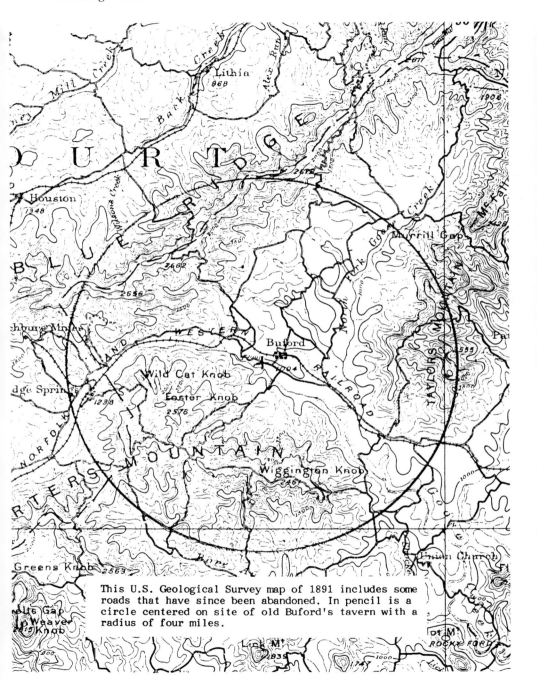

This U.S. Geological Survey map of 1891 includes some roads that have since been abandoned. In pencil is a circle centered on site of old Buford's tavern with a radius of four miles.

Later, the route was used by those going to the spas or "sweet springs" of West Virginia. Over time the route came to be called the "Sweet Springs Road." No one knows for sure how Black Horse Gap got its name. One legend says that Buford was riding in the mountains near there when his black stallion was suddenly struck in the head and killed by a hunter's stray bullet.

This path through the gap was improved by the Bufordville and Fincastle Turnpike Company and completed as a commercial toll road in 1835. On the flat spot, the turnpike owners set up their tollhouse, known as Mountain Gate. The toll collector lived there. It was not a tavern, although he would let travelers spend the night if need be. Fences made of piled rocks held animals overnight.

When the railroads began to serve more communities, stagecoach traffic diminished. Some sheep ranchers and cattlemen would still drive their herds between Bedford county and the Shenandoah valley, but people mostly rode the train. Soon the tollhouse no longer mattered and finally no one lived at the Gate at all. The house deteriorated and yielded to the elements.

David T. Thaxton acquired the land in 1863 from the Burns family of Botetourt. Others also owned it over the next century. In 1981 the site left private hands; the U.S. Forest Service bought it and the surrounding 368 acres for a reported price of $114,207.

The confusion about the Black Horse Tavern location probably started in the 1930's when some young people from the neighboring village of Villamont came upon the abandoned site of the toll house. One of them recalled hearing about a Black Horse Tavern in this direction, somewhere or other. They assumed that this was the place, so they named it the Black Horse Tavern. Then, when the boys of the Civil Conservation Corps (CCC) were clearing fire trails there, they used that name too. The name has persisted to date.

It is doubtful that in 1819 there was enough traffic going up and over the mountain to justify a tavern at the spot. Black Horse Tavern did indeed exist. But not here. It was to the west, out of Bedford County, into Botetourt County, down past the foot of the mountain, near Hollins and Cloverdale.

Two Pennsylvania couples started their Beale treasure search by looking for the tavern. A Galveston couple also felt that the supposed location of the Black Horse Tavern was important. They concluded that a tavern would have needed to be near a spring and that there would be a big rock near it. Instead of being at the crest of a hill, they suspected that it would have been down the slope towards Montvale. Using this logic, they visited a likely spot — the spot of the former tollhouse — and saw that others had been there before them. They found a machine-made hole, perhaps 10 feet wide, 30 feet long, and 6 feet deep.

Experienced treasure hunters know that it is illegal to go dig anywhere you want. There is no such thing as land that "nobody owns." Unless you own the land, you need permission to disturb property. Government land has its own special rules.

The Mountain Gate area is now U.S. Forest Service land and abuts the U.S. Park Service land of the Blue Ridge Parkway. Green "USNPS" markers show the boundaries of the Park land. On the National Park Service land, no digging is allowed and no permits for digging are available. The Forest Service will consider permits, but no one can remember an example of a permit actually being issued.

Digging for treasure is prohibited on Federal and City of Bedford property. Six Pennsylvanians were reminded of these restrictions in a costly way. Two couples and two men, all members of the same church, made three secret trips to Bedford to search for the treasure. At night or during Federal holidays when they assumed that fewer rangers would come by, they dug seven pits. In 1991, U.S. Magistrate Glen Conrad made them pay restitution to fill in the pits and warned that they would be jailed and each fined $5,000 if they dug again.

But there has been digging in private lands near the Park lands. The map on page196 shows some of the known dig locations. Many holes were covered up after hunters failed to find the "vault." They come in, make a quick dig, and then are gone.

There are mysterious holes near the Fincastle crossover. After exploring the area, one man said it looked "devastated, like Iwo Jima." It appears that in this remote area some people don't wait to get approval. They just dig and hope they don't get caught. One man says, "It's a covert operation, like in Vietnam."

Another prospective treasure spot is on the old route to Buchanan that goes up and over the mountains near Bobblet's Gap. Some seekers think that Black Horse Tavern was here. About a mile or so from the ridge is a rambling house that has underneath its aluminum siding an 1820 log building. Several hunters have homed in on this site. The owner has graciously let them dig. One dug a fair-sized hole and uncovered as his only prize the lid of an antique washing machine.

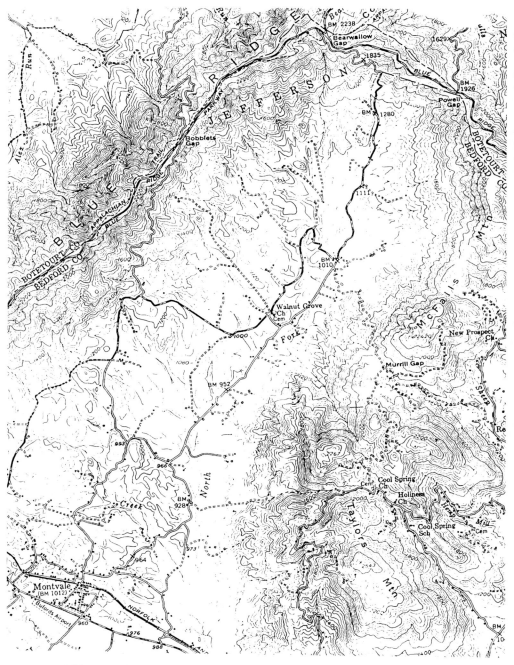

This 1950 Geological Survey map of the U.S. Deparment of the Interior shows contours and major topographic features.

Joseph Durand, encouraged by the Cheyenne legend passed down by his family, has researched the Beale story and concluded that the site is near Bobblet's Gap, just over the line into Botetourt County, on U.S. Forest Service property. His interest concentrates on a 65-foot deep cave, which could be the treasure site or may have been an old mine. He and Bedford farmer Jimmy Luck have been seeking permission from the government to dig, but after several years, no permit has yet been granted.

About forty years ago, Margaret McGhee Ballard dreamed that the treasure was on land she owned — near Bobblet's Gap. She persuaded her daughter, Peggy Maupin, and grandson, Harry, that it might be there. Peggy said, "We went out there. We watched as Harry dug, and dug, and dug. We found nothing." That spot is now federal property, part of the Blue Ridge Parkway land.

The Parsons case ignited interest in a different area: near Mountain View Church. This is four miles south of Montvale and US 460, near Porter's Mountain. One evening, a western Virginia couple who enjoy hiking and treasure hunting began trudging around Porter's Mountain. Later, they emerged some miles from where they had left their car. They didn't find the treasure. They did find that snakes were around the rocks even at night.

Mountain View Church is high on Wiggington Knob. It is reached by negotiating a twisting, gravel road that follows alongside a rocky stream. About a mile away is a microwave relay tower. There are some homes here and there alongside the mountain road.

The date of the founding of the church or its cemetery is unrecorded. The brick exterior of the church is a 1981 renovation and covers the original white weatherboard. The structure itself was dedicated in 1892 and built on a half acre of land donated by M.M. Giles, next to an earlier site and cemetery. On that old site once stood a log building which was used as a school and meeting house and whose date of origin is not known. Baptist records report that the "mission station" Sunday school was flourishing as early as 1868. No earlier references have been found. Three pastors met in that old building in 1891 and organized the new church, which was to be used by Baptists, Church of the Brethren, Methodists, and Presbyterians. Only the Baptists have used it with any regularity.

The cemetery of Mountain View Church is in two sections. A few hundred yards away is the modern graveyard with modern headstones.

Nearer the church is the old graveyard where the headstones are just rocks, painted white. Long ago, such simple markers were used for slave graves. But church officials say that no blacks were buried here. It is near these rocks that Parson's backhoe started to dig. Ten years later, the scars of the dig have been covered by time.

Behind and below the church is a stream, that starts with a trickle and gains momentum as it twists down the mountain, spilling and splashing over a rocky route to finally join Goose Creek miles below. A horse would have a hard time going up or down a stream like this one without injuring a leg.

A different route did exist long ago. An 1887 map shows a parallel route up the mountain, slightly west of the present road. It ran on the crest of the terrain, rather than next to the stream in the hollows. It may have been easier to negotiate. Maybe Beale took this path if the church was his destination.

Another church on another mountain has also fascinated treasure hunters. It is the Cool Spring Church over on Taylor's Mountain, four miles northeast of Montvale. Sharon Dooley, who lived near it, recalls hearing about people wanting to dig under a giant boulder that sits in front of the church. The Reverend Cyndi Grubbs was told that folks had in the past inquired about obtaining permission to dig in the church basement.

Cool Spring Church is on an isolated and high spot of land. Parishioners come up a narrow, twisting gravel road that roughly follows the path of a stream. That stream, like the one to Wiggington's Knob, is steep, tortuous and rocky. Even the best of trail horses would have trouble climbing it. A few generations ago the area was a world apart from the rest of the County. Lula Jeter Parker, noted Bedford County historian, wrote that back in those days "lack of school and church privileges produced a condition of ignorance and lawlessness."

Times have changed. School buses now bring area children down to the public schools in Montvale. Taylor's Mountain residents are fully involved in the Bedford community.

The Cool Spring Church building is well maintained. Dedicated in 1915, it replaced a log building whose original date is not recorded. The church cemetery is well fenced, with handsome headstones that include the names of Dooley, Orange and Ruff.

Mrs. Jean Kokette's cipher solution locates the treasure on the hillside just below the church. But the very top of Taylor's Mountain is where

Some treasure hunters wanted to dig beneath Cool Spring Presbyterian Church on Taylor's Mountain.

two Kentucky men wanted to dig. They told the landowner that satellite data revealed a major ore lode there. The owner, a civil engineer, replied, "Send me $2500, we'll draw up a 50-50 contract, and I'll let you dig on three spots." Apparently the Kentuckians were not that sure of themselves; after four years, they still hadn't accept the deal.

9.
Two West or Ten East?

Not near Montvale? How about two miles west?

"Buford's" could mean the center of the community of Bufordville: the home of Paschal Buford. Most researchers interpret it to mean Buford's Tavern, where Beale is supposed to have stayed.

The brick Buford home, on the south side of Route 460 in Montvale, is the focus of much interest, because behind the house are the ruins of an old building and a large stone chimney. This chimney has been photographed and used in magazine articles and TV shows to symbolize the starting point for searching for the treasure site. The general story is that these ruins are all that remains of the old Buford's Tavern.

This stone chimney is all that remains of a building behind the 1822 brick home of Paschal Buford.

This may be an erroneous assumption. First of all, the brick Buford house was built about 1822, which is after Beale made his visits to the tavern. But most convincing is the comment made to me by Lucy Buford. Miss Buford, a teacher, lived most of her life in the Buford house. Shortly before she died in 1989, she told me that the ruins were once the home of the local Episcopal minister. The tavern, she said, was about two miles to the west of the oft-photographed chimney.

9 — Two West or Ten East?

If the cipher translation refers to Buford's tavern, then the four-mile radius circle should be centered two miles west of Montvale, near Villamont. A Colonel Holland is said to have visited the area several times. Once, he hired a backhoe to excavate an old stone furnace near Villamont, the present name for an area once known at Ironville.

An 1820 map of main routes of Botetourt County shows just a single road connecting to Bedford County. Other routes either didn't exist or were too crude to be included. The route shown then passed through Buford's Gap, where US 460 does today. So some seekers deduce that the vault is not far from U.S. 460, west of Montvale. There is a spring on the north side of 460 at Villamont.

Mr. Nat Harvey, Resident Engineer of the State Highway Department, recalls that in the late 1970's a man requested a permit to dig up the spring. The Department refused, but did allow digging of some test holes. The man was so certain of finding it that he paid an off-duty Sheriff's Deputy eight dollars per hour to be present to guard the bounty. After five hours of laborious work, the man gave up the search.

E.J. Easterling, a postal worker, drew attention to an area just west of the mill — land which had long been in his family. Easterling, who compiled *In Search of a Golden Vault*, organized a "safari" tour of familiarization of the tract. He indicated that it would take some time and special probing before the exact vault location could be pinpointed. And, through the media, he offered to be a consultant to people seeking the treasure.

Also near Villamont, a Tennessee businessman had an almost surreal experience. He weekended in Bedford about once a year to refine his treasure search. One spring day, he climbed a stony trail to a knoll above Villamont and then paused to check out the area. He put down his video camera and his red tote bag and began gently sweeping with his metal detector. He stopped when he sensed that he was being watched. He had heard nothing, but upon slowly turning around, he was startled to see, staring at him, three weather-beaten horsemen, all wearing big-rimmed dark hats and long, leather coats. Two of them slowly and solemnly passed him by.

The third man clamped his teeth and complained, "That red thing there spooked my horse," and then asked, "What are you doing here?"

The business man felt intimidated and defensively replied, "I'm sorry. Isn't this a beautiful day?"

The horseman demanded an answer, "What are you doing here?"

The treasure hunter responded, "I didn't mean to bother anybody. I'm looking for the Beale Treasure."

Before he could grab his camera to record what he was seeing, the horseman prodded his stead and barked a quick reply, "It's not here. It's over there—" and pointed to the east and quickly disappeared down the trail.

Would a horse really be spooked by a red tote bag?

A cave could hold a treasure. There is one at Ironville that is a favorite, even though Beale says in *The Beale Papers* that he rejected that particular site. North of U.S. 460 and just west of Montvale, the cave is about 100 yards deep. Montvale resident Frank Smith explored it years ago. The only notable thing he found inside was a dead collie that had apparently fallen into a pit from which it couldn't climb out.

Robert Scott Carr, Jr., who lives near Montvale, has guided several people to that cave. Some of the folks wanted to look in the cave itself, while others just stand next to it and use it as a reference point while sighting other landmarks.

Beale may have put his hoard into a cave, boarded it up, and then sealed it with rocks and dirt. Such a cave would not be easily recognized. Bill Rodenburg, a former civil engineer, suggests that careful analysis of seismographic data would indicate where other caves may be.

Barite was mined near Villamont starting in 1866 when the area was known as Ironville. It is conceivable that mining excavations might look like caves. But cartographer Robert Murr notes that limestone breaks down over time. He has found several such cavities that are not on maps. It is possible that any Beale treasure pots that had been atop limestone could have sunk six feet deeper or more by now.

Floridians Claude deGolyer and David Workman and his son have visited four caves in Bedford County; some may be abandoned iron mines.

There is a tale about a different cave, one not far from Walnut Grove Church. It was discovered on a winter day because warm air was coming from the ground. It is said that young men used a rope to lower themselves down into what seemed like a room. At the end of the space was a stream. This tale has not been verified.

One Beale aficionado says the treasure is even further west of Villamont, near the Norfolk & Western railroad track, where it was unloaded from a slow moving train one night. If *The Beale Papers* are true, then this notion is not. The railroad didn't exist in this part of Virginia until thirty years after Beale buried his treasure.

9 — Two West or Ten East?

Some caves resulted from mining; others are natural. The sign says, "Mel. It ain't here."

A Minnesota man suggested that Beale may have taken the easy way to stash his treasure, without having to cover it up or dig a hole. Perhaps he just lowered the pots down into a cistern.

Walnut Grove Church, four miles north of Montvale in Goose Creek Valley, is another suspected site. It has a graveyard atop a knoll just above the church building. Most of the graves are marked with modern engraved headstones. But there are some graves that are marked only by ordinary, unpainted rocks. No treasure find has been reported at this church. But at least one treasure digger has found the church bathroom to be a handy place to wash the dirt off tired hands.

Walnut Grove Church hasn't always been at this site, which is on land that was donated by Rev. G.P. Luck. The present building, erected in 1909, replaced one that had burned down three years earlier. And the burned one replaced another structure that had been dedicated in 1870.

But prior to that, the church was a mile or so further away from Montvale. It was originally Methodist and named Smyrna Church, built on land given by James Bunch. This building served as a school during the Civil War. After this one burned down, the parishioners decided to change its name and rebuild on the new Luck site closer to town.

If the pamphlet author wanted readers to look near this church, the author may have erred. The church is now within 4 miles of Buford's, but back in 1820 and 1822, it was a bit more than 4 miles away.

Walnut Grove Church. The prior church building was further from Buford's in the 1820's than this present Walnut Grove Church.

The church's first site tantalizes Beale hunters because it is near a point where Goose Creek crosses the early road trail between Buford's and Buchanan.

It would make sense to bury a treasure near a stream. Travelers used streams as their road maps, and streams and rivers run fairly level. A stream is a good source of rocks, and a stream will not show hoofprints.

At the third Symposium of the Beale Cypher Association, Miss Jean Hamilton, gave one solution to Cypher No. 1. Her set of directions said to follow Goose Creek Trail to Murrill Gap Trail. "Leave the trail there, and where a small creek meets a larger one, up a mound, near an oak tree" is where the pots are buried.

A New Yorker told a Bedford realtor that the treasure was under a rock, with an "X" chiseled on it, in the middle of a stream. The realtor is keeping the location to herself until she can figure out how to strike a deal with the landowner. He has in the past prohibited any digging and rejected offers.

A middle-aged woman twice hired Kenneth Dooley to use his backhoe to dig for her in Goose Creek Valley. Each time she directed him to a very specific spot, limited to about 10 or 20 feet across. Each time, she was certain that "this was the place." Dooley says that after finding nothing, her reaction was typical of most others. "They shrug their shoulders and go home to save up more money so they can come back again for another try."

The property of Lee Dooley (no close kin of Kenneth), north of Montvale, holds special fascination for Beale buffs. Ruth Daniloff, wife of journalist Nicholas Daniloff (who was held in the Fall of 1986 by the KGB in Moscow on spy charges), visited Bedford on July 26, 1980. She wrote the feature article about the Beale treasure that appeared in the April 1981 issue of *Smithsonian* magazine. Her article had a photo of Lee Dooley, whose land abuts that of Otis Dooley. She wrote that many folks had wanted to search on his land and that he would let them if they guaranteed that he would get 25% of whatever they found.

It is said that some Texas folks spent weeks at a nearby motel and paid for the right to dig on some Montvale land. They rented a backhoe and even a jackhammer. After the hired help quit work each day, the landowner was allowed to use the equipment for tasks on his farm.

Other Westerners were so sure that they knew exactly where the treasure was that they bought a specific acre of land from Dooley. But they found no treasure after all.

The Dooley land could have been a good place to bury a treasure. It is near an established trail. The Creek crosses there. One problem with this idea: it is significantly more than 4 miles from today's Montvale and even further away from Buford's of 1819.

Nevertheless, in the summer of 1986, a middle-aged couple from the Midwest dug at the foot of the Dooley driveway. They seemed to be living in their big white Mercury. They dug with determination, even on rainy days. One would dig, and the other would pull up the bucket of dirt. An observer estimates that they got 15 feet deep. They finally hit water, so they rented a pump. But their metal detector found nothing. Mr. Dooley was concerned about a cave-in and made them fill it back up.

Kenneth Dooley used his backhoe to dig near Route 460 for a small Florida gentleman, who "was as nice a man as you'd ever meet." He visited Montvale several times. At first he came alone. On another visit, he brought along his son, but the younger man wasn't really interested.

On the first dig, the man was "excited and uptight." As Dooley dug, he asked what the man would do with the treasure if he found it. He said he hadn't really thought about that. So Dooley said, "If you find it, you'd better be careful that you don't get a heart attack."

Road name signs were erected throughout Bedford County in 1997.

Each time, Ken Dooley was directed to a specific place and hired for just an hour or two. In all, he dug three sites, all within a quarter mile of each other. The deepest was fifteen feet.

The field can get crowded. Two Floridians went to check out the ruins of Wilkerson's mill, which burned down in 1937. As they neared the ruins, they were surprised to see three men already there, on the other side of Goose Creek. And what were the men doing? Digging.

Some solutions to the ciphers involve clues that relate to animal names. Charles Burton remembers being asked by a hunter who was a California state policeman

9 — Two West or Ten East?

if there was any place or landmark in Bedford "named after an animal that was dirty." Burton said we have the "Peaks of Otter." But the Californian said that wasn't it; otters are clean. Quite independently — and several years apart — Burton heard that same question, only this time from some New Yorkers who had formed a corporation to solve the Beale puzzle. Hogs? Pigs? There is Bearwallow Gap; that's where the Blue Ridge Parkway is crossed by today's road from Buchanan to Montvale.

A New Jersey man told a Roanoke librarian that he had solved cipher No. 1: the treasure is underneath a ladies' privy at the Peaks of Otter. This is well beyond four miles from Montvale.

There has been a growing belief that the treasure is not located within four miles of Montvale, but instead is some ten miles to the east, near the Peaks of Otter. The final letter to Morris from Beale was dated 1822. At that time, Paschal Buford was a man of substance; his holdings included a tavern, water mills, his own home and a large plantation with an elegant house. This plantation, known as Fancy Farm, was far from his tavern — about ten miles east.

The house is at the base of the Peaks of Otter in the rural community known as Kelso Mill, some five miles north of the City of Bedford and a hundred yards north of Northside Supply, the social and commercial enterprise where residents get their pickups serviced and buy gas, hardware, groceries, farm boots and lottery tickets. Northside regulars stop by the first thing each day for coffee and a chance to share comments on world and neighborhood news.

The plantation has been reduced in size over the years, but the house still stands and is a private residence. The book, *Peaks of Otter — Life and Times*, details the history of the area and this house. It was built about 1780 by Andrew Donald, a Scotland-born merchant. Paschal Buford bought the plantation in 1820 for $19,200.

Since this property was "Buford's" at the time of Beale's letters, some hunters begin their four-mile radius search there, rather than in Montvale. There is no record of his actually living there, and it is unlikely that the treasure was buried there. Buford sold it in 1823 and lost money in the process; buyer John W. Scott paid him just $15,000. As far as the Beale Treasure is concerned, Fancy Farm itself is not a treasure site, rather it is merely a geographical reference point.

A four-mile radius centered on Kelso would include part of what are known as the Peaks of Otter. Some treasure hunters are concentrating near the two mountains.

Northside Supply, on Route 43, at base of Peaks of Otter mountains — Sharp Top (L.) and Flat Top (R.).

9 — Two West or Ten East?

Sharp Top and Flat Top — the two Peaks of Otter — can be seen for miles and miles around. Sharp Top, once known as the South Peak of Otter, has a pointed tip which makes it appear taller than Flat Top, though it is actually falls 26 feet short of Flat Top's 4001 feet. The tip of Sharp Top Mountain is four air miles from Fancy Farm, as the crow flies. Montvale can be seen from Sharp Top Mountain, and Sharp Top can be seen from Montvale.

In the 1770's, traders and wagon freighters traveling between Buchanan (on the James River) and Liberty (now the City of Bedford) would pass between the two mountains. The trail has been refined over the years to ease the steepness of the climb. Today, at that pass, the Peaks of Otter Lodge hosts guests with fine food and comfortable accommodations.

Two miles from Northside Supply, a retired Texas doctor with a twinkle in his eye made a vacation out of treasure hunting, while respecting property rights. He narrowed his search with a "sensing probe," which has the unexplainable effectiveness of a dowsing rod. First, he held his swinging, telescoping antenna device, which pointed horizontally, to the treasure mass. After driving around and getting a number of sight lines, he zeroed in on a specific spot.

He would not sneak in and be a midnight miner. With his target firmly in mind, he enlisted the help of a local attorney and made a deal with the land owner. The written agreement allowed the doctor to dig, and he and the property owner would split any treasure (on a specified percentage ratio). If he found no treasure, he would fill up the hole and restore the land to its original condition. If he failed to do that, he would forfeit a $1,000 escrow which he had deposited with the lawyer.

The doctor rented a motor home, hired a back hoe, and invited his son and his brother to join the project. Each day, the hoe operator dug this way and that way. Deeper here, there. After a week of digging, they realized that they had not found the Beale Treasure. But they found a different kind of treasure. There, in the shadow of a mighty Peaks of Otter, away from the mundane routines of life, the three men relished a camaraderie they hadn't had for years.

They refilled the hole, and the doctor retrieved his $1,000 check. Before driving away in his motor home, he stopped by to say good-bye and told me, "That was great. What a beautiful place to spend a vacation. Even after paying for the hoe, it was cheaper than some fancy resort. We had a wonderful time, the best time together in years and years."

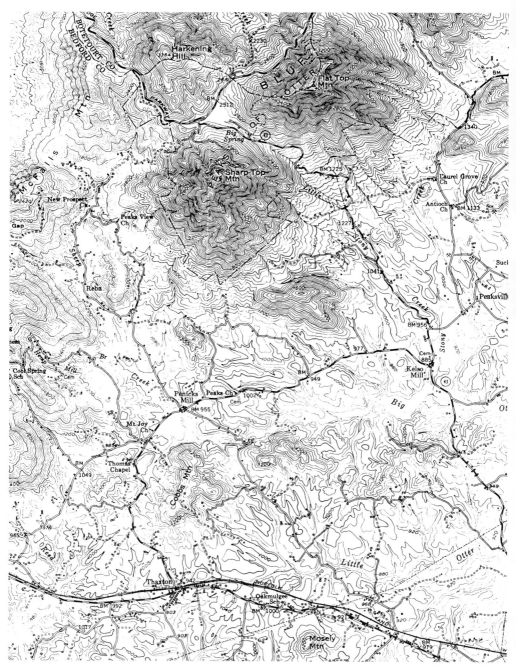

U.S. Geological Survey map shows topographical details around Kelso and the Peaks of Otter.

9 — Two West or Ten East?

A mile north of the doctor's vacation spot, a small, moustached California computer programmer kept an excavating contractor busy for months. Convinced that he had solved the ciphers, he made a verbal deal with the dairy farmer to share any treasure. He believed that the treasure lay beneath a huge boulder which, over the decades, had slid down the mountain slope.

The programmer stayed in Bedford month after month, as the hoe man dug around and beneath the giant monolith, which a farmer described as "bigger than a post office." The digging reached twenty feet down. Could Beale have dug down so deep? Could that rock really have moved to be atop the vault?

This project took longer than expected, and the Californian sought investors to share in the costs, for which they would share the rewards of the search. When I asked, "Don't you think that if it was there, you would have found it by now?" he earnestly replied, "It's there all right. Just a few feet more." The field crew of the TV series *Unsolved Mysteries* captured some of this dig on film, before the man finally gave up and returned home, without the treasure.

There are hunters who reject any mileage limit at all. They think that the deciphered message No. 2 may be incorrect. Perhaps the treasure is in a completely different area of Virginia. Col. Holland derived clues that pointed to Fort Early, in Lynchburg, but dismissed the idea, since the fort was built during the Civil War and wasn't even in existence in 1822. Another man believes that the treasure is in the more western county of Wythe. Or maybe in Kentucky.

One 1970 search centered in a Lynchburg cemetery, 40 miles from Montvale. Cass Ott, a Chicago refrigeration contractor, said he solved the ciphers. He got necessary government approvals, and then he and city workmen dug in a grassy part of the City (Old Methodist) Cemetery. Instead of treasure, they found scraps of horseshoes and coat hangers.

Over the years, the areas that have been most scrutinized are from Montvale west to Villamont, and north and northeast to Blue Ridge Mountains. There is hardly an area that has escaped the eyes, or detectors, or "vibes" of the treasure hunter.

And still there is no solid evidence that there ever was a treasure. Could it be that there never was a Thomas J. Beale? What can be found about the man himself? Who was this man Beale?

10.
The Virginian

According to *The Beale Papers,* Beale was "…a gentleman well-educated, evidently of good family, and with popular manners." The pamphlet quotes Robert Morriss as saying that back in January 1820 Beale had come to his lodging place in the company of two others and said he was "from Virginia, but I am of the impression he was from some Western portion of the State." Morriss said that "all were refined and with courteous manners, with a free and independent air, which rendered them peculiarly attractive." Beale himself "had a friendly demeanor... [and was] extremely popular... particularly with the ladies."

Morriss recalled that Beale was about six feet tall, had "jet black eyes and hair of the same color, worn longer than was the style of the time." He "gave evidence of unusual strength and activity; ....woe to the man who offended him." The author further quoted Morriss: "his distinguishing feature was a dark and swarthy complexion.... I thought him the handsomest man I had ever seen."

A Virginia psychic sees Beale as about five feet, ten inches tall, with dark hair and skin, and fairly good looking. She says Beale was a dynamic, charismatic personality who was a leader of men. He was charming, but an ambitious, driven man who would stop at nothing — even murder. He sought out and associated with politicians and others of power. She says he died in the desert.

Miss Jean Hamilton raised the possibility that Beale could speak German. She observed that the letters to Morris are the work of a "very well educated man." Another suggested that he wasn't an American but an adventurer Englishman.

A fair number of folks believe that there really was a Thomas J. Beale. Some 41% of the attendees at the 1986 BCA Symposium thought that he definitely existed. An additional 24% thought it is probable. One in three thought he is fictitious.

In 1982 an article seriously shook the confidence of many treasure enthusiasts. Investigative writer Joe Nickell wrote in *Virginia* magazine that "one must conclude that both Thomas Jefferson Beale and his fabulous treasure were fictitious and that James B. Ward was the author of the fraudulent Beale Papers." Nickell made a convincing case. He detailed an analysis of the writing style of Beale's letters (of 1822) and of the pamphlet (of 1885) and said the author was one and the same person. This article caused a number of Beale fans to stop any further pursuit. Maybe it is all fiction. Maybe there never was a Thomas Jefferson Beale. Or a Thomas J. Beale. Or a Thomas Beale.

Nickell commissioned a survey of the U.S. Census records of 1810. Those records showed no Thomas Beale in Virginia and no Thomas J. Beale in any state.

Old census data is skimpy by modern standards. It lacks details. For example, the census of 1790 identifies the head of a household but doesn't name the others counted as living in that household. Even in modern times, census takers fail to account for every person. They sometimes miss individuals who are on the move or on the run. So it could be that there actually was a Virginian named Thomas J. Beale who escaped tabulation in 1810.

Other research found two Thomas Beales in Virginia — in Richmond County and King George County. But this was at an earlier date and would make them too old in 1817 to be our vigorous hero.

Further research turned up a Thomas J. Beale in Virginia — who lived at about the right time period. He was son of Margaret and Richard Eustace Beale of Richmond County. But Nickell is skeptical that this Thomas J. Beale was ever connected with an enormously valuable treasure.

This Thomas J. Beale of Virginia was born in 1792, and it appears that he was never a man of great wealth. After his father, Richard E. Beale, died in Fauquier County, Thomas wrote a note assigning his $60 interest in that estate to his brother, James M. Beale. That was in 1835. Other court records show that Thomas owned one horse. Thomas died in 1851, and the estate tabulation of 1855 showed a net value only $21.92. This doesn't sound like a man who was involved with a treasure of tons of silver and gold.

There have been hundreds of Beales in America since 1640 when the first Thomas Beale came from England. And there have indeed been many Beales named Thomas. Their trails appear in records of several states. Among them may be the Thomas Beale that the author describes in the 1885 pamphlet.

There was a Thomas Beale born near Winchester, Virginia, in 1784 to Sarah and Samuel Beale. Carl W. Nelson, Jr. reports another one living in Kentucky: that one signed an indenture in December 1818 selling 70 acres of land to Charlotte Atwell.

Kentucky records also show a Thomas Beale acquiring 9,812 acres of land on Salt Lick Creek in 1819. He gave his home address as "Maco, China"! This same Thomas had acquired 1,000 acres in Kentucky in 1787. He sounds like an intriguing fellow.

Some of the older U.S. Census files may help sort out these possibilities. The census of 1790 identifies these heads of households in Virginia named Beale:

Thomas : In upper Lunenburg County.
Household of 11 whites and 26 blacks.

Taverner: Shenandoah County.
Household of 8 whites and 17 blacks.

Taverner: Upper Lunenburg County.
Household of 8 whites. Household had 12 buildings.

Two Taverners; could be father and son. But let's keep after the name Thomas. Not too rare a name, Thomas Beale. There were a number of them who fought in the American Revolution. The Patriot Index of the Daughters of the American Revolution (DAR) lists these veterans:

Thomas Beall, Sr. Husband of Sarah Antrim.
Died age 82 in 1801.

Cpl. Thomas B. Beale. Husband of Margaret Heugh.
From Maryland. Died age 38 in 1801.

Capt. Thomas Beale. Husband of Sarah Todhunter.
From Pennsylvania. Died age 68 in 1803.

Pvt. Thomas Beale. Husband of Huldah Flagg.
From Massachusetts. Died age 79 in 1806.

Thomas Beale. Husband of Lucy. From Maryland.
Died 1818.

Thomas Beale. Living in North Carolina in 1820.

Capt. Thomas Beale. Husband of Verlinda.
From Maryland. Died age 80 in 1823.

But none of these men fit the story. The two who were alive in 1822 were probably too old to carry out the rigorous western adventure, and neither was "from Virginia."

Another source tells of more dealing in Kentucky in 1837 in the name of Thomas, who was then said to still live in China. He sold 1,000 acres on Obion Creek.

The Innis book tells of a Captain Thos. J. Beall heading from Harpers Ferry to New Orleans down the Ohio and the Mississippi aboard the ship, Smyrna, in 1816. There was indeed a Thomas "J" Beall who graduated from West Point in 1811, but he was from Maryland and not Virginia. The "J" stood for Jones, and during the War of 1812 he was an officer in the U.S. Army.

No, Thomas Beale was not a rare name. Could any one of these be our man?

Others say that a Thomas Beale fought in the War of 1812 at New Orleans. This Beale was said to be from Virginia.

There are references elsewhere to a Thomas Beale of Fincastle, Virginia who went to New Orleans, Louisiana. Rosa Yancey, a historian of Lynchburg, Virginia, wrote in 1935 that a "Thomas Beale, before going to New Orleans, ... fought a duel with Mr. Risque, of Lynchburg, over Miss Judy Hancock. Mr. Risque was shot in the stomach, but recovered." Ruth Daniloff, writing in the April 1981 issue of the *Smithsonian* magazine, said Thomas J. Beale had "a pistol fight with a Fincastle, Virginia, neighbor over a woman" in 1817. This man sounds like he might be our hero. At least there is a geographical tie. If he buried a treasure in Bedford, at least he knew the area; Bedford is near both Fincastle and Lynchburg. There

The town of Fincastle is the seat of government for Botetourt County, Virginia. This courthouse — the third one here — was built in 1847.

may be clues about the treasure man tucked away in the records of Fincastle, Virginia.

Fincastle, was a small but important town, about 20 miles from Buford's of Bedford County. It has no river, but it was on the route to the West. It was "the last western outpost at which might be found some of the gaiety of the East, as well as supplies," wrote Robert Stoner in his *Seed Bed of the Republic*. He noted that Lieutenants Lewis and Clark, of the famous Lewis and Clark Expedition, both had sweethearts there.

The town is west of Bedford and the Blue Ridge Mountains, towards the Shenandoah Valley. Since 1770 it has been the government center of Botetourt, a county that once made up an enormous portion of all the land claimed by Virginia. This county spread as far west as the Mississippi River. It included all of Kentucky and much of what is now Illinois, Indiana, Ohio, and West Virginia. When Virginia ceded land for the new state of Kentucky in 1792, Fincastle's political importance began to decline.

Today Botetourt is a normal-sized county, and today Fincastle is a subdued and quaint village of about 500 residents. No trains go through Fincastle. There is no airport. The nearest interstate highway is miles away. The town exudes historical significance, quietly.

Julia (Judy) Hancock lived there. She was the beautiful and intelligent third daughter of Congressman Col. George Hancock and kin to John Hancock. Researcher Richard Greaves wrote that she was just sixteen when duelists Beale and Risque faced each other in 1806 or 1807. While the date of this duel is uncertain, this could well be our Beale.

Men have dueled when competing for a fair maiden's attention. The reason for this duel is uncertain (and the fact that Risque was married and his wife was living does little to clear up the mystery). The pair might have been competing for the attention of fair Julia. Perhaps Risque was defending the honor of Julia, who was like a sister to his wife. Or maybe the men were reacting to insults to their manhood or pride. Whatever the reason, the duel did not result in either man winning Miss Hancock's fair hand. She chose the dashing, redheaded frontiersman, Lt. William Clark, who had visited Fincastle several times.

Just after the United States acquired the Louisiana Territory, it was Clark and an associate, Meriwether Lewis, who in 1804 were sent out to explore across the United States to the Pacific and back. The Lewis and Clark Expedition was the first to survive the arduous trek. They arrived back in St. Louis in September 1806, after having been gone more than two years. Clark returned to Fincastle "to make love to Judy," wrote John Blakeless in his book *Lewis & Clark*. Miss Hancock was smitten. The other residents welcomed Lewis and Clark in a more formal fashion. They addressed the men with commendations and gratitude for their historic accomplishments.

Clark was promoted to General. Julia married Clark in 1808. They moved to St. Louis, and she became involved in life of the upper strata in the new territories. More about Clark later.

Beale's life was not so prestigious. Richard Greaves says that Thomas Beale was born in 1773 in Shenandoah County and moved to Fincastle in the 1790's to enter into business with his brother John.

William Clark returned from the Lewis & Clark Expedition and married Julia (Judy) Hancock of Fincastle.

Let us check official records in Fincastle to see what is said about the Beale family.

The trail of records of Thomas Beale leads to the brick courthouse on the square at Fincastle, a town of narrow streets. The courtyard is entered by passing through an unusual, wrought-iron gate that rotates like a turnstile. A brick walk ends with a few steps up into the air-conditioned Clerk's office.

Yes, there really was a Thomas Beale here. There is a deed showing that he owned a piece of real estate. There is a will of which he is a beneficiary.

These records also show that Thomas picked a good man as his mentor. Brother John was an enterprising fellow who was also "Commissioner of the Peace" in Botetourt County in 1791. He was a successful merchant and plantation owner. When he later died, in 1809, his estate included 31 slaves and assets worth $16,000. In those times, that was great wealth. The entire United States government budget was only 500 times as much as that. So Thomas Beale had a taste for wealth, but there is no evidence within the courthouse records to suggest that he was a frontier adventurer.

Thomas Beale himself owned a piece of land in the town, Lot Number 9, on Main Street, just a block from the courthouse. Furthermore, he was a merchant, and bought wares from as far away as Philadelphia. He sold the place in 1806 for 120 pounds. Here is how he signed his name on the deed. He didn't lack flourish.

Fincastle files also hold the will of Taverner Beale, who died in 1810. It makes bequests to a number of people, including Thomas. This will raises more questions about Thomas Beale. The will also provides insight into Taverner's attitudes toward his family when he signed it in 1806. His treatment of Thomas seems odd.

It was Taverner's wish to distribute his estate in unequal shares. He made generous provisions and bequests to: "Charles Beale,... my son James Madison Hite Beale,... daughter Catherine Jordan,... daughter Elizabeth Steenbergen,... son John, ... and ... daughter Mary Higgins." But then the will reads "& no more of my estate I give to my Thomas Beale 5 shillings only." In those days, 5 shillings was not even equal to a week's wages for a carpenter or mason.

Taverner did not make clear what he meant in 1806 when he said "my Thomas Beale." My what? My son? My grandson? My ward? It is puzzling that Taverner would treat Thomas so differently from other males in his family.

Perhaps Taverner had given something to Thomas earlier and felt no need for further gifts by bequest. A grandson or ward might get only a token bequest. Or maybe he had disdain for Thomas. Could his son's duel have soured Taverner? Perhaps there was another reason.

There was a suggestion that Beale may have been part Indian. This notion is consistent with the descriptions of Thomas J. Beale as having dark skin, black hair, and dark eyes. The man who raised this possibility is Jacques Boegli, an experienced government engineer. He didn't stake his reputation on this as fact, but he identified some bits of information that warrant consideration.

Boegli studied the genealogies of the Hite families and Beale families and historical stories and tales about the Hite family's encounter with Indians in the Carolinas. Interestingly enough, he found that years later some of the family returned to Virginia, bringing with them an illegitimate child that had either a slave parent or an Indian sire. It is a complex story, but an interesting one. It involves both the Beale family and the Hite family. In it, Taverner's mother became his mother-in-law!

Taverner Beale was born in 1742, the son of Taverner Beale, Shenandoah County's delegate to the Virginia General Assembly. His mother was Frances Madison Beale, kin to James Madison, the fourth President. When his father died in 1756, Taverner was just 14. Frances remarried about a year later to a 38-year-old man named Jacob Hite.

Frances is believed to have had two daughters by Jacob, Anne and Eleanor. These girls would be half-sisters to our Taverner and almost a generation younger than he.

Jacob had lost his wife earlier and already had children. One of Jacob's daughters was Elizabeth. Youthful Taverner and Elizabeth — who had become his step-sister — grew to love each other. Ultimately they married. By this act, Taverner's own mother became his stepmother-in-law! The newlyweds stayed in Virginia; not so for the Hites.

Around 1773 Jacob Hite took his family — including Taverner's mother, Frances Madison Beale Hite — to near what is now Greenville, South Carolina. The American Revolution had not yet begun.

The move to Carolina turned out to be a disaster for them. The Hites had sided with the colonists. Indians nearby were being inflamed by the English. In 1777 or 1778, Jacob and his son were killed by Indians, possibly Chickamauga Cherokees. Frances, her small children, and a woman slave were taken captive by the Indians.

After the Revolutionary War, Taverner went searching for his mother and half-sisters. They had disappeared. In about 1784 or so, Capt. George Hite brought back a woman slave and "an Indian son." No one recorded who he was. The boy may have been sired by an Indian. The mother may have been the slave, one of the Hite girls, or Mrs. Hite herself.

That boy was then raised and educated at a farm in Winchester, where Taverner was living. Some diaries do report seeing a boy at Maj. Isaac Hite's farm there. This mystery boy could be the son of a number of people. But two possibilities seem most likely.

The child was born about 1780 or so, when the Indians had the women in custody and no white men were there. The father was probably Indian.

If the mother was one of the Hite girls, he would be a half-nephew of our Taverner. If he was the son of Mrs. Hite, he would be a half-brother. Either way, the boy would be young enough to be Taverner's son.

This is supposition, of course. But if either of these women were the mother, Taverner would likely have had some interest in or feeling of responsibility for the boy. Was this boy the Thomas who was later short-changed in Taverner's will because he was not really Taverner's own son?

Rosa Yancey's account of the Indian child contradicts all of this. She wrote in 1935 that George Hite brought back a woman slave who had married the son of an Indian chief and that the slave's child was... a daughter.

11.
New Orleans & Burr

Taverner Beale's Thomas might be our man. Let us track this Thomas Beale and see what he did with his life. This information will shed light on whether he could be a finder of fortune or not. The Fincastle records are helpful. But there are even more things to be learned down in New Orleans.

New Orleans does indeed have official records of a Thomas Beale. And not just one Thomas Beale, but two: a father and son. Both of those Beales came from Fincastle, Virginia.

Beale was attracted to New Orleans as were many others. Traders. Adventurers. Swindlers. Pirates. Schemers. Missionaries. Planters. Entrepreneurs.

New Orleans offered opportunity. It was the focal point of Gulf trade. It was growing fast. It was and still is many things that Fincastle was not

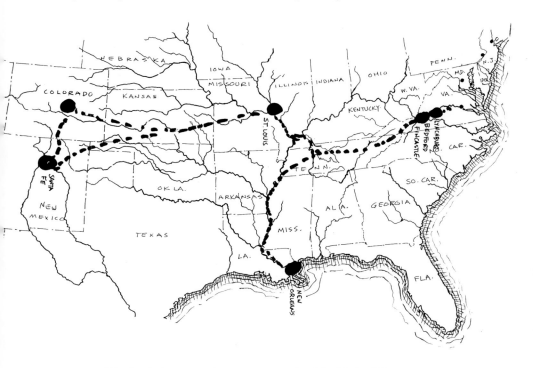

The Beale treasure story spans much of the United States.

and still is not. It was big then and is even bigger now. Early settlers were Spanish and French. It was a cosmopolitan place of many languages, with French and Creole being most common. It was raucous. Early in the century, Daniel Adams wrote, "The city is unhealthy, particularly to strangers..... The state of morals here is deplorably low." Adams did acknowledge that "New Orleans is advantageously situated for commerce, at the mouth of one of the noblest rivers in the world, whose branches extending in almost every direction, waft to this port the products of various climates."  This Mississippi River city was a beachhead of European culture in America that flourished as an economic center of the South. Its economy boomed after the U.S. bought Louisiana in 1803. It looked like a place where ambitious men could make money.

Strange events in Washington would echo through New Orleans. These events would draw to New Orleans men who wanted money, power, or excitement. The pied piper was Aaron Burr. He lured a number of men to the port city. Beale may have been one of these recruits.

Beginning in 1804, Vice President Aaron Burr changed his life from being the second highest powerful official in the United States Government to virtual traitor almost overnight. Burr had been bristling under the steady criticism coming his way from Alexander Hamilton, Secretary of the Treasury. So in July, 1804, Burr challenged Hamilton to a duel. They met. Burr's shot hit home; Hamilton died. The public was stunned. Many of Burr's own political party recoiled and disassociated themselves from him. They dropped any idea of renominating him and dumped him in favor of George Clinton. It was at this time that Burr began developing a secret scheme to create a new political empire for himself. (Meanwhile he ably presided over the U.S. Senate until his term ended in March 1805.)

Burr started lining up men to help him achieve his fantasy. Many were attracted to his allusions to potential riches and great power. Other adherents were just adventurers. He enlisted a number of men for what he termed "service on the Mississippi," but what was really a grandiose scheme. One recruit was U.S. Army General James Wilkinson, who owed him something. Burr, as Vice-President, was instrumental in getting the general appointed as Governor of the Northern Louisiana Territory.

On two occasions Burr met with Wilkinson (who had been receiving a large "pension" from Spain as late as 1800), and they conspired to build an empire in the Southwest. They planned to conquer Mexico and annex the southwestern part of American territory. They agreed on a method of using substitution ciphers for secret messages. Burr wanted New Orleans to be the capital of his Second American Republic. So he was there in the spring of 1805 to measure public sentiment and build support.

But by the fall of 1806, Burr's dreams had begun to evaporate. The country learned that he was up to no good. Ally Wilkinson turned against him and told President Jefferson about Burr's plans. The President called for Burr's arrest, charging him with fomenting revolt in the Orleans Territory. Wilkinson then tried to cover his own duplicity by offering a $5,000 reward for Burr, dead or alive, and putting New Orleans under martial law to flush out Burr's allies.

UNITED STATES, ORIGINAL AREA AND ACQUISITIONS OF TERRITORY, 1790 TO 1910

Burr's followers backed away from him and started pursuing other possibilities. He was alone.

The former Vice-President was arrested in Mississippi Territory and taken to Richmond for trial before Supreme Court Justice John Marshall. There was damaging testimony given by patriotic Commodore Truxtun. Wilkinson also testified against Burr. But Marshall ruled that the government failed to prove its charges, so Burr was released. The public was outraged.

Wilkinson was exposed and almost charged. Incredibly, he was allowed to return to his command of the Army. He kept his post but was no longer trusted. Theodore Roosevelt later wrote of the irony that "Wilkinson, the double traitor, the bribe taker, the corrupt servant of a foreign government, remained at the head of the American Army." He died in 1825, where his heart was, in Mexico City.

But America moved ahead — in spite of people like Burr and Wilkinson. New Orleans flourished. Maybe Burr had helped lure Beale to New Orleans; maybe not. For whatever the reason, Thomas Beale had come from Fincastle to seek his fortune.

He went overland at first, down through the valley, into Tennessee, then past Nashville and on to Memphis. (No one seems to know if it was Beale's presence there that earned the street name made famous by W.C. Handy's "Beale Street Blues.") There he probably boarded one of the flat bottom boats or barges that carried tobacco. It was a long drift down the Mississippi to Baton Rouge and New Orleans. It was not an easy voyage. Snags, punctures, tedium, and discomfort made the journey uncertain and tempers impatient. Fights among passengers and/or the crew were not unusual. But Beale made it.

Thomas Beale arrived in the city sometime before 1808. Rosa Yancey wrote that he left Fincastle shortly after his duel with Mr. Risque. One legend says that as he departed, a brother called after him, saying "tis a tis."

Beale found New Orleans bustling with wheelers and dealers. There were cotton traders, fur traders, sugar buyers, and even slave traders. Commerce included loot pirated from Spanish ships. Privateers who worked the Gulf of Mexico would sail in past Grande Terre Island and drop anchor in Barataria Bay, about thirty miles from the city. They dealt with impatient buyers or transferred booty to smaller craft that would go upstream to New Orleans itself.

Ringleader of the illegal trade was a clever, French-speaking man, the youngest of eight children, named Jean Lafitte. His brazen flaunting of laws — anybody's laws — and his obvious success, made him a local celebrity. It seemed that Jean would acquire the stuff, and older brother Pierre would sell it. Brother Dominique provided the muscle — and expertise with artillery.

Beale learned that Jean Lafitte had attracted a lot of attention in 1805 when, at age 23, he sailed up the Mississippi to New Orleans with 12,600 pounds of British silver he had seized. The Lafittes opened a warehouse in 1807, and by 1811, Jean was the acknowledged leader of all Baratarians and privateer ships using that Bay. From his house on the high spot of Grand Terre, he was master of all he surveyed.

Of course Beale was aware of Lafitte. And Lafitte would later get to know of Beale. The Lafittes had a "blacksmith" business in the city, which many suspected was an outlet for smuggled and pirated goods. This place on St. Phillip Street was within walking distance of Beale's business, a hotel.

In New Orleans, the Lafittes owned this blacksmith shop.

Beale was an entrepreneur, earning a reputation first as a businessman and later as a planter. He owned and operated a hotel and rooming house on Chartre Street. It is unclear when he acquired it or how he paid for it. He seemed to have the knack of raising money. And he got to know the movers and shakers of the city.

Far from New Orleans, Britain was fighting France. After Britain blockaded France and began seizing American ships and sailors, the United

States declared war on Britain on June 18, 1812. A number of sea battles ensued. Fewer trading ships got through to and from the port of New Orleans. Cotton bales piled up, and prices dropped. Sugar imports slowed, and costs rose.

William Claiborne, governor of the new State of Louisiana, seemed more attentive to squelching privateers and the smuggling of slaves — importation was outlawed in 1806 — than to the war with England.

When Lafitte held an auction of nefarious wares in the city in 1812, Claiborne became even more determined to stop illicit, privateer business. He urged the Navy to take action, and they made news by seizing several privateer vessels and their goods and arresting the Lafitte brothers. But Jean and Pierre escaped. The district attorney filed suit against them, and Pierre was soon recaptured and jailed in July of 1814.

But New Orleans faced a bigger problem: the British were coming. They had landed troops in Maryland, and on August 24th, they reached Washington and torched the Capitol and the White House.

12.
Lafitte & Jackson

Now, the British planned to invade Louisiana, to seize New Orleans, work their way up the Mississippi, and then take over St. Louis, and thereby dominate the great Louisiana Territory by controlling all traffic on the Mississippi, the Ohio, and the Missouri Rivers. St. Louis was of strategic importance, even though it was then a thinly populated frontier town, settled primarily by fur traders and government officials. It was the gateway to the natural resources of the vast new West.

On September 3rd, 1814, the British tried to recruit Lafitte, with his skilled cannoneers and well-armed sailors, to join them in attacking the U.S.A. They shared their planned strategy and offered him $30,000 for his support. While he stalled to answer, he decided to help the U.S., hoping to trade for the release of brother Pierre and gain some relief from Claiborne's efforts to put him out of business. He wrote to an important city official, revealing the details of the British plan and offering to use his fighting men — and his cannons — against the British. He knew that his friend would pass the information on to the governor.

But Claiborne would not deal and instead dispatched Commodore Patterson and Colonel Ross to Grande Terre to wipe out the privateers. Jean Lafitte must have heard of Claiborne's plan. Local citizens learned on September 6th that Pierre had been broken out of jail. Jean dispatched his best ships out of the Bay and began evacuating most of his people of Grande Terre, leaving brother Dominique You with a small force to defend the island.

Patterson and Ross, with an overwhelming force, reached Grande Terre a few days later, but Jean, Pierre, and most of their people had long gone. You surrendered in the face of hopeless odds. The U.S. force then seized sixteen craft and jailed the 80 Baratarians, including Dominique You.

But then, upon the arrival of U.S. Army General Andrew Jackson, sentiment about the Lafittes changed. Claiborne finally knew that the British were a far greater threat than the privateer smuggling. And even Jackson, who had first shrugged off the Lafittes as "banditti," decided to take seriously Lafitte's inside information about British strategy. He realized that he needed those guns and experienced cannoneers of Lafitte to repel the impending British attacks on New Orleans. Politics — and war — make strange bedfellows, indeed.

Lafitte's information helped General Andrew Jackson plan his strategy against the British for the Battle of New Orleans.

Citizens of New Orleans mobilized to supplement Jackson's government forces. The government relied heavily on its militia then; only 33,424 people were in the entire U.S. regular Army. Most of them were entangled elsewhere, so not many of them were available to Jackson. Thomas Beale became a leader of one of the newly organized, supplemental fighting teams that included various notable citizens. Beale was later described by Vincent Nolte, a German-born international trader, as "a native of Virginia, and then residing in New Orleans, where he had some reputation as a fine marksman."

When Jackson reviewed his forces at Fort St. Charles in 1814, there were lines of regulars and the 7th infantry and some marines. Then, according to Alexander Walker's 1856 book, *Jackson and New Orleans*, these forces were "preceded in their march by a company of sharpshooters, with long rifles, blue hunting shirts, and citizen's hats, who advanced with unusual vivacity and rapidity, eager to be the first on the field to meet the foe."

"This was the famous corps of Beale's Rifles. It was composed of picked men, leading merchants and professional characters of the city, who had formed themselves into a volunteer corps, and solicited the post of danger in the coming contest. One of the officers of this corps was Judge Joshua Lewis, of the First District Court of New Orleans, who laid aside the judicial robes to fulfill the duties of patriot and soldier. The members of this gallant corps were in the flower of youth. The neatness of their equipments, the intelligence of their countenances, and the ready promptitude of their movements, showed that they were no ordinary soldiers. They were all expert in the use of the rifle." Their captain was Thomas Beale.

In one early shoot-out, Beale's corps showed its bravery, but nonetheless had some of their number captured by the British. Vincent Nolte had met many people he disliked. Beale was one of them. He wrote that Beale was " a great braggart" and during that first battle "had completely disappeared, so that he was supposed to be dead; for that he would hide, and leave his little command in a lurch." Nolte wrote in his biography that he himself had served in the grenadiers as a loyal and brave soldier.

The really big Battle of New Orleans came after the war was already over, but neither Jackson nor his adversaries knew it. In January 1815, before either group had learned that a treaty had already been signed in Ghent, the British attempted to assault the embanked troops and artil-

JACKSON AT NEW ORLEANS.

Cannons of Lafitte and rifles of Beale helped Jackson win at New Orleans.

lery of Jackson. The Americans won a lopsided victory. Two thousand British were killed or wounded, compared to only two dozen Americans. Jackson became a national hero. Nolte didn't like him either. Beale was in good company!

In March, General Jackson accepted the gift of a sword as token of admiration from Beale and his men. Jackson thanked them and, recalling the memorable 23rd of December, said, "The members of the New Orleans Rifle Company — a spartan band — survived the carnage of that night ... [and] ... maintained their gallant reputation. It was to spirits like these that Louisiana owes her second independence."

Lafitte's cannons and Baratarian men, directed by Dominique You, had been a major factor in American victory. Jackson publicly expressed his gratitude for their help, even though Jean Lafitte had not been personally been on the battlefield. Some historians believe that if it hadn't been for pirate-privateer Jean Lafitte, Jackson would not have notched a great victory and would not have been elected seventh president of the U.S. All of New Orleans — and especially the Lafittes — took notice when, on February 6th, 1815, President James Madison issued a public proclamation of pardon for all the Baratarians, including the Lafittes. As in our modern day, acquittal does not assure that the government will give back what is yours.

Some less notorious Baratarian successfully petitioned Louisiana legal channels to retrieve some of their stuff seized by Patterson Ross. Indeed, a number of them were soon back to sea in the Gulf, plundering Spanish ships again. But the Lafittes were not recovering what had been seized from them. The lives of the Lafittes did not return to normal. They tried to make people think they were destitute. Perhaps it was Claiborne's influence that the Lafittes were getting nowhere.

But Jean Lafitte was wily and resilient. It is reasonable to suspect that he would be back in the pirating business. He would survive. Or thrive, probably.

He was not exactly a hero in the city, but he was always a topic of gossip. There were rumors that he had relocated on the mainland, or maybe on an island off the shore of Texas. Beale lost track of him. The war was over. Beale focussed on his own life.

Later, in April 1815, Beale and Nolte clashed again, although a bit obliquely. Beale was a friend of English-born Joseph Saul, who was Cashier at the Bank of New Orleans and a special enemy of Nolte. Saul's son (described by Nolte as a "stupid and yet conceited booby") insulted Nolte by spitting on his back. Nolte challenged him to a duel. At the appointed hour, Thomas Beale served as second to young Saul. Nolte lost the duel, suffering a bullet in the leg. He was confined to bed for fourteen days.

The episode didn't interfere with Beale's life. His business empire grew, and his family grew. Though Protestant, he married a Catholic woman, Celeste de Grandpre, daughter of the one-time governor of Baton Rouge. No marriage records have been found, but the courts have never questioned the legality of this union. Celeste gave birth to a baby girl in December 1815. They named her Eliza.

On the river, the new, steam-powered boats had nourished traffic even during the war. By war's end New Orleans had grown to be home for 33,000 people — more than twice the population of Richmond, capital city of Beale's former home state of Virginia. Now Gulf trade resumed without restraint. Cotton prices tripled. In 1817, 2,000 flat bottom boats and barges arrived from upper country.

But not all was good news. Yellow Fever flourished in port cities. New Orleans was badly hit in 1817; 800 people died. But the economy continued to expand.

Beale bought a plantation for $21,000. He hoped to become less dependent on suppliers and middlemen; food for his hotel would be produced by his plantation. (The city of New Orleans has since spread out to include this land. The plantation was long and pie-shaped. The location is not far from the present Audubon Park, and it borders on Nashville Avenue as its western boundary. It would be about eight blocks wide at its widest end and nearly three miles long.) By 1819 the plantation had 15 horses, 100 hogs, and 380 sheep. Beale also owned 29 slaves.

He paid $5,000 cash for the plantation and agreed to pay the rest over three years. Having often used credit to finance his business ventures, he had now amassed substantial debt. (A creditor in Philadelphia claimed in 1810 that he had never been paid $2,864.89 for things that Beale had bought from him in 1801.) Clearly he was not adverse to taking chances in business. Perhaps, like so many others, he gambled.

Then there were two Thomas Beales in New Orleans.

13.
Widow vs. Widow

A son, Thomas Beale the Younger, showed up in November 1818. Eighteen years old, he arrived "without any property and without a dollar."

Celeste had also contributed to the family expansion by giving birth to a second daughter, named Celeste, in September.

A casual observer would believe that Thomas Beale was a rich man. The elder Beale looked like a great success. Yet underneath that big image was a too-small net worth. Financial troubles hit Beale. For whatever reason, he was overextended. Facing bankruptcy, Senior decided to shelter the family assets from creditors. He sold all his land, his property, and his 29 slaves to Junior, in exchange for $124,400 in notes. (Appraisers later figured that the value didn't exceed $45,000 — far, far less than the $124,400 "paid.") The $124,400 then is equivalent to about $3 million today.

Father and son signed their names to an agreement in April 1819. Copy from Notorial Archives of Orleans Parish, Louisiana. Courtesy Zuma Salaun.

Junior lived in the hotel and helped manage it. Beale Senior lived on the plantation and came to the city from time to time to supervise or give orders. Business was good, but some of the hotel guests failed to pay their bills when they became ill or died. Yellow fever surged again in the city in 1819. New Orleans was hit harder than before: 2,190 people died.

In January 1820, a boy was born to Celeste, named James William. Beale was glad to have a second son. By August, Celeste was pregnant again. Then the Beale world changed.

In September 1820, Thomas Beale, Senior, died.

His widow was left with heavy debts. She had a brood of three small children, with a fourth on the way. Her only assets were the mortgage I.O.U.'s signed by Junior. Although Beale was buried in the Protestant cemetery on Friday, September 8, 1820, a certificate filed in 1855 on behalf of the then-35-year-old James William adds confusion; it says his father died in September 1818. It is not known if Beale died somewhere else and then was reburied in 1820, or if the affidavit reference is a clerical error.

The Beale Papers pamphlet says that Robert Morriss hosted a Thomas Beale in Lynchburg twice: in January 1820 and again in January 1822. Presuming that Morriss had good memory, and presuming that the pamphlet author had accurate recollection of what Morriss said, then Thomas Beale, Senior couldn't be our man. He died in New Orleans before that second visit to Virginia.

Celeste gave birth to her baby, whom she named Octavine, in May 1821, too late for Thomas Beale, Sr. to see his last child. Celeste and her children continued to live on the plantation. Junior managed the affairs of the plantation in an economical and upright way. He also completed a new hotel, the Planters & Merchants, at 15 Canal Street.

Young Beale advertised that the hotel had "upwards of an hundred and twenty apartments, sixty of which are single bedded rooms, the balance containing more than one bed each." He claimed that the "dining room is sufficiently large to accommodate, with comfort and convenience, two hundred and fifty persons at table." As to decor, the hotel "is furnished throughout in the most elegant style." Many furnishings came from the old hotel. Besides rooms and food, "The Wine and Liquor Stores ... are very extensive and contain a full and constant supply of the very best. Orders by the demijohn, 1/4 cask, 1/2 pipe, or pipe, are respectfully solicited.... no pains shall be spared to give every satisfaction."

Business was good for the first two years, and Junior helped support his stepmother and his half-brothers and sisters. One witness said that

Beale's Hotel in New Orleans.

he was "an industrious and economical young man." He sold 11 slaves to get some cash. He paid off some of his father's debts.

Meanwhile New Orleans was a-buzz with news that some of Laffite's lieutenants had attacked a U.S. ship. Later reports said that Laffite was so embarrassed that he sailed away on his ship *The Pride* and disappeared. Lafitte could have drowned in a storm.

Records are incomplete and make it impossible to account for all of Lafitte's doings — or of young Beale's time and whereabouts. It is conceivable that he had time to go west and/or to go to Virginia twice. We do know that in the fall of 1823 Thomas Beale, Junior became ill. He was attended by the same doctor who had cared for General Jackson. But the ministrations were in vain.

Young Thomas Beale died at the Merchants and Planters Hotel, in New Orleans, on October 22nd. It was 1823, the year after the last letter from Beale was sent to Morris.

Then began prolonged financial confusion.

Celeste bought part of the plantation from Junior's estate in 1824, indebting herself by giving mortgage notes in return. Ultimately the plan-

13 — Widow vs. Widow

tation was sold to Daniel Walden for $23,900 to pay debts. Celeste moved with her children to Baton Rouge. On the advice of her brother, Celeste refused to pay the notes. She charged that Junior's estate had no right to sell the plantation to anybody because it was rightfully hers.

Enter Chloe Delancy, of Fincastle, Virginia. (Some documents call her Clory Delancy or Delaney.)

Through New Orleans attorney Thos. F. McCaleb, Chloe claimed to be the natural mother of Thomas Beale, Junior, and the sole heir to his estate. She petitioned the court to force Celeste to honor those mortgage notes and make payments to the estate of Junior. So these Beale widows battled it out through their lawyers. But they weren't both widows in the legal sense. The papers of the court arguments reveal more facts about this, and about the origin of Thomas Beale, Junior.

The probate court "agreed that Chloe Delancy, of Fincastle County, Virginia is the mother of the late Thomas Beale, Junior, and that he was the natural son of said Chloe Delancy, and Thomas Beale, Senior, late of New Orleans, deceased."

However, Chloe's claim gained her little. The court ruled in 1828 that the 1819 sale from father to son was "simulated" to defraud creditors and further, that Junior was not of legal age at the time. The deal was not, after all, a deal. Junior, therefore, never really owned the plantation or the hotels. Celeste's I.O.U.s were also cancelled. In-laws and grandchildren argued that the court should not have allowed the sale of the plantation to pay debts and that it belonged to them. They contested the ruling for a quarter of a century.

One thing was not contested. All did agree that Thomas Beale already had a son when he married Celeste.

This relationship is confirmed back in Fincastle, Virginia.

Children of Fincastle County, an index compiled from court records by Charles Burton, lists a Thomas Beale as son of the unmarried Chloe Delaney. His father is unidentified. The Fincastle records further noted, "Thomas the Younger went to New Orleans but was dead 11-12-1824." So Thomas Beale, Junior was born out of wedlock.

U.S. census data of 1810 and of 1820 confirms that there was a Chloe Delaney or Delancy living in Botetourt County. We do not know how she paid for her New Orleans litigation.

The record does not say if Chloe was white or black, slave or free. If she was a black slave, Thomas could have been of darker skin than his father. If she was white, but his father was part Indian or slave, he could have had darker skin than his mother. She must have had legal standing to have been able to appeal the handling of the Beale estates, so she was either a free slave, a mulatto, or white.

During his boyhood, Thomas Beale the Younger would have been, at best, an awkward citizen of the Fincastle community. His uncertain and unapproved ancestry might have made him yearn for a life where he could make his own reputation and enjoy greater acceptance. Like on the Western frontier. There he might have felt he could be free to pass himself as a white — or as an Indian — and to be accepted to lead ventures into Western and Indian lands. Or he might want to go where his father was: New Orleans. There, mixed heritage was more common and less of a stigma.

This unusual family background may explain why Beale confided in Robert Morriss. It seems strange that Beale would have trusted a man he only met while at his lodging house. But for Thomas Beale the Younger, this makes some sense. He had no family to confide in. He had no wife. He had no children. He may have been alienated from the mother he left behind in Fincastle. His father was dead. He only had step-brothers and sisters that he barely knew. He could well have felt as though he did not have any family. He may have been close only to the men who had been with him on the western venture.

Beale's middle name might reveal something about his background. How did "Jefferson" get into his name? Was it given at birth or adopted later?

Thomas Beale, Senior was born before Jefferson became famous. (President Jefferson, born in 1743, helped write the Declaration of Independence, was Virginia governor in 1779, became President in 1801, and died in 1826.) Yet Taverner did name a son James Madison Beale, after Senator Madison, whose son later became the fourth president.

Of course, either Senior or Junior could have taken the name of Jefferson on his own, just because he admired Thomas Jefferson or merely liked the name. Yet no papers have been found to show that the middle name was actually Jefferson.

The primary source of information about the treasure and its participants is the pamphlet, published in 1885. This publication never once calls the hero Thomas Jefferson Beale. Nowhere in the pamphlet does he have a middle name. Just "J." So who turned the "J" into "Jefferson"? When? Why? Did the Harts do that?

As early as 1927 Beale treasure aficionados referred to the hero as Thomas Jefferson Beale. Someone, sometime must have merely guessed that the "J" stood for Jefferson.

Ever since that assumption was made, stories and articles have called the man Thomas Jefferson Beale. And because of the magic of the Jefferson name, there has been speculation that Beale knew Jefferson.

The Innis book refers to Beale's "friend and namesake Thomas Jefferson." Thomas Jefferson had a summer home now called Poplar Forest in Bedford County. Jefferson designed the octagon-shaped house himself, and he relished the time he spent at this estate of more than 1,000 acres. The Innis documentary fiction also speaks of Beale visiting former President Jefferson at Poplar Forest. Some believe that Beale used Jefferson documents as code keys. In fact, there is even speculation that Jefferson himself created the codes.

Thomas Jefferson built his retreat, Poplar Forest, in Bedford County.   Drawing by Revelle Hamilton.

Most of the treasure hunters and many of the treasure writers have not seen the pamphlet itself. They perpetuate an error — or assumption — made earlier.

In any event, there was indeed a Thomas Beale — and not one, but two — a father and son. Two Thomas Beales lived in New Orleans and both were from Fincastle, Virginia, about 20 miles from Buford's and the suspected site of the buried treasure in Bedford County. Thomas, Jr. was illegitimate. Thomas Senior has had his lineage questioned. Senior signed his name "Thos." or "Thomas." Younger usually signed his name "Thomas." None of five signature samples found contained a "J."

One of them — the Beale described in the pamphlet — brought back a treasure. Odds are that he is the one who dueled with Risque.

Father. Son. "J" or no "J." Who dueled with Risque in Fincastle?

Was the duel, as Greaves said, in about 1806? If so, it must have been Senior, because Junior was only six years old at the time.

Or was the duel in 1817, as Daniloff said? If so, it could have been the 17-year-old Junior. Senior was living in New Orleans. If Senior was only passing through Fincastle, would he fight a duel over a 16-year-old girl? Junior, then 17, might. But wait — if the lass was Judy Hancock, and it was in 1817, she was no longer 16; she was married and living in St. Louis. Then again, the duel might have been about honor, and not a lass.

For the moment, let us put aside the question of which Beale dueled and when.

What does matter is that the duel involved James Beverly Risque. And it is Major Risque we should get to know better. For Risque and his family are linked to the Beale story and pamphlet in very special ways.

14.
Man of Connections

Major James Beverly Risque is a pivotal character whose ghost haunts the Beale treasure. Major Risque was a talented man who had American generals in his circle of friends — and family. He dueled with Beale. He knew Robert Morriss. He was related to James B. Ward. A look at his life will give insight into the veracity of the treasure.

Risque was an attorney who began practicing law in 1794 in the town of Fincastle, Virginia. He bought property there, and then in June 1797 he was appointed "Attorney for the Commonwealth" (the equivalent of District Attorney) for Botetourt County.

He was respected for his mind and his skill. Botetourt residents placed him high on their list of important citizens. He was one of seventeen men who were proposed to serve on a Board of Visitors for a new "College of Washington in Virginia" in Lexington. This 1796 proposal fell through. Aging George Washington had just made the largest gift ever given by anyone to a private educational institution — $50,000 — to the Liberty Hall Academy, which had been in Lexington since 1782. That institution was renamed Washington Academy. By 1820, it had increased its faculty to two professors and fifty students were enrolled. Today it is named Washington & Lee University.

Risque resigned as Commonwealth Attorney so he could devote his full time to private pursuits. He built his law practice by specializing in criminal cases. He was a man who enjoyed the fine art of arguing. He liked to control whatever situation he was in, but mostly he wanted to win. And win he did, earning a reputation as an outstanding lawyer.

In 1799, citizens were saddened as the new nation lost two of its greatest heroes. Both George Washington and Patrick Henry died that year. It seemed like the end of an era.

But Risque was widening his horizons. He fell in love with Eliza Kennerly, daughter of Samuel and Mary Talbot Hancock Kennerly, kin of John Hancock. James and Eliza were married in a June wedding in 1799. Eliza's sister, Harriet Kennerly, was there — as well as members of the Kennerly and Hancock families. Because the Kennerly girls' mother died early, they grew up in the home of uncle George Hancock. Eliza and Harriet had become like sisters to cousin Julia (Judy) Hancock. After the wedding, Risque considered little Judy to be his sister-in-law.

The Risques talked of family and future. James sensed that the growth of Fincastle was slowing down. Recently, a big part of Virginia had been taken away to create the state of Kentucky. He had heard of a new town on the James River, fifty miles from Fincastle, named Lynchburg. Chartered in 1786, it had only five houses in 1793. But just six years later, there were almost 500 residents. He decided to keep an eye on progress there.

In the spring of 1801, former Virginia Governor Thomas Jefferson took the oath of office as our third president. It was anything but a landslide victory. Aaron Burr had received the same number of electoral votes as Jefferson, so the House of Representatives had to break the tie. After voting 35 times, the House chose Jefferson to be President, and Burr Vice President.

In the fall, in Fincastle, Eliza gave birth to her first child, a girl. The Risques named her Adeline Eliza Risque.

The United States grew much larger by acquiring the vast Louisiana Territory from France in 1803. The Risque family expanded too. Little Ferdinand Risque was born that year. William Clark teamed up with Meriwether Lewis and headed for St. Louis and then off to explore the uncharted Louisiana Territory.

Risque's family responsibilities continued to grow — little Harriet was born in 1806 — and his wife was giving more of her attention to her children. Risque usually was able to keep pressures under control, until one day an encounter with neighbor Thomas Beale strained his patience too far.

The men traded insults and allegations, challenging the very essence of the other's integrity or manhood. They agreed to a duel.

They dueled. Beale shot Risque in the stomach. It was not a mortal wound, but it did make a hole in his body, "a silk handkerchief being drawn entirely through him."

The traumatic event was burned in Risque's memory. His family would talk about it for generations. A few years later the Virginia Assembly passed the first laws outlawing dueling.

When Beale left town, Risque was glad to see him go. But he would never forget him.

With Beale gone, Risque put his energy into living. Real estate interested him, since he was certain that land would grow in value. For most of his adult life he was involved in land deals. He bought — and sold — several pieces of real estate in the first decade of the nineteenth century.

His wife was party to these transactions, including the sale of a parcel on Catawba Creek in April 1808 for the price of 2,350 pounds.

But then his wife Eliza died, depriving the Risque children of their mother's love. Slaves helped raise them. Risque yearned for companionship. He immersed himself in his work. He continued to buy land, acquiring 52 acres from Eliza's uncle George Hancock in 1810.

In 1812 the United States declared war against Britain, an event that would have significant consequences in the life of James Risque, an event that would bring Risque in contact with General Andrew Jackson, a man with links to both Aaron Burr and Thomas Beale.

Back in 1805 Burr had been rejected by his party. As he began secretly planning an empire, he visited Jackson, who was then a Supreme Court Justice of Tennessee. Burr tried to get Jackson to help expel the Spanish from the West. Jackson liked the notion and envisioned a greater United States. When Jackson heard that Burr's true intent was to start a new, separate country, he was furious — and was ready to do battle with Burr if necessary.

Risque and Jackson were brought together when, following the declaration of war with Britain, Risque joined a battalion of Virginia volunteers to serve as bodyguard to General Jackson. He attained the rank of major. It was the Battle of New Orleans that made Jackson an American hero. It would be interesting to know if Risque's service included the Battle of New Orleans. If so, did he encounter his old nemesis, Beale, there?

When the war with Britain ended, Risque started anew, but not in Fincastle. He opted for a better future at Lynchburg. The young city on the James River was a center of trade for tobacco grown in the surrounding region. Hogsheads of tobacco were carried by bateaux down river to Richmond and the markets of the world.

Lynchburg had escaped the ravages of the war. The British had entered Washington in 1814 and even set fire to the White House. But they never got to Lynchburg. Also unharmed was Thomas Jefferson's summer home, Poplar Forest, in Bedford County.

In 1815 former President Jefferson was in Lynchburg to greet the hero of the Battle of New Orleans. He sat with General Jackson at a public banquet in the city. Later, they stopped for drinks at Bell's Tavern. Jefferson was a great booster of the city and once said, "I consider it as the most interesting spot in the State...."

After moving to Lynchburg, Risque sold off his last piece of land in Botetourt County in 1815. In his new locale, Risque used his skill to further his reputation. He built up his law practice in the young and growing city. He got to know more and more people. He learned of more and more opportunities. He took advantage of those opportunities, and he prospered.

He owned slaves. They did his menial and manual labor, and sometimes they served as collateral for loans. He once pledged six slaves for a $1,300 bond. In 1815, he pledged ten slaves for $2,713, a loan he paid off just a year later.

He also acquired valuable real estate in the city and nearby counties. His town house was at a choice location: the plateau on the north corner of Court Street and 12th Street. The building later was used for the Lynchburg Female Seminary. Today the land is the site of the First Baptist Church. Risque further increased his holdings in the city by buying a large plot on Sixth Street.

About seven miles out of town, and three miles from Poplar Forest, was Risque's other residence, a farm that he called "Hunter's Hill." From 1817 to 1829, he assembled parcels totalling more than 500 acres on Dreaming Creek near the road from New London to Lynch's Ferry, thereby enlarging his plantation. This property served five generations before being subdivided just after World War II to finance the college educations of some of Risque's great-great-great-grandchildren.

His interest in land extended far afield. He even bought 100 acres in Chesterfield County.

But Lynchburg was his milieu. Risque became one of the more prominent citizens of Lynchburg, visually and politically.

He was a small man, yet as he walked to the courthouse, he was anything other than "low profile." He had an air of elegance. He was one of the last to wear knee britches and his hair in a queue. Fastidious, he demanded elegance in his home. He imported a pair of "large plate, giltframe, looking glasses" from France to enhance the interior.

He was active in local politics, strongly supporting the philosophy and policies of Jackson. When the General came through town he and Major Risque found time to play cards. The table is today treasured by a Risque descendent.

His stellar reputation was tarnished by some complaints that he was slow to pay his bills. He would eventually pay them. But only when he was ready.

People knew Risque, and Risque knew people. Robert Morriss, an active businessman, and his wife Sarah, were well known. The couple owned parcels of land on Second, Fifth, and Seventh Streets in Lynchburg, as well as a tract in Campbell County not too far from Risque's own plantation. Morriss was ambitious and enterprising. He owned a yard goods store, was treasurer of a proposed toll bridge, had an interest in a mill, and even served as chairman of the town council for a time. Robert and Sarah had no children and lived in a big house.

But not all of his ventures went well for Morriss. Mrs. Cabell, writing in 1857, noted that when the affairs of Morriss weakened, the couple continued to live in their big home and "there established a house for boarders." A visitor to Lynchburg could stay with Morriss overnight — or for months.

The Beale Papers says that from January to spring of 1820 Thomas J. Beale stayed in Lynchburg at the place of Robert Morriss. We don't know if Risque and Beale crossed paths then — or if they intentionally avoided each other. If Risque had dueled with Senior, and the visitor was Junior, Risque may not have cared. And if the visitor was an impostor — and he knew who it really was — he may have played along with the game.

That year was one of big events for Risque. Daughter Adeline married a 21-year-old attorney named Giles Ward, who recently moved from Torrington, Connecticut. Ward was bright and articulate, with an interest in theater; he became president of the Lynchburg Thespian Society.

Mixed news came from St. Louis. Julia Hancock Clark died at the age of 31. Risque felt close to Judy, and her death depressed him. But there was a happy twist too. His sister-in-law, Harriet Kennerly Radford had lost her husband, John Radford, when he was killed by a wild boar. Risque learned that Harriet was going to marry widower General Clark. He was twenty years older than she, but both were very happy that they would no longer be alone. Clark adopted her three children, though they kept the Radford surname. Risque let all his acquaintances know that his new in-law was the famous General William Clark.

On the cold day of January 27, 1822, Risque's daughter, Adeline Ward, gave birth to her first child, a healthy, blue-eyed, baby boy. This was James Beverly Risque's first grandchild, and he was especially proud that the parents named the little boy James Beverly Ward.

Lynchburgers were pleased that year too. More business flowed their way. Work began on the Lynchburg-Salem Turnpike, which would reach west into Bedford County to the town of Liberty and continue onward, through Buford's Gap, past Big Lick and on to Salem. Paschal Buford was delighted. The new, eighteen-feet wide artery would increase the traffic for his tavern.

Lynchburg hotels flourished as the town grew. In 1823, Morriss took over the management of the Washington Inn, about five blocks from Risque's town house. The Inn was a popular place to eat, meet or stay. Visitors included politicians, famous and near famous. Host and hostess Morriss expanded their circle of friends and acquaintances to include folks of all ages. Robert Morriss made friendships that continued into his final years.

Robert and Sarah Morriss were known to most of Lynchburg's society. Giles Ward knew them so well that his little boy would call Sarah Morriss, "Aunt Sarah."

14 — Man of Connections

The Franklin Hotel was built in 1816. Robert Morriss was manager here after he left the Washington Inn.

The 1824 Presidential election produced no majority winner. First reports showed that Jackson, hero of New Orleans, would be the next president of the U.S. He did earn more votes than any other candidate, but not a majority. The House of Representatives made the decision. They passed over both Henry Clay and Andrew Jackson and instead awarded the sixth presidency of the U.S. to John Quincy Adams.

On July 4th, 1826, both Thomas Jefferson and old John Adams died. People of Bedford and Lynchburg especially mourned the loss of Jefferson, who was considered one of their own. Earlier in the year, Risque had experienced opposite feelings when he learned that the nefarious General James Wilkinson had died in exile in Mexico City, a few days before New Year's Eve. Risque knew that Jackson, whom he so greatly admired, considered Wilkinson to be a traitor. Jackson's initial dislike began in 1813, when Jackson and 200 militia men marched in winter cold from Tennessee to help in the battle of Mobile. Unwilling to share any glory, Wilkinson rejected their help and made them turn around and march all the way home to Tennessee. Jackson's distrust grew more intense as Wilkinson's true character became better known.

It wasn't until 1828 that Jackson won on his own plurality. Risque was proud when "his general" was inaugurated as the seventh President of the United States on March 4, 1829.

Daughter Harriet Risque went out to St. Louis to visit her Aunt Harriet and Uncle William Clark. While there, she met a tall and handsome Army officer named George Christian Hutter, 37. The son of a German immigrant, Hutter had been building a distinguished career in the Army. He was based at the Jefferson Barracks, south of St. Louis. The couple fell in love and were married in 1830 in the home of General Clark. Hutter gave her a pearl necklace as a wedding present.

The next year Harriet Risque Hutter delivered her husband George a little boy, named Ferdinand Charles Hutter. Grandfather Risque was pleased to have another grandson.

Aaron Burr died in 1833 in a New York City hotel. John Dos Passos wrote that Burr never escaped "from the strait-jacket of self worship." Few mourned for him.

George and Harriet Hutter decided to settle in the Lynchburg area. Hutter chose well in 1841 when he bought the Sandusky plantation, once owned by John M. Otey. The elegant 1808 brick house sat on a hill overlooking Lynchburg and was about halfway between Lynchburg and Risque's Hunter's Hill plantation.

Risque was proud of his Hutter in-laws and his Hutter grandchildren. But he especially doted on that very first grandchild, James Beverly Ward, the only child of Adeline Eliza Ward.

James B. Ward, then a young man, was a bit gangly with his long legs. Most education of the times was by tutoring. Being a former military man, Grandfather Risque felt that the lad could benefit from a more disciplined education, away from home. In 1838 he and son-in-law George Hutter encouraged grandson Ward to apply for admission to the U.S. Military Academy at West Point in New York state. Risque wrote a glowing letter of recommendation for grandson James Beverly Ward.

Young Ward was admitted to the Academy in July 1838. It soon became apparent that West Point was not the place for him. His grades were deficient, and he left the Academy after eighteen months.

If Risque knew how his grandson had fared up there on the Hudson in New York, he would have been disappointed. He was used to winning. Perhaps he was never told.

Risque grew ill and died in 1840. His vision about Lynchburg had come true: the city was now booming, with a population of 6,400 people. His aspirations for success had come true too. By most measurable terms, he was a successful man. He left a proud reputation that his descendants admired. For the next consecutive five generations, at least one heir was given the name James Beverly.

He also left his heirs nine slaves and substantial money, real estate, fine silver, and furnishings. Son Ferdinand Risque, who already had been given some land, got title to the slave Peter, who had been loaned to him when he was in Missouri. Ferdinand Risque became an attorney in Georgetown, D.C. Son-in-law George C. Hutter was willed some property to help discharge his debts. Son-in-law Giles Ward was given Risque's library and law books. Daughter Adeline Ward and husband Giles Ward got to live on the farm. His special grandson James B. Ward was bequeathed a gold watch and a mulatto slave boy, George, who was valued at $450.

After his grandfather's death, James Beverly Ward, with the watch in his pocket and with the Academy in his past, looked westward. This young man would prove to be a critical figure in the Beale treasure story. He is the only person whose name is on *The Beale Papers*. His life gives still more insight into the veracity of the pamphlet.

15.
James B. Ward

Uncle George Christian Hutter knew of the potential of the west first hand. He had been there. As an army officer, he served in Missouri. He told James that the frontier offered great opportunity, and he would help James get started with a job.

The trip would be uncomfortable and hard. There was no railroad, no through stage. However, it sounded interesting, challenging, exciting. Ward decided to go. It was 1840.

Ward may have sold his slave, George, to pay for the trip. Or he may have taken him along. We can guess his route: travel by horseback, over the Blue Ridge, down the valley and into the tip of Tennessee. Then overland to Nashville, where a horse trader would convert his horse into money. Then board a river boat to ride down the Tennessee to Paducah and the Ohio.

At Cairo, near Fort Massac, he could have boarded a steamboat to go up the Mississippi toward St Louis. Steam power had brought modern times to the Mississippi. Steamboats were safer than the earlier days when boilers might explode and sear or kill people. There was still some risk, but since travel was much faster than by other boats or by horse, it was worth the risk. It cost twice as much going upstream as downstream (12 cents vs. 6 cents per mile), but it was the way to go.

The official capital of Missouri after 1826 was Jefferson City, on the Missouri River 125 miles west of St. Louis. The economic and cultural capital was St. Louis, located just a few miles south of the mouth of the Missouri River. The army installation, Jefferson Barracks, was south of that.

Ward had heard about Jefferson Barracks, where Chief Blackhawk had been imprisoned in 1833. Uncle George had served with the regular army as a lieutenant during the Black Hawk War.

This was also General William Clark's base as territorial governor and later as Superintendent of Indian Affairs until he died in 1838. St. Louis was home for Senator Thomas Hart Benton, a man who once brawled with Andrew Jackson. (During that brawl, Benton's brother shot and wounded Jackson in the shoulder. But the men later became good friends and political allies.) In the U.S. Senate Benton was a strong champion of

Jefferson Barracks was established about 1826, on the Mississippi River south of St. Louis.

Jacksonian Democratic policies. He advocated western expansion, favoring low land prices to stimulate settlement in the territories. He believed that westward expansion was the nation's "manifest destiny." Missouri ranks Benton as one of its greatest native sons, along with Mark Twain.

Ward debarked at Jefferson Barracks. He was glad to have the trip behind him. Knowing that St. Louis had been the center of French fur trade, he could see strong evidence of that heritage. There were streets with French names, and some people still spoke French. St. Louis was exciting — still a frontier settlement. There were Creole descendants of the first French colonists. There were Indians and half-breeds and vagrants. There were rifle-toting backwoodsmen from Kentucky, Tennessee, and Virginia. There were boatmen who floated the commerce on the Ohio and the Mississippi. There were some fine homes. And it was growing fast as new residents moved in. Each day more people arrived. Some were just passing through: traders, settlers, and adventurers who stopped there only long enough to gather provisions and supplies before heading west: .

Major George Hutter had arranged a job for nephew James as an assistant paymaster. It was routine work, but it did associate Ward with "real" money — the kind Army men got. And shopkeepers welcomed their business. This was a time when gold and silver coins were in short supply. Until just a few years earlier, people had used — and trusted — paper money notes that were issued by state banks. But not in 1840. The United States had paid off its national debt in 1835. Sales of territorial land had helped produce a $40 million surplus, and part of these funds had been deposited into state banks. But then the banks made bad loans that they couldn't recover, so they couldn't redeem their paper money with gold or silver. Faith in banks and paper money collapsed. Many banks closed down, and the economy had been partly paralyzed in 1837. No one wanted state bank notes, which became known as "broken notes." Any paper money was suspect. And the supply of coins was not adequate to serve all the needs of the economy.

Perhaps the glitter of all those payroll gold coins sparked the idea of a treasure fantasy in young James Ward. Actually, there was something more important to captivate his fancy. Ward discovered other Virginians in St. Louis. There was a family from Bedford County: Colonel John Buford Otey, his wife Angeline, and their daughter Harriet. The colonel was a cousin of Mrs. Paschal Buford.

James Ward became strongly attracted to Miss Otey. He proposed. She accepted. In an Episcopal ceremony at the town of St. Charles, they married. Now James had a wife Harriet and an aunt Harriet. It was 1841. He was nineteen years old.

It was a dramatic year in yet another way. President William Henry Harrison set a new record for the least time in office. He was inaugurated in March, caught pneumonia, and died in April. John Tyler became the first Vice President to succeed to the Presidency. His policies conflicted with those of the dead President, so most of the cabinet quit. There was uncertainty in the air.

But the Wards began a family nonetheless. Harriet gave birth to a boy. They named him James Beverly Ward, Jr. This first member of a new generation carried the given names of his great-grandfather Risque. Ward, Sr., had been an only child. He appreciated all the attention he received while he was growing up, but he wanted a big family. Harriet would ultimately deliver eleven babies, and the Wards would have twenty grandchildren.

When Risque died, his daughter Adeline Ward inherited rights to Hunter's Hill, the family plantation. Living there, she missed her only child, James. He missed home too. She urged him to return to Lynchburg. James did not need much prodding.

The young Ward family — James, Harriet and baby James — did come back to Virginia, bringing exciting memories of Missouri frontier life that they would always remember.

Other members of Adeline Risque Ward's family also returned to the Lynchburg area. The family network grew with interwoven cousins, in-laws, and babies. It was special to have James home. Sister Harriet Hutter "came home" to live at Sandusky, just a few miles from Risque's Hunter's Hill. The "Risque sisters," Adeline and Harriet, could spend more time together. James and Harriet Ward had their second child, Ella, in June, 1844 and two years after that another girl was born, Adeline.

Then came war with Mexico. Most of Virginia was unaffected, but the Wards and the Hutters felt deeply involved. Uncle George was serving as a captain in the Sixth U.S. Infantry.

Trouble had started brewing in 1803 with the Louisiana Purchase when the border between the U.S. and the Spanish territory was not clearly defined. Then in 1835 some Texans declared their independence from Mexico. The Mexican army tried to squelch this uprising and stormed the Alamo, killing all within. The next year General Sam Houston forced General Santa Anna to surrender.

In 1845 President James Polk and Congress decided that the United States should annex Texas. Mexico and the U.S. went to war about the boundary.

U.S. General S.W. Kearny marched into and occupied Santa Fe in 1846. A year later Army General Winfield Scott, with Captain Robert E. Lee on his staff, landed troops at Vera Cruz and battled westward to occupy in Mexico City in September 1847. Rumors whispered that the U.S. Army seized gold and silver from the Mexican treasury. It wasn't until the U.S. and Mexico agreed on peace terms in February 1848 that the region finally calmed down.

But then came news from the West that sparked everyone's imagination: gold had been found in California. In September 1848, Easterners had not only heard about the gold; they had gotten a chance to see some of it. A U.S. Navy Midshipman was first to bring samples to Washington and then to Wall Street. This Navy man, a grandson of Commodore Thomas Truxtun, was one Edward F. Beale. This Beale was no close kin of the Beales of Fincastle. There is no doubt about this Beale gold. Hundreds saw him with it, and history confirms it. Edward F. Beale, USN, was a man with actual pieces of gold.

Dreams of riches lured Easterners to head for California and try their luck at prospecting. In 1849 some 80,000 "forty-niners" went west. One of them was bachelor Dr. David C. Ward, a distant cousin of James Beverly Ward.

The year 1850 brought both good and bad news to the Wards: a birth and a death. Harriet delivered the couple's fourth child, a boy, on Valentine's Day. Ward's father, Giles, died at age 51. With no husband and no other children, widow Adeline would have to depend upon James.

The family needed money. James and his mother raised $900 in cash the next year by selling a family slave, Leander, his freedom.

The Bufordville Oteys, Ward's in-laws, encouraged James to have a business. The Virginia and Tennessee Railway, with offices in Lynchburg, began laying tracks through Bedford County and announced plans for a station at Buford's. The area was expected to experience an economic boom, with considerable new construction. There would be a need for lumber.

The Wards went ahead with the idea of having a business. In March of 1852 James and Harriet contracted to buy for $300 a sawmill and land on Goose Creek in Buford's, in Bedford County. The sellers were Lucy and Benjamin H. Franklin, and their signatures were certified by Justice of the Peace Paschal Buford. Buford's son-in-law was trustee for the deed of trust (mortgage).

Later that year the first train made its way from Lynchburg, through the County, and on to Big Lick. Everybody came out to see this mobile marvel of hissing steam and belching smoke. This historic trip fueled further optimism about the future of Bufordville.

During these months James Ward visited Goose Creek Valley to check on his mill. He heard the rhythmic squeaking of the wheel and the splashing of the water. He hoped this venture would be a real moneymaker. Sometimes he would also stop in and have refreshments at Buford's tavern. It was then owned by Paschal Buford and had been built in 1822 to replace the one owned by his father.

Harriet Ward's little son, Ferdinand, died in infancy. Her sixth child, Annie, was given the middle name of Morriss, in honor of family friends, Robert and Sarah Morriss.

Ward's business dealings escalated, and he started to have financial problems. The Wards borrowed $800 to buy a steam engine "and appurtenances" for the mill. John Otey showed his support by co-signing the note. Ward was granted credit for some other items, again with Otey as a co-signer. He paid off the mortgage on the mill in 1855, but another creditor had to go to court soon after to force Ward to pay $198.67 that he had owed for eight months.

The Wards found 1856 a very trying year. Their responsibilities mounted as a daughter, their seventh child, was born. They experienced a profound tragedy: their fourteen-year-old son, Junior, died in a hunting accident. They were grief stricken. The body was buried in the family cemetery on the Risque plantation.

And the business venture was not working out. Business had not boomed, and the mill was not as profitable as they had hoped. There were three court judgments against Ward for debt problems. Finally Harriet and James gave up their mill, after just four years. They signed the mill and its acreage over to Simeon Buford for $300.

Ward then obtained $200 credit from Snowlins and Murrill, Lynchburg merchants, but it was a debt that he didn't pay until forced by the court in 1858. Baby number eight, Charles, arrived the next year.

16.
Civil War

A friend told Ward that the Masons would be starting a new lodge and would welcome new members. Lynchburg would have two: the Marshall Lodge and the new Hill City Lodge. Ward knew that just about every important man in town was a Mason, and he wanted to be in that circle. But it was a bit far to travel to meetings, and family finances were strained. Some day, perhaps.

The struggles of the Ward family continued but soon were overshadowed by the issues and differences between the North and the South. Abraham Lincoln, who opposed slavery, won the election vote of 1860. South Carolina then declared that the Union was dissolved. A rapid series of events brought the United States into war with itself.

Southern states seized federal properties, arsenals, and installations. Rebels fired upon a federal ship as it was bringing supplies to Fort Sumter in January 1861. Jefferson Davis was inaugurated as President of the new Confederate States of America, which proclaimed itself to be a separate nation.

After Lincoln was inaugurated as President of the U.S.A., Confederate shore batteries pounded Fort Sumter into surrendering in April. Lincoln called the Confederate actions an "insurrection" and called for volunteers.

Virginia legislators interpreted Lincoln's call as an intent to invade the South and seceded from the Union. Robert E. Lee resigned from the U.S. Army and became a leader of the Confederate armies.

Southern men stepped forward and volunteered to defend their homeland. James Ward, now 39, was unable to join the Confederate Army because of an old bone fracture. But he was able to ride to remote places and bring supplies to the railroad. He planted more vegetables than usual at Hunter's Hill to help feed his family.

The Confederate flag of stars and bars.

Uncle George Hutter, 68, decided to forego a commission in the Confederate forces and stay home at Sandusky. His three sons — first cousins of Ward — went to war. J. Risque, Edward S., and Ferdinand C. Hutter all became Confederate officers.

"Aunt" Sarah Morriss, family friend and wife of innkeeper Robert Morriss, was staying with the Wards when she became seriously ill and died in May, 1861, at age 77.

The Southern forces represented themselves well at the first battle of Bull Run at Manassas. Many were killed and more were wounded. Lynchburg — far from the scene of battle — began to serve as a hospital area. The injured were brought to the city by train. Even warehouses became makeshift hospitals.

In 1862 the Ward's ninth child was born. Ward did join the Freemasons, as an apprentice. He enjoyed the camaraderie and prestige. He was embarrassed by a court order requiring him and a friend to make good on a $125 debt.

In 1863 Confederate General "Stonewall" Jackson died after being shot by his own men in error. The body was brought by train to Lynchburg. People lined the streets to watch the funeral cortege move through town. The casket was placed on a packet boat, which then headed up the James River towards Lexington and its final resting place. There was much sadness. The South had lost a hero.

Ward was saddened again when Robert Morriss died at age 85. A notice in the paper appeared January 8, reporting that he had died five days earlier "at Roslin, the residence of his niece, Mrs. David Saunders." (The Saunders were part of a prominent family that had first acquired land from John Lynch, Jr. in the earlier days of Lynchburg.) Ward was one of many who felt he had lost a wise and trusted friend.

Lynchburg remained out of the way of battle. Though it was one of the more prosperous cities of the Confederacy, there were no sounds of battlefront gunfire here. But there was a compassionate awareness of the effects of the war among its citizens. Thousands of wounded soldiers were brought in by train throughout the war. During the single month of May in 1864, more than 10,000 wounded were brought to Lynchburg for care. The people of the city did all they could, but hundreds and hundreds of young soldiers died and were buried in Lynchburg cemeteries.

The war took a heavy toll on Harriet Otey Ward's family. Her half brother, Charles C. Otey, was killed in action in 1862 and buried in

Bufordville. Harriet's second cousins, from Lynchburg, Samuel, Van Rensselaer, and George Otey were killed.

She was grateful that James had been home. He attended his lodge meetings in Lynchburg when he could and qualified as a Master Mason.

Lynchburg had been spared the destruction of battle for more than three years. And then the city was threatened: Union General David Hunter, with 15,000 men, was in Lexington. General U.S. Grant ordered him to move on Lynchburg. Spies alerted C.S.A. General Jubal Early to rush to help defend the city.

On June 15 Hunter's army swarmed over the mountains, between the Peaks of Otter, and camped north of Liberty in Bedford County. He stayed at Fancy Farm, the elegant brick home once owned by Paschal Buford. Then his army began to march eastward. The stream of weary and hungry Federal soldiers stretched for miles.

By June 17 the front ranks of Federal forces had neared New London, outside of Lynchburg, not far from the Risque plantation. Ward and his family braced for the worst. Residents feared that if marauding soldiers didn't kill, maim, or rape, they would surely take food and steal valuables. Folks tried to hide their jewels, their silver, their trinkets. Wells were favorite hiding places. Others buried their things. The Wards left their home and stayed with friends farther away. Not far from the Risque plantation, Poplar Forest seemed vulnerable. Once the summer retreat of Thomas Jefferson, his heirs had sold it in 1828. Ownership passed by inheritance to the wife of Edward Sixtus Hutter in 1852. As Hunter's men neared New London, Aunt Matilda, an old "Mammy" of the owners, hid bags of sugar and the family silver service in her austere cabin.

There were some brief battle encounters. Early had his troops ready to counterattack the next day. Hunter and his aides took over Sandusky, placing owner George C. Hutter, 71, under house arrest. Here were two military professionals, two graduates of West Point, with Hutter being a nominal prisoner of Hunter. What did Hutter say about Lynchburg's defense?

We don't know what was said, but one thing is clear. Hunter concluded that he would not take the city. Frequent train movements and other ruses made him believe that he was outnumbered. His army was tired and low on ammunition. He decided to abandon Lynchburg and withdraw.

The next morning, Hunter let Hutter have his house back. But he left 117 wounded and sick Federal troops in the Hutter barn. Confederate Dr. Edward Craighill cared for them as best he could.

Union General David Hunter stayed a night at Major George Hutter's Home, Sandusky, before abandoning plans to attack Lynchburg.

As the Union army headed west, Confederate sharpshooters shadowed them for miles, picking off many Yankees as the swarm of soldiers retreated, then bivouacked west of Liberty, and finally streamed past Buford's and on towards Big Lick, Salem, and West Virginia.

Lynchburg was relieved. And Ward had yet another reason to celebrate. His tenth child, Otey Beverly, was born July 12.

In spite of their failure at Lynchburg, the Federal troops overpowered the Confederate forces all through the rest of the South. Atlanta fell in September. In April 1865 Robert E. Lee and his Army of Northern Virginia surrendered to General Grant at Appomattox. General Johnston surrendered to Sherman at Hillsboro, N.C., on April 29. Then, on May 10, C.S.A. President Jefferson Davis was captured in Georgia.

The war had taken a terrible toll on the country, especially in Virginia, which had been the primary battleground. Virginia lost many of its finest young men to death and disease. The economy was in shambles. Goods were hard to get. Confederate paper money was worthless. Gold and silver coins were rarely seen. Many wealthy people had lost most of their assets. Slaves could not be sold; they had been freed. Yet the South began to rebuild.

It was a difficult time for many families. Ward was still struggling financially. On three occasions in 1866 he was cited by the courts and ordered to make good on certain debts. Undoubtedly he was grateful for what the farm provided for his large family.

Finally in 1867, after 27 years of marriage, Harriet gave birth to her last child, her eleventh. But little Mary Beverly died at birth. That same year forty-five-year-old Ward accepted another disappointment. His membership in the Masons was suspended in October. No records have been found to explain why, but he probably couldn't pay the dues. Most of the South was in economic doldrums.

Lynchburg recovered more quickly from the war than most other southern cities. Its buildings were intact. The railroad tracks in the city had not been torn up. Its major product — tobacco — was in strong demand. Capable and enterprising veterans rebounded too. Harriet Otey Ward's second cousins flourished; John and Kirkwood Otey succeeded in insurance, and Peter Otey became a banker, a railroad president, and finally served in the U.S. Congress. The three sons of George Hutter came home and made their mark in engineering and, for Ferdinand, in accounting and Internal Revenue service.

The Wards hosted a festive occasion in 1869: daughter Adeline married in Lynchburg. The groom was an Alexandria man who had served in the Confederate Army and was badly wounded and held prisoner. The Wards were proud of him and happy for their daughter. The family grew again the following year: eldest daughter Ella also married a veteran, again in Lynchburg. Her groom fought for the South with the Louisiana troops. Ward heard his new son-in-law talk about the big cities of Louisiana.

On some Sundays James and Harriet Ward would take their buggy on the seven-mile trip to Lynchburg to attend Episcopal services at St. Paul's Church. Years earlier the Thespian Society and Ward's father, Giles, had given benefit performances that raised funds to help build that church's first edifice.

In 1870 a death occurred that sent Lynchburg and the South into mourning. It was the death of their beloved leader, General Robert E. Lee. Even Northerners, who respected his integrity, mourned.

In the next few years the Ward family spread out with two weddings, both in Florida, and more grandchildren.

James Ward celebrated his 54th birthday while the United States celebrated its 100th, in 1876. Lynchburg's premier railroad, then known as the AM&O, was not so ecstatic: it lost money and went into receivership. Many workers lost their jobs.

About the same time, President Rutherford B. Hayes visited Lynchburg. He had last been here when he served under General Hunter in 1864. Heavy rains also visited the area, flooding the James River and destroying parts of the canal.

Soon thereafter an unusual wedding took place. Ward's first cousin, J. Risque Hutter, married Charlotte Hutter. The bride was a first cousin of the groom. The wedding took place at the estate of Lottie's family, Poplar Forest.

After Harriet's father, Col. John B. Otey, died, the Wards relinquished any claim to his real estate. They sold their interest for $45 to other relatives. It wasn't much, but the cash was useful.

In 1879 Ward lost one of the important mentors of his life when Uncle George C. Hutter expired at the age of 86. His Sandusky estate would be divided among his children at a later time.

Ward's son, Charles Bell Ward, was then working with Adams Express. Ward was happy about that. He was not happy when people asked if he was related to James A. Ward, the bartender, or James Ward who worked for the bakery.

Lynchburg's economy got some serious news in 1882. The railroad revealed that it would move its headquarters out of Lynchburg and set up offices to the west in Roanoke, the town which had changed its name from Big Lick just the year before. Yard and office workers worried that they might have to move or — worse — lose their jobs. Storekeepers feared losing business and fretted about the future of the city. There were rumors that the move would not help the railroad's finances and that it would have problems, even in Roanoke. But the railroad management stuck to its plan.

The city suffered yet another loss in 1883: a fire consumed almost an entire block of downtown Lynchburg. Even the new brick *Virginian* building — home of the newspaper and print shop — was destroyed. Its walls collapsed during the conflagration, killing five volunteer firemen. The publisher resolved to stay in business.

Another merger occurred in town, though not one as profound as the railroads: Adams Bros. Co. joined J.G. and E.O. Payne. The principal store was at Upper Basin and 159 Main. And this company's name was about to get tangled with the Beale story.

On March 26, 1884, James B. Ward, at age 62, wrote to the Library of Congress asking for a copyright for *The Beale Papers,* "as agent for the author." His letter did not identify the author. He wrote the letter on the stationery of Adams Bros. and Paynes Feed Store. He submitted only the title page, not the whole pamphlet.

17.
The Agent

On March 31, 1885, a copyright for *The Beale Papers* pamphlet was granted to Ward.

That same year, copies of *The Beale Papers* were offered for sale in Lynchburg for fifty cents a copy. The pamphlet had been printed by the Virginia Job Printing House, at 1001 Main. This facility, owned by Charles and Joseph Button, also printed *The Virginian* each day. Ward was the man who acted as the pamphlet's marketing manager.

In the pamphlet the author states, "The gentleman whom I have selected as my agent to publish and circulate these papers, was well known to Mr. Morriss; it was at his house that Mrs. Morriss died...." That describes Ward. There are no documents showing how Ward marketed the pamphlets. There was a brief news item in the paper, noting that it created quite a stir.

The city had a party in 1886. Lynchburg was 100 years old.

Some years passed. There were more weddings. There were more grandchildren. Ward worked for the Campbell County court. He became interested in genealogy. He looked over grandmother Kennerly's family papers. He retrieved a partially-used ledger book that had been discarded by the court and in 1892 he carefully copied the Kennerly family history into the old ledger book. He had good penmanship. No evidence has turned up showing that Ward was capable of creative writing.

At the age of 70, he got an official appointment. Campbell County designated him as "Road Surveyor," whose duties included road inspection and evaluation.

More years went by, and Ward was feeling his age. His tall frame got leaner than ever. His face thinned out, accentuating his ears and his white moustache. He was unable to get around like he used to. His joints hurt. His wife died. He accepted the invitation of his daughter, Adeline, to come live for a while in her home at 105 Harrison Street. It was just a few blocks from St. Paul's Episcopal Church.

About 1903, a man from Roanoke came looking for him. The man said his name was Clayton Hart and that he wanted to talk about the pamphlet. He wanted more details about the Beale story. Ward told him that most of the pamphlets had been destroyed in a fire at the printers. He said that he could add no details about the Beale story, because everything he knew about it was already in the pamphlet. He gave no more details. Honorable man that he was, Ward also never publicly disclosed the name of the person for whom he had served as agent.

Clayton Hart talked with Ward's neighbors to measure his veracity. Hart learned that these neighbors had high respect for him and believed, as George Hart later wrote, "that Ward would never practice deception."

In 1904 Ward, enfeebled, formally resigned as Road Surveyor. He was 82.

Finally, after a long illness, Ward died on May 16, 1907, at his daughter's home, at age 85. There was an Episcopal funeral service conducted by Dr. Colston of St. Paul's. There was a large gathering of family. He would have liked that. The flower bearers included four granddaughters. Among the pallbearers were three grandsons and Christian Sixtus Hutter, of the Poplar Forest Hutters.

James Beverly Ward's body was taken to the family cemetery at Hunter's Hill, where he was buried along with his son, his father Giles Ward, and grandfather James Beverly Risque.

The name of James B. Ward is on *The Beale Papers* pamphlet. But, did he assemble, write, and publish the it? For many years, most Beale fans presumed that he did. They wanted to solve the ciphers and find the treasure.

They believed the story, so it mattered not who actually created the pamphlet. Most had never seen its full text. Instead, they relied on articles or stories that quoted parts of it, or articles that were based on other articles.

Of course it is possible that Ward fabricated the story. He had background and experience that could be the basis for a good tale about an adventurer bringing gold back from the West. Make-believe and drama were not new to him; his father had even been president of the local Thespian Society. Father Giles also set a good example for his son as a literate man, an editor, a lawyer. James knew something about adventure, having personally been "on the frontier" at St. Louis — albeit briefly. He was familiar with the area around Buford's. He had heard stories about his grandfather's duel with a flamboyant character named Thomas Beale. He knew the Morriss family and their lodging house background. So it is possible that James Ward created the story which is related in the pamphlet; it could have been a product of his imagination. Perhaps he and his wife Harriet worked it out together. She had been in Missouri, she grew up in Bufordville, she knew Lynchburg.

17 — The Agent

Did the Wards do it all, or part, or not at all?

Would a sexagenarian — man or woman, with many children and many grandchildren — have the solitude needed to create a complex tale? Harriet was a homemaker and mother to many children, with little time to do creative writing. Did they merely receive the ciphers and the Beale letters and then write the narrative? Because James had a poor track record in managing his personal financial affairs, we can doubt that he financed the publishing venture. If he couldn't afford it, someone else probably put up the money. Perhaps the only thing Ward wrote was the letter to the Copyright office.

James Ward was an intelligent and likeable man. He was persuasive and charming. He had the likability needed to win political appointments in Campbell County when he was well along in years. His neighbors thought that he could not practice deception.

Perhaps we should take his word at face value. In March 1884 he wrote a letter to apply for a copyright "as agent for the author." The pamphlet itself did not name an author; it just identified Ward as the copyright holder.

Then, too, *The Virginian* reported in May 1861 that Mrs. Morriss had died in the home of James B. Ward. The pamphlet author says "the gentleman whom I have selected as my agent to publish and circulate these papers.... it was at his house Mrs. Morriss died." If Ward were the author, it seems strange that he would talk about himself this way.

If the entire story had been Ward fiction, he might have wanted to keep his name out of it. He might not want his neighbors or friends to learn that he was guilty of a hoax. Yet, Ward made no effort to disassociate himself from the pamphlet. His name is there for all to see. If he had made it up, and didn't want to admit it, he could have gotten someone else to hold the copyright and thereby remain anonymous. But if we can believe the pamphlet and/or believe Ward's application letter, then Ward was just the agent. Someone else was the author.

18.
Author Wanted

The Beale Papers could be a true story. Or, it could be fiction; a clever, determined person could have made it up. A writer of fiction need never have met Morriss, well known around Lynchburg as a businessman and hotel keeper. Furthermore, there was printed in 1858 *Sketches and Recollections of Lynchburg, by the Oldest Inhabitant*, a book that described not only Morriss' career but also his character and manner.

A fiction writer could have mined popular literature for inspiration and details. Both Mark Twain and Edgar Allen Poe wrote books that involved treasure and intrigue. Both would surely have been available in Lynchburg in 1880.

Mark Twain's *Tom Sawyer* was first published in 1876 and enjoyed popularity right from the start. In this tale, Tom and his friend Huckleberry see Injun Joe dig up a treasure chest. Later Tom and friend Becky are lost five days in a cave, where Injun Joe was. After Joe dies, the boys return to the cave and find the chest, containing $12,000.

Edgar Allen Poe's The Gold Bug *told of ciphers and buried treasure.*

Poe's *The Gold Bug*, first published in 1843, has been widely circulating ever since. Its central character believes that he will find a treasure buried by Captain Kidd in a seven-foot deep hole. This treasure hunter is an amateur cryptographer. The secret location of the hoard is revealed in a coded message — comprised of a series of numbers. The solution comes from substituting letters for numbers, using a key.

Both these classic tales have a hidden treasure. *Tom Sawyer* has a cave. *The Gold Bug* has a substitution cipher. The Beale story has a hidden treasure, with its location defined by a substitution cipher, and discusses a cave.

The Beale Papers and Poe's *Gold Bug* share some other story ideas, too. The very first two sentences of *The Gold Bug* are "Many years ago I contracted an intimacy with a Mr. William Legrand. He was of an ancient Huguenot family, and had once been wealthy; but a series of misfortunes had reduced him to want." Now compare that idea with this early part of the Beale story: "The following details of an incident happened many years ago.... Robert Morriss ... was eminently successful ... however ... reverses came when they were least expected ... and left him nothing to save."

Innis wrote that "some think *The Gold Bug* was based upon the Beale Treasure story." Yet *The Gold Bug* was published decades before *The Beale Papers*, and even decades before Morriss supposedly turned the papers over. Poe died in 1849.

Similarly, a writer can also write a story about gold and the West without ever having been near Santa Fe. Libraries everywhere have books about the subject. Printed lore is rich with fascinating details about places and men of adventure.

Students of history could have learned that gold had been found in Colorado, north of Santa Fe, in 1858. There was yet was another source: *Life in the Far West*, by George Frederick Augustus Ruxton, which was published in 1859. This is ten years after the California find, and almost forty years after Beale's purported discovery. The 1880 book, *New Colorado and the Santa Fe Trail* by A.A. Hayes, could be inspiration for a story about gold north of Santa Fe. Certainly in 1882 an author could write about gold found in Colorado.

There are clues that should not be ignored in our search for the author of *The Beale Papers*. They have to do with the what was going on in Lynchburg at the time the pamphlet was being prepared.

The pamphlet probably had its beginnings in the early 1880's, well before Ward's application for copyright. If we accept the pamphlet's account as truth, then we must believe the author when he says that he got the box and papers from Robert Morriss in 1862 and when he says he wrote the pamphlet "more than twenty years since the papers came into my hands." Even a fiction writer would need two or three years to work out this intricate story and the ciphers. Fiction or fact, the manuscript was probably completed about 1883.

There are theories about to whom Morriss told the story.

Morriss died in January, 1863 at the home of his niece. Perhaps she or her husband got the papers and tale from Morriss. Another roomer could be the one. Or maybe the author was a relative or a friend that merely dropped by from time to time. The pamphlet says, "Inviting me to his room... [Morriss] ... gave me...." And later, "[T]he papers upon which this history is based were delivered into my possession," and "the box and contents were placed in my possession."

The original papers and letters from Beale have never turned up. If the author was a hoaxer, then Morriss never had any papers to pass along. If Morriss was the hoaxer — or if Morriss told the truth — he would have passed the papers to the author.

Factual or fictional ... the author wanted more than just casual privacy. He or she wanted absolute privacy. He may have feared that public revelation of his role would jeopardize important parts of his life — such as his family's prestige in the community, his profession, his career, or his reputation for integrity. The author could have wanted privacy whether the story was true or not. If he was a hoaxer, of course he would want anonymity. Even if Morriss really had given him the papers, the author may have had some reservations and not wanted to risk looking foolish. So either way, he wanted to keep his name out of it.

An author of fiction may have gotten into this venture because he worried about his financial security and hoped to make some money outside of his job. (As is often the case, the most capable and most responsible people are the ones who worry most about losing their jobs.) His job may well have been secure, but he may have lacked confidence that his boss was satisfied with his work. He may have had access to inside financial information and saw that his firm was in such bad financial shape that his job might disappear.

Creating a fictional *The Beale Papers* would be a challenging task which could not be accomplished in a few weeks. The ideas of the story probably rattled around in the creator's mind over a period of many months, or even years. Most likely, the work went on a bit at a time, when there was privacy or quiet at home late at night, or when he was away on business and at night in his hotel room.

Many of the names, places, and ideas relate to James Ward's life experience. He could have had a role in developing the story if it were fiction.

Fact or fiction, the author had some association with James Ward. They could be relatives, close friends, or merely acquaintances. They could have met at a store, restaurant or inn. Perhaps they were both Episcopalians who met at church. Maybe both were Masons. Or they could have swapped stories at a bar. They could have been of different ages.

They may have crossed paths in or around Lynchburg. In 1880, there were just 7,485 white residents, of whom approximately 1,500 were Episcopalian. Ward was one of those, as were 450 other adult males. If the author were also Episcopal, there is a high likelihood that they would have known each other.

One scenario goes like this: The two got to know each other, and the younger man enjoyed hearing Ward's tales of his true experiences, along with embellishments he may have added. As they talked, a story evolved that could have been part fact and part imagination. The younger man suggested that they put it into print; maybe they could make some money on it. Ward liked the idea, but he was short of cash. The younger man agreed to help out — and maybe even pay the printing cost — if Ward would protect his privacy. Ward was to get a share of the income or be paid outright to be the agent.

The adventure story may have originated with the Wards. The other person refined the details to fit history. Then they developed the three ciphers. One described the size of the hoard in the vault. This was to be the teaser, so a deciphered solution was provided. Another cipher was purported to list the associates of Thomas Beale who were to share in the treasure. But the most important cipher was the one labeled "No. 1." It would give the directions to where the treasure is buried. This was intentionally the toughest one. And tough it is. Some of the best code experts have failed to crack it so far. Could it be random gibberish that was designed never to make sense?

After it was all carefully written down, the pamphlet was printed. Employees at the print shop may have seen only Ward. If Ward paid cash, he could have taken delivery of the pamphlets. His later remarks imply that the bulk of the pamphlets remained at the printer. This was either by choice or because full payment hadn't been made. Ward did take some sample copies home, along with the original manuscript. He sent just a printed sample title page to the Copyright Office.

It is possible that the pamphlets were printed well before 1885, with no date. Sample copies of the pamphlet show that the date on the title page is in a slightly different place on each copy. This suggests that the date was added on a later press run. The undated pamphlets could have been printed in 1883 or 1884, prior to receipt of copyright.

At last, in 1885, some pamphlets were sold. The price printed on the cover was fifty cents. The Lynchburg paper commented that the pamphlet created quite a stir.

Then the author started having misgivings. His job seemed to be going well after all. He feared that if people should learn that he was involved with some kind of hoax, he could lose his dignity, his reputation, or his job. So he told Ward to sit tight. He withheld the supply of copies. The story faded quickly; very few copies got into circulation.

Ward would later tell people that not many copies got out because most of the pamphlets were destroyed in a fire at the printers. There was indeed a big fire at the *Virginian* building, but that was back in 1883. Maybe these were undated pamphlets.

We can wonder why additional pamphlets were not printed after the fire. There were some copies around. Clayton Hart got a copy of the dated pamphlet a few years after publication. If it had been a good idea to publish the pamphlet in the first place, it could have been reprinted. Maybe it was never done because of lack or money, or misgivings on the part of the author.

There are several theories as to why so few copies got out. Richard Greaves thinks that children of Paschal Buford were annoyed that a treasure story involved their father and his tavern. Paschal's son, Rowland, was Bedford County Clerk and a prominent citizen in 1885. Greaves speculates that the Buford family pressured Ward to withdraw the pamphlet from circulation.

There is another notion: the pamphlet wasn't selling. Some copies have been found where the cover price of "fifty cents" was crossed out and "25¢" was written in. Maybe the pamphlet was a publishing turkey. The author or publisher may have died, so the project died, too.

In any event, the Beale story didn't really get wide distribution in 1885. There are no tales of treasure hunters for the period of time between 1885 and 1897. It seems that all was quiet for a dozen years.

In fact, other than the author, the earliest recorded seekers of the Beale treasure are the Hart brothers, Clayton and George.

18 — Author Wanted

It was in 1897 or 1898 that Clayton Hart was approached by his boss, Newton Hazlewood, Chief Clerk in the Audit office of the Norfolk & Western Railway at Roanoke, to type up copies of some sheets that he said were codes about a treasure. The numbers were on sheets of papers, not pages from a printed document. There were eight sheets of notepaper, two sheets headed simply "No. 1," three sheets headed "No. 2," and three sheets headed "No. 3." Hart was told that the numbers had come from a pamphlet that had been published and sold in Lynchburg.

Innis interviewed Clayton Hart's brother, George, and wrote in *Gold In The Blue Ridge* that "Hazlewood said that he tried to persuade Ward not to publish the pamphlet...." In his comments George Hart, father of a judge and a man with a reputation of unquestioned integrity, indicates indirectly two very significant points. First, Hazlewood knew Ward. Second, Hazlewood knew what was in the pamphlet — before it went to press.

If Hazlewood was the author, why, after a dozen years of anonymity, would he let the story out? His job was secure after all. His mood may have changed. He may have yearned for recognition for his efforts. He may have wanted the satisfaction of knowing that he had created a very clever puzzle: he let someone see his original cipher sheets.

Innis also reported Hart saying that Hazlewood had told him that, after the fire, Hazlewood got the original papers back from Ward so that the pamphlet could not be reprinted. It seems implausible that Hazlewood would spend money to buy the papers from Ward if he merely disapproved of the Beale pamphlet. Ward would have given them to him, if they had been Hazlewood's papers to begin with.

We can speculate that Newton Hazlewood had the opportunity and the motivation to be involved with *The Beale Papers* pamphlet. He had lived and worked in Lynchburg, as did Ward. He was an Episcopalian, as was Ward, and he lived near St. Paul's church. He was a Mason, as had been Ward. He was familiar with Buford's, as was Ward. He had a job with a firm that was indeed in financial difficulty in the early 1880's. He was literate and had a reputation to protect. He was skilled in working with numbers. He traveled and he spent many nights away from home.

Let us see what we can learn about this man, Newton Hyde Hazlewood.

19.
Trusted Friend

Newton Hyde Hazlewood was a keen-minded, career-oriented professional who had lived in both Lynchburg and in Bufordville. Apparently he knew Ward before the pamphlet went into print. He was a tall man — in his later life a bit heavy around the chest and neck. He was somewhat bald on top and wore a closely cropped beard. To most folks he seemed formal of manner.

Hazlewood was learned and articulate. He had a collection of books and was especially proud of his complete set of Shakespeare. He once taught Latin at a school near Baltimore. While there, he met his future bride, Mary Marriott, a native of Howard County.

Mary was a small and pretty woman, even in her old age. Some thought she was just a "man's woman" — always looking pretty. But she was indeed a mother! Mary had twelve pregnancies, one of which was a set of twins who died in infancy. Seven of those children survived their parents. Fortunately Mary had help with running her large household. The Hazlewoods employed two indentured girls for housework and a hired yard man.

Newton was born in Campbell County in 1840, son of Charlotte and Henry Hazlewood. Newton's father was the first postmaster of Castle Craig, a small village on Ward's Road south of Lynchburg. Newton was named for the great scientist, Sir Isaac Newton. He grew up on the family's 200-acre farm, where they raised tobacco, sheep and cattle.

In 1852, the first Virginia & Tennessee train came to Lynchburg. In November of that year the first train of passengers and freight made a run from Lynchburg to Big Lick. Another line was built between Lynchburg and Petersburg. After the Southside Railway was built between Lynchburg and Chatham, the mail was dropped off at Lynch Station. Newton would sometimes help his father get the mail there and bring it back to Castle Craig. He didn't know then that he would later have a career in railroading.

When the Civil War began in 1861, 21-year-old Newton joined the "Old Dominion Rifles" (Company C) of the 28th Regiment Virginia Infantry; he served under Capt. Thomas M. Bowyer. He was mustered into service on May 25th by Lt. Col. Langhorn.

His regiment marched north and fought in the first battle of Manassas (Bull Run). Newton's acumen and courage earned him an early promotion to 3rd Sargeant in August, as his company transferred into the Artillery as "Bowyer's Battery."

Later Hazlewood served under Captain Richard Johnson and then in "Latham's Battery." A dependable fighting man, he was promoted to 1st Lieutenant in December 1864. His even temperament was particularly evident during those war years. He was a man who could be calm under pressure. One who served with him said, "I never saw him flicker."

Later in life his associates called him "Captain." This may have been an honorary title of respect like the "colonel" or "major" titles frequently imputed to people of status in the South at that time. Like all Americans, Newton found the war a traumatic experience. After the war, Newton maintained a strong tie to the William Watts Camp in Roanoke, where he and other veterans shared their experiences.

The railroad industry provided Newton with his career. He worked for the railroad for 42 years. Most of those years were spent in a supervisory capacity as chief clerk in the audit department.

He began working for the railroad as a clerk in Lynchburg. Two Lynchburg railway companies — the Virginia & Tennessee and the Southside — merged in 1870 and adopted a grand name: the Atlantic, Mississippi, and Ohio. Most folks called it the AM&O. President of the firm was Con-

Railroad service between Lynchburg and Big Lick (now Roanoke) enhanced the Bufordville economy in 1852.

federate hero General Mahone. By 1873, Hazlewood was living in the heart of Lynchburg and had joined the Masons.

The nation celebrated its anniversary in 1876: one hundred years of independence as a nation. Newton and Mary also celebrated. Mary gave birth to a son, William. This son was always very special to Newton. Later in life, when Newton signed his will, he selected William, from all his children, to be executor.

The year was not without strains and worries. The AM&O went into receivership. Newton had worked on some of the financial figures. He knew that the business was shaky. With the future of the company in doubt, Newton was nervous about his job. He began thinking about how to survive if his job disappeared some day. He and his small family were living on Madison Street, not far from St. Paul's Episcopal Church.

The railroad's problems grew worse. A fire broke out and destroyed the main Lynchburg roundhouse shops. The railroad struggled for economic survival. The next year it was bought by the E.L. Clark Co. The new owners changed its name to Norfolk and Western Railway (N&W) and vowed to do whatever would be necessary to make it profitable. Employees wondered who would be retained and who would be let go. Newton was told he was still needed. He breathed more easily, but knew that no job is ever guaranteed.

The new management wanted to consolidate the various lines at a central point. The area known as Big Lick seemed logical: east-west lines crossed the north-south lines there. The bosses chose Big Lick over Lynchburg and started planning to move there. The business people of Big Lick were delighted, and the 669 residents voted in 1882 to adopt the more prestigious sounding name of Roanoke.

Newton wanted to live closer to where he'd be working, but he also thought it wise to have a small farm — to help support his burgeoning family. He scouted Bedford County and chose Bufordville because he loved its beautiful countryside and because it was just a short train ride to work. Bufordville would be important in the lives of the Hazlewoods. It would also be important for seekers of the Beale Treasure.

In 1883 he bought a parcel of 59 acres. It was a beautiful tract. It included a knoll where he would build the house. It was convenient: its northern edge abutted the railroad tracks, and it was a short walk to the Bufordville station. It had highway potential too: the southern boundary was the East-West turnpike. Newton bought a horse and a cow and hired a "colored man" to do the manual work, cut firewood, tend the garden, and carry out other chores. Neighbors rented part of the land to grow corn.

19 — Trusted Friend

Bufordville took the new name of Montvale in 1890. This is the station plaza area about 1895.

The Hazlewood home was filled with children. Besides their own offspring, the Hazlewoods had provided a home for their two indentured nieces, Alice and Lottie. When their mother Margaret died, the Overseer of the Poor bound the two girls out to Newton "to be taught the art and business of housekeeping" until each became 18, at which time he was to pay each $10.

Newton missed his Lynchburg friends when his N&W office moved to Roanoke. He had enjoyed his Lodge meetings and getting together with professional comrades. He was home on weekends, but spent the week in a rented room in Roanoke.

His job often took him "on the rail," away from the area on business. From time to time he had to be in Lynchburg to audit the railroad activities still located there.

In 1884 the New London Academy became a public school. The Academy had a reputation for providing superior education. Even though it was far from Bufordville, Hazlewood enrolled two of his sons, Will and Frank. They became boarding students. Newton wrote to them often and frequently sent them a bundle that included clothing that he had bought for them.

His letters reported news about the family and the farm, sometimes written on Norfolk & Western paper. He urged them to go to church, "study hard and improve your time. Be obedient and careful." The usual sign off was, "Very fondly, your father, N.H. Hazlewood."

Newton's oldest son, Newton, Jr., married in 1887 and took a job with Norfolk and Western, too. Sadly, that happy event was closely followed by two unhappy ones. Newton's father died in 1889. His will stipulated that his widow could "remain in quiet" at the family's Campbell County farm if she wished until her death or remarriage. Then the farm was to be divided equally among the children.

In 1892 Newton's mother died. As executor, Newton's job was to implement her will. Most of the parental assets had already been allocated in the father's will. Charlotte left Charlie $100; Walter would have received $10 (but he died before his mother); Jamie was left a heifer; sister Ella received the mother's house and its contents; and Newton received $10 cash.

Newton's association with the Beale treasure first became known outside the family in the summer of 1897 when he asked Clayton Hart to make several copies of eight sheets of paper with numbers on them. Hazlewood reportedly told Hart that the numbers in the pamphlet had been changed to protect those to whom the treasure rightfully belonged.

The numbers Hart typed differ slightly from those printed in the pamphlet. More about that later.

George Hart wrote that Hazlewood wished Clayton success in finding the treasure, saying, "Even though I have never made any headway in the matter of deciphering the figures, I remain reasonably confident the treasure lies buried where originally placed."

Innis learned from George Hart that the reason why Hazlewood had tried to stop Ward from publishing the pamphlet was that he thought it would be unfair to the legitimate claimants to the treasure. Hazlewood always had been an upright and honorable man.

Clayton Hart went to Lynchburg, located a copy of the pamphlet, and brought it home. He and his brother tried to decode the ciphers. They tried to deduce where Beale could have buried the treasure. They even enlisted a young clairvoyant to help them find it. The brothers broke their first ground in Montvale in the spring of 1903.

The Harts did not find it.

In 1905 Newton gave four acres of his land to Newton Jr., who had become a station agent. Junior built a house on the property, but shortly thereafter sold it and moved to Danville, where he made a career with Coca Cola.

Son Frank and his family moved from Roanoke to Bufordville/ Montvale in 1914, to a house on property adjoining the Hazlewood homestead. Frank's wife died, so his sister Mary brought up Frank's children.

The family farm shrank further in 1905: N&W acquired 2.62 acres of land — to permit changing the track curvature near the farm.

In 1906, while in Baltimore with son William, Newton signed a simple will. In it he directed that the proceeds of his Royal Arcanum life insurance be paid to his widow and that she live in the family's house until her death or remarriage, and then his assets should be divided "equally among my six children." He noted that Newton Jr. had already been provided for.

Newton kept working until he died. There were no pensions then to provide income in old age. He continued to be one of the first in the office each morning. He stayed in a room in a private Roanoke home, but routinely ate breakfast and picked up his mail at the Stratford Hotel.

One payday morning, he didn't show up for work. Puzzled, his boss sent a clerk over to see what was wrong. Hazlewood was found on the floor — in his sleeping clothes. He had apparently died before going to bed or just after he had gotten up. The landlady said that he had been complaining of shortness of breath. Coroner Dr. R. Gordon Simmons examined the body, concluded that the cause of death was due to heart disease, and ruled out an autopsy. His body was sent to Montvale on train Number 3.

An Episcopal service was conducted at Christ Episcopal Church by Rev. Archer Boogher. Besides his wife and seven children, thirteen grandchildren attended the funeral. Two special railroad cars brought about a hundred friends and associates from Roanoke. The body was interred on a knoll, about 100 yards from his house where, a few weeks earlier, he had remarked that "this is the spot" where he'd like to be buried.

The family homestead burned down in 1938.

Hazlewood had the opportunity and the intellect to write *The Beale Papers*. He knew the content of the pamphlet before it was published.

However, if the pamphlet's record of the treasure's history is accurate, several details weaken the possibility that Hazlewood was the author. Hazlewood's parents were not in the Lynchburg city orbit, and so they may not have been well known to Morriss. Hazlewood himself was perhaps too young to have been close to Morriss.

The pamphlet says that Morriss gave the letters and papers to the author in 1862. At that time, Morriss would have been 84 and Hazlewood just 22. Hazlewood had enlisted in 1861 and was a battlefield soldier away at war; he would have had scant opportunity to be in Lynchburg.

But in the 1880's Hazlewood could have had some involvement. He was living and working in Lynchburg. He may well have known Ward, and he may well have been a friend of the unidentified author.

Who, other than Hazlewood, was close to Ward and could have authored *The Beale Papers*? Kin of Morriss, a niece or a nephew, or a Saunders? There has been a suggestion that the Hart brothers dreamed up the whole thing. One especially interesting possibility is a cousin of Ward, a man who had many experiences similar to those of James Beverly Ward.

20.
Hidden Talent

The author of *The Beale Papers* alludes to Ward as a potential "beneficiary" of the author's decoding efforts. Ward could have been a beneficiary — either as a business partner or a family member. Ward's father was dead. His wife was too busy and his children were too young to write something like this. But he did have cousins.

The author also alludes to Ward as a "gentleman." This is a term of respect usually used when one is speaking of someone older. The author could have been younger than Ward. The author explains that the gentleman was "ignorant of this episode in Mr. Morriss' career, until this manuscript was placed in his hands." The author also claims he obtained the papers "in the second year of the Confederate war," which started in 1861. A newspaper reported that Robert Morriss died in January 1863 "at Roslin, the residence of his niece, Mrs. David Saunders."

The author admits that "All knowledge of this affair was confined to a very limited circle — to the writer's immediate family, and to one old and valued friend." The friend may have been just a sounding board or an editorial critic. But if the story was fiction, then that friend could be a real collaborator, helping to fill in the story details — or to prepare the ciphers.

The author says that Morriss had confided in him because their families were friends. He explains he was "young and in circumstances to afford leisure for the task" and that Morriss had confidence that he would carry out Morriss' wishes. If the author became unable to carry out Morriss' desires, the author would be honor-bound to pass the whole matter along to someone the author trusted. A close cousin could have been trusted by the author. Ward was close to at least one cousin who had the experience and intellect to write *The Beale Papers*.

James Ward had four close cousins in the Lynchburg area: the children of George C. Hutter, three boys and a girl. All were younger than James. They were capable, educated people. However, the girl, Adeline L. Hutter, was only 16 in 1862, probably too young to have earned the confidence of Morriss.

The three male first cousins — J. Risque, Edward S., and Ferdinand C. Hutter — had each served as Confederate Army officers. All were proficient in mathematics. All undoubtedly knew about the story of a duel involving their grandfather, James Beverly Risque. As boys — and as adults — they too lived in the Lynchburg area, but a few miles away from Ward.

Both J. Risque and Edward S. Hutter graduated from Virginia Military Institute (V.M.I.) in Lexington, as did Harriet Otey Ward's cousins, Kirkwood, George, and Peter Otey. Both Hutter boys were born at Sandusky, the home of George C. Hutter which once belonged to the Oteys.

J. Risque was the youngest Hutter boy. A successful military man, he eventually earned the rank of full colonel. In 1861 he joined the 11th Virginia Infantry as a captain. He was wounded and captured in Pickett's Charge in 1863, exchanged in January 1865, and recaptured in April 1865. His imprisonment was at Johnson's Island, near a town in Ohio coincidentally named Sandusky. The young prisoner must have thought this ironic. After the war he worked as a surveyor in Bedford and Campbell counties. In 1877 he married his cousin, Charlotte Hutter, at Poplar Forest. They had eight children and lived at the old homestead, Sandusky. J. Risque was just 21 when Morriss purportedly gave Beale's papers to the author.

Edward Sixtus Hutter was the middle brother, two years older than J. Risque. He rose to the rank of major in the artillery and fought in numerous battles. His surrender at Danville was more than two weeks after Robert E. Lee's. Back in Lynchburg he rejoined his wife, Nannie Langhorne, and began his family, which would eventually number twelve, and his career as a surveyor. He lived in town on an estate with an elegant Greek Revival house called Rivermont. He developed land above and below the house in the Daniel's Hill area and helped start the Rivermont Company. One of his partners in that venture was J.H. Adams, president of Adams Bros. Paynes Company. As a civil engineer, Edward helped design the Rivermont Bridge that was built in 1890-1891. He was a man of ability and experience. But one published sample of his literary skill and style was incompatible with *The Beale Papers*.

Ferdinand C. Hutter was the oldest of the three brothers. With his background and circumstances, he could have had ample opportunity to receive the papers from Morriss and then later write the pamphlet.

F.C. Hutter was nine years younger than cousin James Ward, yet had special reason to be close to this cousin. Both attended West Point, though neither completed the course work. Ward worked briefly in St. Louis, and F.C. was born there. Both had served as assistant Army paymasters as young men. They even looked somewhat alike. Both were tall and lean.

In the pamphlet, the author says of Morriss in 1862, "Inviting me to his room, with no one to interrupt us, he gave me an outline of the matter. About this time, however, affairs of importance required my presence in Richmond." In 1862 F.C. Hutter was a Confederate Army officer, assigned to government offices in Richmond. He was 31. He had no family obligations at that point, so Morriss could have assumed that he was free to pursue the subject.

For many years after receiving the papers, the author says that he tried and tried to decode the ciphers and finally did solve No. 2. But the others defied him. Finally, he gave up and decided to let the public have a go at the confounding puzzle. He sounded tired and disappointed when he wrote the pamphlet, saying, "I have been reduced from comparative affluence to absolute penury, entailing suffering upon those it was my duty to protect [his family], and this, too, in spite of their remonstrances."

Whether *The Beale Papers* is based on truth or not, the author finally wanted to be totally and irrevocably removed the matter. He wanted complete anonymity. He wanted out.

James Ward agreed to follow it through, to be the front man, to be agent for the author. In March 1884 Ward applied for the copyright. The pamphlet had gone to the printer.

Ferdinand C. Hutter, after "some months in delicate health," died February 21, 1885. He was 53.

Ferdinand Hutter's tie to the Beale story is a circumstantial "maybe." There is no evidence that any member of the Hutter family was involved in either the creation or publication of the pamphlet. A Hutter family genealogist was totally unaware of the Beale treasure story and had never heard any hint of a family member creating any fictional treasure tale. But let us take a closer look.

Ferdinand Charles Hutter was a grandson of James B. Risque. He was the oldest son of Harriet Risque and Major George Christian Hutter. He was born in 1831 at Jefferson Barracks, Missouri, where his father was then based. His parents had been married there the prior year, in the home of Harriet's uncle, General William Clark. George had served in the Blackhawk War.

The family later moved to near Lynchburg when Major G.C. Hutter bought "Sandusky," an estate with a fine brick home built in 1808. This house was located some four miles from James Beverly Risque's "Hunter's Hill." His mother, Harriet, was able to visit with her sister, Adeline Ward, who lived just a few miles away at Hunter's Hill. She could stay in touch with relatives nearby when George was off during the Mexican War.

Ferdinand won an appointment to West Point but did not finish. After leaving the Academy, he worked as a clerk in his father's Paymaster department of the U.S. Army. In Lynchburg in 1859, he married Belle Goggin of Bedford County. He was 28. She was 18. It was a terrible shock when she died three months after the wedding.

Ferdinand worked for the Army in Charleston until the South seceded from the Union in 1861. Then he resigned from the U.S. Army, came home, joined the Confederate Army and began serving as a second lieutenant in the Beauregard Rifles. His brothers — both graduates of V.M.I. — were commissioned in the Confederate army. His father, then 68, would soldier no more. He stayed at Sandusky and cheered his boys on.

Ferdinand's younger brothers were in the field, closer to the shooting war. Edward became commander of the arsenal at Danville, while Ferdinand was doing staff work at the center of the Confederacy. He was a captain in the first provisional army, and then a major in the regular army, serving at the headquarters in Richmond. As a paymaster, he signed the first paycheck for Major General Robert E. Lee (for $1,323).

He met Mary Lyons while in Richmond. She was the daughter of a former Senator of Virginia's House of Delegates, James Lyons, who was then a Virginia Representative in the Confederate Congress. They married there in April, 1864. The Lyons family home, La Burnham, was one of the more handsome homes in the city.

Back in Lynchburg the Union was preparing to assault the city in June. The forces of Union General David Hunter had skirmished their way through Bedford County. Hunter then decided to pause and regroup just short of Lynchburg.

Hunter and his generals, Crook and Averell, commandeered the house at Sandusky as headquarters. Crook's officers included Col. Rutherford B. Hayes and Maj. William McKinley. They helped themselves to stored food. They used the large brick barn as a hospital for 117 of their wounded men.

Suspecting that Lynchburg's defense force was too strong, Hunter and his army canceled their Lynchburg plans and headed west.

20 — Hidden Talent

James Ward learned about this episode a few days after it happened and was relieved that it had not happened to him. For George Hutter and his daughter, this was a profound and very personal historic event — not unlike being burglarized and held hostage in your own home.

A year later the war was over. All three Hutter boys had survived. Sandusky survived. George C. Hutter could not have then known that he had been host to two future American presidents.

The war's end brought Hutter's military career to an end. In civilian life he worked for the Internal Revenue Department in Lynchburg as Chief Clerk to Capt. J.H. Rives.

Ferdinand and Mary had five children. The eldest, James L., was born at Sandusky in 1865. The couple established their own estate adjoining Sandusky. They built a new house, with some financial help from Judge Lyons. They named it Igloe, probably after Iglau, a leatherworking town in Austrian Moravia, where Ferdinand's great-great-grandfather Johann Ludwig Hutter had managed a tannery for the Moravian Brethren.

There are no records to confirm that Chief Clerk Hutter (of Internal Revenue) ever got to know Chief Clerk Hazlewood (of Norfolk & Western Audit). But the Wards, the Hutters, and the Hazlewoods all lived in the Lynchburg area and all were Episcopalian. Also significant is the fact that Hutter and Hazlewood were both members of the Masons in Lynchburg at the same time. It seems likely that the men knew each other. They may have even been good friends.

Ferdinand was a government employee, and his job responsibilities probably ended at sundown. During the evenings he could well have had the time to wrestle with puzzles, to read, or to write. In Lynchburg he was a proud, respected, and trusted member of the community. He treasured his privacy and his family name.

Christian Sixtus Hutter died in 1875. Uncle Chris was married to Emma Cobbs, the only child of the man who had bought Poplar Forest from the heirs of Thomas Jefferson. The children of Emma and Chris would later inherit Poplar Forest. Ferdinand's brother, J. Risque, who was married to Charlotte Hutter, would also participate in that estate.

In 1879 Ferdinand's father, George, also died. The Hutters, Risques, and Wards mourned the passing of old Major George.

In July 1881 news came that President James A. Garfield, who had been inaugurated in March, had been shot at a Washington railroad station. His assailant claimed he acted because he wanted Vice-President Chester

Arthur to be President. Garfield died in September, and Arthur did succeed to the Presidency.

Soon after that, Hutter heard that his 33-year-old cousin, John Pickerel Risque, had been killed by Indians in Arizona. His death came as he was returning home with a party that had been inspecting some sort of mine. This news came as a shock. Hutter had always found John's adventures fascinating.

In 1882 Ferdinand and Mary decided to move into the city. Life would be more convenient there. Mary thought it would be easier for the children to get to school. They bought a home at 14th and Pierce. They added an adjoining lot the next year.

At the end of 15th Street, not far from the Hutter home site, was a short street that for years had no name; after 1877 it was named Roslyn. It is unclear whether or not this street, road, or area had ever been spelled Roslin. The question is likewise open: is this where Robert Morriss died?

In Richmond, Ferdinand's brother-in-law, James, Jr., was carrying on the Lyons family tradition of serving in government. He was in his second term as a Delegate in the Virginia General Assembly. The Hutters were proud of him and did all they could to protect and boost his reputation.

Ferdinand's health waned, so he retired early. The local tobacconists regretted his departure from the Revenue Office. They had found him to be man with a high sense of honor.

Ferdinand C. Hutter died of heart disease in 1885. He had not yet reached his 54th birthday. He was survived by his wife and five children, ranging in age from five to twenty. Even his mother, Harriet, survived him. His estate was formally settled in 1888. The court awarded the title of the house and its contents to his widow, Mary Lyons Hutter.

Later owners of their former country estate subdivided the land, put in a road named Igloe, and changed the name of the estate to Longmeadow. The house today is the home of TV evangelist Dr. Jerry Falwell.

The author's narrative is clear regarding his family's feelings about the matter of the Beale treasure. They were unenthusiastic. After his death the author's widow would more than likely wish to forget it. If that was the case, the author's trusted friend and confidante may have felt that the honorable thing to do was to protect the family's reputation. He could have decided to retrieve the original papers from the printer and terminate distribution and further printing of the pamphlet. This could be another reason why there were so few copies circulated.

If the valued friend had been Newton Hazlewood, this would explain why Hazlewood had "sheets" instead of pages from a pamphlet and why, as Innis reported, Hazlewood said he had gotten the original papers from Ward so it couldn't be reprinted "after the fire." There would be no Beale letters today in the hands of the Hutters.

If Hutter was the author, much of *The Beale Papers* has a ring of truth to it. The circumstances of and the feelings expressed by the author seem to fit what we know about F.C. Hutter's situation. If the tale was his fabrication, he would probably have been less honest about himself so as not to reveal his identity. So, if much is true, then is all of it true? The author — whoever he was — could have been honest in all his statements. He could really have gotten the papers and the story from Robert Morriss.

We wonder if Morriss made up the story. Was Morriss himself so gullible that he was duped by someone else? He didn't seem to know very much about this lodger who called himself Thomas J. Beale, "from Virginia."

21.
Fiction or Cover?

The Beale Papers may be true, partly true, or entirely false. Consider these four ways of classifying the pamphlet.

1. Pure creative fiction. Published in order to make money. Or, as Dr. Brian R. Ford of Spirit Lake, Iowa wondered, "The cyphers constitute a practical joke or an instrument of revenge used against the descendants of Thomas Beale by the descendants of Major James Beverly Risque."

In 1885, the fiction writer had freedom to have his characters do what he wanted — especially if, like Beale and Morriss, they were long dead and buried and couldn't contradict his story. He didn't need Beale to be in Lynchburg in 1819-1822. Morriss never told a treasure story to the author.

The author intended to mislead us. His ciphers No. 1 and No. 3 are pure gibberish. There is not now and never was a treasure.

If this is the case, the author was brilliant, deserving of what I might call "The Golden Beale" award.

Trying now to find the Beale gold and silver is a fool's errand. The challenge is to identify the author.

2. A cover story. There really was a treasure, but it was illegally acquired. Beale was fiction and/or Morriss's tale was fiction. Ciphers No. 1

21 — Fiction or Cover?

and No 3 are pure gibberish. The author or authors — the collaborating perpetrators — created the story solely to "launder" their treasure. In this case, the treasure has probably been retrieved and the game is over. It is probably too late to recover the treasure.

However, valid questions demand answers: where did the treasure come from, who got it, and what happened to them?

Two plausible cover stories come to mind: one about the Mexican Treasury and the other about the Confederate Treasury. More about that in a moment.

3. Mostly true. The story is basically true, but Beale was an impostor and Morriss was duped. The author was accurate and honest. The treasure did not come from where Beale said, but a treasure did exist and the ciphers are legitimate. Beale never returned. The treasure may still be there. Or it may have been found.

Two plausible "mostly true" stories can be considered: one about a fugitive pirate, and the other about a former slave.

4. All true. The pamphlet was created to make a profit and to share an opportunity. Beale was real. Morriss' story was truthful and accurate. Treasure was from Indians. The author was honest, and the story is accurate, except for typos and memory lapses. The ciphers hold useful messages. A treasure did exist. Beale and his confidants must have died. It may have been found or it may still be there.

Consider now the notion that it was a cover story.

22.
Mexican War and Confederacy

A German researcher believes that *The Beale Papers* story is a fabrication, published to hide the truth of where the treasure came from and to "launder" the loot. He opined that the gold and silver were stolen, and that several murders had been committed to prevent the perpetrators from being identified. They wrote *The Beale Papers* to legitimize the cache, so they could then "discover" and claim the loot without fear of prosecution.

One story bandied about is that Robert E. Lee was involved and that the gold and silver had indeed come from the Southwest, but it had been looted from the Mexican government treasury during the American victory over Mexico in 1848. As the story goes, an important U.S. Army officer in the conflict was none other than Robert E. Lee, and he contacted Beale who did the actual looting and then moved it with some slaves, they say. Then Beale made up the Indian mines story.

Up North, at Santa Fe in that war, the United States enjoyed an easy "victory" in August 1846. The town had been trading more with the United States than it did with the rest of Mexico. When General Stephen Watts Kearny and 1700 men in his "Army of the West" neared Santa Fe, the Governor disbanded his defense force of citizens — who lacked conviction — and left town. Kearny strolled in and shortly thereafter redirected 1,000 of his men to leave and help the American cause elsewhere.

American forces met serious resistance much further south. In early 1847, Gen. Winfield Scott led a force of 12,600, which had been brought by the Navy to the Mexican shore near Vera Cruz. On his staff was Robert E. Lee, then a 39-year-old captain. In a series of painful battles, they fought their way inland and occupied Mexico City on September 14, 1847. There they stayed until the peace treaty of Guadalupe Hidalgo was signed in the spring of 1848. Lee was promoted, but his activities are not well reported.

In fact, Lee's biographer, A.L. Long, is virtually silent about what Lee was doing in those months. The *Memoirs of Robert E. Lee* of 1886 say, "Colonel Lee managed to kill dull time during his long detention in the City of Mexico," and as to details, "no such information [is] extant."

The conquerors of Mexico had the time and opportunity to seize assets of the national treasury and mint. Such things have been done before.

Captain Robert E. Lee served under General Winfield Scott in the Mexican War.

Consider if the U.S. Army would loot the Mexican treasury — or allow someone else to loot it — when the treaty stipulated that the U.S. would pay Mexico $15,000,000 as compensation for ceding to us an enormous land area in the Southwest. That concept is not unknown in the world of finance and hostile takeovers and buyouts. A corporate raider borrows money to buy a cash-rich company and then, after getting control, turns around and uses the target's cash to pay off the loan. One can wonder, however, if the Mexican Treasury contained anywhere near as much as the $15 million the U.S. needed.

Military organizations tend to generate records and diaries, even during the chaos of war. It is one thing to remove tons of gold and silver from a vanquished enemy, but quite another to ship it thousands of miles (on and off ships and river boats and trail wagons) and then bury it without some sort of telltale incidents or audit trail. Bureaucratic secrecy nets ultimately spring leaks.

It is hard to believe that Lee, a man whose integrity has never been questioned, would be party to such a scheme. Winston Churchill described Lee as "one of the noblest Americans who ever lived." More about Lee later.

The idea persists that *The Beale Papers* was fabricated to allow the perpetrators to claim legitimate ownership, by "finding it." There is speculation that the treasure was neither Indian nor Spanish, that it was not from 1819 and 1821, but rather was the legendary "missing Confederate Treasury" of the 1860's.

As the South was retreating during the War Between the States, President Jefferson Davis and members of his cabinet of the Confederate States of America (CSA), abandoned Richmond on early April 3, 1865, and boarded a special train. They headed southward, hoping to establish a new capital 140 miles away at Danville, Virginia, bringing with them the assets of their treasury.

J. Frank Carroll, in his *Confederate Treasure in Danville,* calculated that the assets leaving Richmond totaled about $600,000, including 200,000 Mexican silver dollars (8 reales coins) and jewelry which had been donated to the Confederate cause by southern ladies.

At Danville, the CSA officers and men unloaded the train and set up offices. Some gold and silver coins were disbursed to citizens and soldiers who traded in their paper currency for the real money. The bulk of the assets were stored in several buildings, and some were believed to have been buried.

The dream of a Danville capital was soon shattered, as news came that the Union forces continued to win battles and were rapidly approaching.

Davis and his entourage felt forced to move further south. So a week later, the Confederate hierarchy made a hasty retreat from Danville, using the same train. Carroll reports that, "In the fear and confusion, no one noticed, even cared, that forty-nine kegs (of Mexican silver dollars) from the Treasury Office had been left behind." This would mean that Danville became the resting place of 196,000 coins, or about 9,555 pounds of silver.

A veteran F.B.I. professional questions this. Brent Hughes, who retired after 37 years with the Washington FBI laboratory, researched the trail of the Confederate Treasury when and after it left Richmond. He doubts that so much silver was abandoned at Danville. He wrote in his pamphlet, *The Confederate Treasure Train,* that by the time the trip southward was over, very little was left because coins of one kind or other were indeed dispensed at every place the train paused or stopped, and there is no void in the audit trail nor is there record of a major dispersal at any one point.

Eight months after Hunter's aborted attack on Lynchburg, Lee recommended on February 22, 1865, "Everything of value should be removed from Richmond." A message from Lee to the CSA Secretary of War in Richmond said, "I think Lynchburg or some point west the most advantageous place to which to remove stores from Richmond." No other city was named.

Lynchburg was a safe haven: though it had once been a key Union objective, it had been spared by Federal General David Hunter back in June 1864.

President Jefferson Davis had the authority to direct that the Treasury assets from Richmond be split by taking some to Danville and having some sent west to be stashed in a safe, remote, rural spot somewhere

22 — Mexican War and Confederacy

near Lynchburg. Treasury assets would be hidden, to be available for the Confederacy to help pay its bills and continue to finance the war.

Carroll reports that when Davis and his group arrived at Danville in early April, 1865, the commander of the Danville arsenal was Major Edward Sixtus Hutter, a native of the Lynchburg area and brother of Ferdinand Hutter. No evidence links the Hutters to the diversion of the Treasury, so neither Hutter may have been involved with this shipment.

A handful of people, the right people, could move those assets to Bedford County and pull it off. They would have to disguise what they were doing, to avoid attracting attention. Try this scenario:

The participants were men who believed in the Confederate cause, who knew each other well, and who trusted each other, as brothers, cousins, or classmates. One officer would ride with the treasure at all times. The group included one — military or civilian — who was familiar with both Lynchburg and Bedford County. He would set things up at the receiving end. One understood railroad procedures.

The Treasury assets at Richmond were loaded into the Richmond-Danville RR train late in the evening of April 2nd. Two officers took turns on watch inside the special Treasury car, which was coupled at the end of the train. After the train pulled out at 11 PM and began rumbling towards Danville, the key man relabeled many of the boxes, kegs, and bags.

At about 4 AM on April 3rd, the train stopped at Burkeville to take on water for the engine. Just about everyone on board was asleep while the

Main railroad lines in Virginia in 1861.

This view is part of a Confederate Engineer's Bureau map of 1864, based on "surveys and reconnaissances by W. Izard, Lt. Eng. P.A."

train waited. Standing nearby was a train from Petersburg, headed for Lynchburg, with its end car containing pine box coffins (empty) and crates (empty), guarded by an officer from Petersburg who was in on the plan. The officers frantically rolled out kegs, slid out boxes, and tossed off bags, which were then put aboard the Lynchburg train, as the Richmond train resumed its trip to Danville, but with one less officer.

They put the containers of gold and silver into the coffins. As the train chugged towards Lynchburg, the coffins were labeled to indicate war dead to be buried at Bufordville. The crates (still empty) were labeled for Big Lick.

At midday, the Burkeville train arrived at Lynchburg. There, the tail end car took on supplies — bags of shot and other material — bound for

22 — Mexican War and Confederacy

Big Lick. That car was shunted and added to the end of a westbound Virginia & Tennessee (V&T) train scheduled to leave that afternoon.

In early evening April 3rd, the V&T train left Lynchburg, headed west. As it moved along, the supplies from Lynchburg were put into the empty crates.

It was dark when the train slowed and pulled onto a siding at the Thaxton Switch. People aboard were informed that they had to wait for a possible eastbound train to pass by. Or maybe they made a long stop at Bufordville to take on water.

In any event, the advance man was there waiting, with a sturdy wagon drawn by two horses. He helped the key men to off load the long pine boxes. Only a few curious bystanders watched. But as the coffins were put on the wagon, they bowed their heads. Too many young officers had come home that way. "The boys will be buried tomorrow," they were told.

The key men drove the wagon to a remote farm, owned by relatives. They pushed the wagon into an earthen-floor barn.

Perhaps the "coffins" were emptied and refilled during the night. Treasure came out, and dirt was put in. They buried the treasure right there in the barn. The hole was topped off, and hay, straw and trash were scattered over. In the barn, or in the cemetery, this share of the Confederate Treasury was safe from the Yankees!

The next morning, in an unpretentious ceremony, the coffins were laid to rest on family land. But on the 9th of April, a cloud of confusion settle over the scheme. General Robert E. Lee surrendered. Was the Confederacy finished?

Those few men who knew about the stash would keep it secret, just in case.

Events of 1865 shook both the North and the South. Lee surrendered at Appomattox. President Lincoln was assassinated on April 14. Major E.S. Hutter surrendered at Danville on the 27th. General Johnston, farther south with CSA remnant forces, gave up on the 29th. Jefferson Davis made it to Georgia, but was captured on May 10th. By year's end, the 13th Amendment formally freed all slaves. .

Attorney Richard Harman raised this point: with the surrender, "public accountability ended. But given the status of Honor in Virginia, it is possible that whoever felt responsible for the Treasury would not have touched it until matters made clear what would develop."

Though reunited, the Nation was unstable. Southern states were distrusted and under military scrutiny. Lincoln's successor, Andrew Johnson, was nobody's hero. Congress impeached him, but the Senate acquitted him in 1868. There was a money panic in 1869 and a shortage of ready gold.

Would the South rise again? Would patriots of Virginia need these hidden assets to fight again?

Hopes faded when Robert E. Lee died in 1870. The War really was over.

Those key men who knew of the treasure wrestled with a dilemma. What should be done with the buried Treasury? Give it to the reunited Nation? Give it to the state of Virginia? Divide it among those who know about it?

They could have chosen to claim it themselves. They talked of using it to help their beloved Virginia recover from the war's economic devastation. They would create a cover story, to "launder" the gold and silver. It had to be a carefully constructed story, without obvious flaws. Several men would collaborate on creating the Beale Treasure story, brainstorming intricate plot relationships, consistent with historical facts and basic logic. Three sets of ciphers would serve their purpose. One set would be "solved," establishing the fact that there was a treasure to be found.

This creative writing effort could take years. At last it was printed and then, finally, in 1885 offered to the public. Now, the world would know that the treasure existed, because the "solved" ciphers said so.

Would any outsider find the treasure? Unlikely. One set of ciphers nobly alluded to naming legitimate claimants of the treasure. The third set of ciphers would tell exactly where it was. Neither of these two sets of ciphers were legitimate, nor solvable. They were only serving to help create the cover. They remain today unsolved because they were never real messages.

But the collaborators worried. Suppose someone did find the cache. When they dug it up, they would find many Mexican silver coins and many U S. gold coins, most dated in the mid 1800's, well after 1822. The story of "Beale" would be exposed as a lie.

Perhaps the collaborators retrieved and divided up the Confederate Treasury shortly after the pamphlet was published. Telltale dated coins were melted down with a blacksmith's forge. No report surfaced about a big treasure find. They were home free!

They no longer needed to have pamphlets circulating. Perhaps they feared that it would trigger too much attention, the cover might be exposed, and they might be implicated. All unsold copies were yanked back and destroyed.

If they did retrieve it, they would need to be patient: spend it or convert it slowly, so not to draw attention. They could start or strengthen their family businesses, improve their homes and farm buildings, and disperse assets to neighbors and friends. Theirs was a low profile "Marshall Plan" which made grants or sweetheart loans for projects of promise.

There are other views of *The Beale Papers* story, of course. There are two interpretations which presume the story is mostly true and that there was a treasure, but that Thomas J. Beale was an alias. Both of these interpretations presume that Morriss believed his visitor and that Morriss told the truth to the pamphlet author.

One version implicates Jean Laffite. The other version links Thomas Jefferson.

23.
The Pirate or The Slave

The man who visited Morriss could well have been someone using the real Beale's name. The impostor could have known that Beale was dead and that he would be unrecognized because not only was the real Beale dead, but so were the treasure companions who could expose his charade.

I have not found a physical description of the Fincastle/New Orleans Thomas J. Beale which could be compared with the description by Morriss.

That man who stayed at the house of Robert Morriss in 1819 could very well have been someone else — someone posing as Thomas J. Beale, someone who knew that the real Beale was involved in far away New Orleans and that there was little chance of anyone knowing the difference. Then, when he returned in 1822, the impostor would have been even more confident, because he knew Beale was dead.

One man who knew these things about Beale and who also had access to much gold, silver and jewelry was the privateer, Jean Laffite.

Beale and Laffite were about the same age. Morriss described his visitor as tall and handsome and suggested he had a charismatic personality. He said that Beale had jet black eyes and dark and swarthy complexion. Others have described Jean Laffite as tall and handsome and also possessing a charismatic personality. Historian Robin Reilly says he was "tall, elegant, and well mannered.... accepted by many of the best Creole families as a gentleman." Virginian Esau Glasscock met Laffite in 1809 and wrote a letter to his brother describing the man. He wrote that Laffite had black eyes. But one feature did not match Morriss's portrayal. Glasscock said Laffite had

Jean Lafitte

23 — The Pirate or The Slave

light skin. However, this does not negate the potential match. During the decade from 1809 to 1819 Lafitte may have acquired the kind of deep tan which Morriss ascribed to Beale: "...as if much exposure to the sun and weather had thoroughly tanned and discolored him."

Laffite himself was not in New Orleans when "Beale" was on his treasure-burying missions in Virginia.

Some say Jean and brother Pierre drowned in the Gulf, not long after leaving Galveston Island.

Where was Jean Lafitte in the years 1816 to 1822? Did he spend any time on land in the U.S.? Could he have parked any of his loot in Virginia? He probably was capable of organizing such a venture. But would he?

Wanda Lee Dickey, a Park Ranger at the Jean Laffite National Park, wrote that "During the winter of 1815-1816 Laffite went to Washington and Philadelphia in an attempt to regain property (seized at a Grande Terre privateer rendezvous by a U.S. Army-Navy expedition in September 1814) ...but none was returned." His trip to Washington could have been by sailing ship, going the long way down and around the tip of Florida and up the east coast. Or he may have merely reversed the route taken by Thomas Beale when Beale moved from Fincastle, down the Mississippi to New Orleans. Such a route could have acquainted Laffite with Virginia.

The scene shifts back to the Gulf, to an island just off shore of Texas, Galveston Island, what had been the home base for the privateering busi-

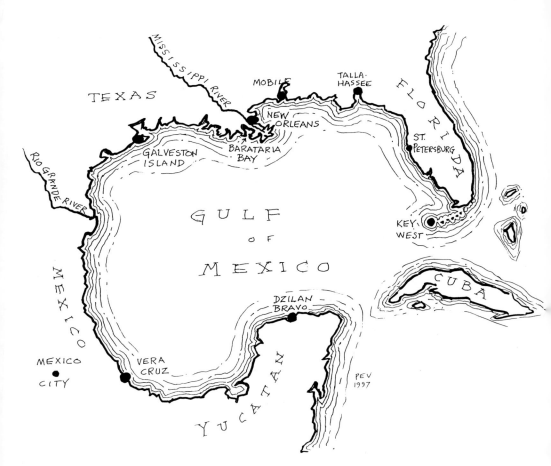

Privateers plundered British, French, and Spanish ships coming and going in the Gulf of Mexico.

ness of Luis Aury, a follower of the Hidalgo revolutionists, in 1816. But after Aury suffered defeats at sea, Laffite and his followers seized control of the place in 1817 and called his town Campeachy. They thrived by preying on Spanish commerce. They may have also preyed on U.S. interests.

In the fall of 1819, smugglers who had been robbing in southwestern Louisiana were chased and caught by the United States schooner *Lynx*. The ringleader alleged that he was on Laffite's orders. In a show of atonement, Laffite assuaged the U.S. by burning down his pirate village in the spring of 1820 and moving elsewhere on the Gulf of Mexico.

One story has it that he moved to the tip of the Yucatan, where he retired at the age of about forty. The tourist guidebook *Fodor's Mexico*

1976, describes this fate of Laffite: "...the lonely north coast fishing village of Dzilan Bravo holds unique interest.... [The] one-time Mayan seaport is believed by many to be the final resting place of Jean Lafitte. There is even a tombstone in the sunsplashed little graveyard there, adorned with a crucifix and the roses of La Belle France, inscribed JEAN LAFITTE 1780-1827. And according to the light-eyed, remarkably Gallic-looking villagers who [claim him] as an ancestor ... [he] gave up his freebooting career... to retire to the simple life in Dzilan Bravo, the denials of some historians notwithstanding."

Unless he was in failing health, it is hard to believe that an ambitious man of forty would suddenly retire and adopt a life without challenges. Other sources described Laffite as being dark eyed. Are his bones really there? Folklore of New Orleans has it that "Lafitte is buried in everybody's backyard!"

We can wonder if Jean Lafitte spent time on land in the United States before he died and was buried in the Yucatan. Was he ever anywhere in America other than the Gulf Coast? What happened to him after he left Galveston in 1821? At least one historian thinks he might have moved to mainland U.S.A.

Robin Reilly, in his history of the Battle of New Orleans, *The British at the Gates*. writes: "For eleven years Jean Lafitte escaped from history. He reappears in June, 1832, in Charleston, where he married for the second time, under the name of John Lafflin. Ten years later he was trading as a manufacturer of gunpowder in St. Louis.... [H]e died (1854) at the age of seventy-two. His brother Pierre, also retired under the name of Lafflin, had died at the age of sixty-five ten years earlier." If the treasure had been theirs, did they retrieve it?

But if *Fodor's* is right or if they drowned in the Gulf, then the treasure could still be there.

It is unclear why Laffite would choose Virginia for his treasury vault and why he would confide in an innkeeper with whom he had stayed just twice. Was Morriss the only man he dared trust? Surely Laffite had other allies, men he had worked with or possibly one of his brothers. Yet as Lord Byron has written, "Tis strange, but true; for truth is always strange, — Stranger than Fiction."

Like politics, history makes strange bedfellows. Jean Laffite was a man who made his own rules, a man who lived outside the laws of the United States, and yet, and yet... there is today, near New Orleans, a National Park honoring Jean Laffite.

In 1817, when Beale set out for the western plains, Thomas Jefferson was in the autumn of his years. The ex-President, then in his seventies, could well have envied the vigor still enjoyed by young men, men like Thomas Beale.

P.B. Innis suggested that Beale knew Thomas Jefferson. She wrote that as he was about to leave from Big Lick, "Beale thought with pride and pleasure of his talk the previous day with the great Thomas Jefferson at Poplar Forest, Jefferson's retreat near Lynchburg."

Thomas Jefferson relished his time at Poplar Forest.

There is no hard evidence for this, but we can speculate that he knew "Beale." One theory goes like this: the "Beale" of the treasure was not the Thomas Beale of Fincastle and New Orleans, but actually the illegitimate son of Thomas Jefferson.

In *The Beale Papers,* Morris is reported as describing his visitor as "about six feet in height with jet black eyes and hair.... [H]is distinguishing feature was a dark and swarthy complexion." Could this be "Tom Hemings," a son of Jefferson's slave Sally Hemings?

Jefferson's primary home was Monticello, near Charlottesville. But he also designed and built Poplar Forest, a summer retreat in Bedford County. Jefferson often visited there to supervise construction from 1806 to 1810, and savored living there whenever he could after that. Slaves could be transferred between his homes.

In *Thomas Jefferson, An Intimate History*, author Fawn M. Brodie reports that Sally was with Jefferson in Paris when he was Minister to France and that a son was born shortly after they returned to the U.S. (in 1789 or 1790). That son (whom we might call "Tom Hemings") may have been one of Jefferson's several slaves named Tom who could have been counted as slave or free and who disappeared from the Jefferson Monticello slave list in 1811 and who was not on his Poplar Forest slave list of 1810. Then "Tom Hemings," twenty-one, ventured out to seek his fortune, perhaps to the West or even New Orleans, where a man's skin color counted less than ability, intelligence, and ambition.

23 — The Pirate or The Slave

Tom Hemings had potential for leadership. He may have inherited his mother's hair, eyes and skin, and if he were Jefferson's son, he could have Jefferson's tall build, good looks, and brain. One scholar of Jeffersonian history recalls that Tom's skin color was "sable." Recall the Pawnee report of seeing men "blocker than the Indians" in 1817-1818.

If Tom were a favored slave, he would have been afforded access to books and good educational instruction. Young Tom could have been aware of the art of secret messages and been capable of creating ciphered messages. Thomas Jefferson once invented a code machine, and after leaving office, he retained a copy of the State Department code book he had used back when he was Ambassador to France. Young Tom might have seen it, held it, or at least been familiar with the concept of substitution ciphers, where a number represented a letter or a word. The ciphers in *The Beale Papers* have the superficial appearance of such a coding system.

At the time of "Beale's" important letters to Morriss, Tom would have been thirty-one or thirty-two, in the prime of his vigor. He would have been familiar with the Lynchburg-Bedford area and thus chose to stash the treasure there.

Tom's respect for the ex-President would not allow himself to reveal who he really was — even if he knew. While staying in Lynchburg, he may have slipped over to see his mentor-father to tell him what he had been doing. Thomas Jefferson died in 1826.

Hemings, Lafitte, or some other "Beale" pretender went back west and never returned. Morriss didn't get the key. Maybe "Beale's" associates did him in, came back and retrieved the treasure... or they too may have met the same fate as "Beale."

Puzzles like the Beale treasure story can trigger innumerable speculations and sub stories. The reader may imagine his own. Now, you the reader may decide and sift out what is fiction and what is true.

Drop the puzzle now. Or continue — to wrestle with ciphers, to find the key, or to discover more facts and more clues that could lead to the truth.

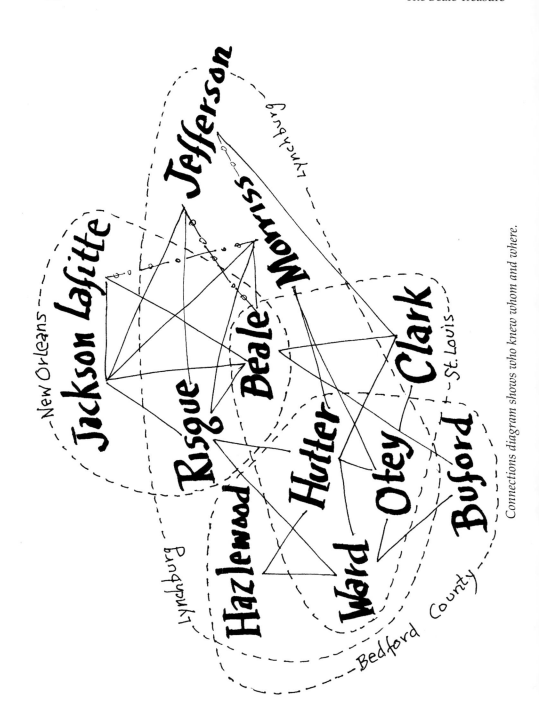

Connections diagram shows who knew whom and where.

24.
Finders Keepers

So far, we have no incontrovertible proof of Thomas J. Beale and his treasure. Nobody has found a "smoking gun." The best evidence so far is circumstantial, built from remnants of information that have survived since 1820 and 1885. We yearn for something more definitive, such as:

1. A written admission by the author, or letter by a relative, stating that the story is fiction, with the letter's handwriting and paper authenticated as genuine.
2. The original cipher sheets and original letters of Beale, with the handwriting and the age of the paper authenticated.
3. The solutions to the ciphers, leading to the vault or site, which is found and verified, even if found empty.
4. The discovery and revelation of the treasure.

The treasure has already been found, some say. Former Bedford County Sheriff Carl Wells has said, "It's long gone bye."

Stan Czarnowski, a Pennsylvania steelworker, spent seven years in his quest to find the treasure. The *Valley News Dispatch*, of Pennsylvania, said that he made 36 trips to Bedford. Finally, in the early 1970's, he found a vault beneath the floor of a six-foot-deep ice house in rural Montvale. The vault was roughly lined with stones. Inspection of the debris led him to conclude that someone else — perhaps 50 years earlier — had already dug there and retrieved the treasure.

A middle-aged woman said that she had not only decoded the ciphers but had also found the treasure vault site. Her search had brought her to Bedford before, but this time, in 1986, she was proud to have solved the mystery, but disappointed by what she found. "I found the vault," she said, "but it was empty. No gold or silver. Just a few bones."

Mel Fisher dug in a different place, and he, too, said he had found "the vault" and it was empty.

A long-time Montvale resident heard tell that Beale buried his treasure in Lynchburg, forty miles away, in the basement of a house where it was found by an obscure tinker who later became a very wealthy Lynchburg merchant.

A very explicit story of discovery came in 1982. Boyd M. Jolley wrote in *Treasure* magazine that the treasure was found near Taylor's Mountain and removed by "Mark Green" (a pseudonym). He had gotten the details of the story from "Lamar Cross" (a pseudonym). The pseudonyms were used to protect the privacy of the men.

The article said Green had found the key in an old family bible. His solution led him along a small creek and "marker rocks that Beale had drilled holes in."

Green and his confidantes went on a major recovery mission with heavy equipment. They posted a guard to keep snoopers out. He says that residents were aware of the attempt, but not of its success.

Cross told Jolley that Green found two chambers, one under the other. The upper one was below a six-foot rock ledge. Then, twenty feet further down, was a second chamber. Water in the chambers was drained off by the team. Inside were gold nuggets, gold coins (some not U.S.), silver bars, and a jeweled brush and mirror, as well as sworn wills of Beale's associates.

The described location is not far from Cool Spring Church, a very quiet area, reachable only by a narrow gravel road. Even the sound of a small car can usually be heard a mile away. Very little escapes the notice of the residents. They would have heard the commotion of vehicles or equipment coming and going. Two different people who live nearby said that Green couldn't have been there at all. Besides hearing noises, they would have seen the tracks of the equipment or evidence of the digging. They heard nothing. They saw nothing. They don't believe it.

Thomas Beale himself could have retrieved it. Dr. Stephen Matyas once outlined this plausible scenario: Beale and his associates decided to exclude their confederate Morriss, after all. Beale reclaimed the key that he had left in St. Louis. He and his men quietly returned to Buford's, dug up the treasure and divided it among themselves. They pledged eternal silence, lest Morriss demand a share or others seek out their mine.

Joseph Durand, according to a 1993 news article in the Roanoke *Times*, said, "It is my contention that the 1819 shipment was hidden in the mountain gap near Bobblet's Gap ... [and that] ... the 1821 shipment was stolen by locals." His premise is that the men delivering the second load were killed by local farmers. Only the first shipment remains to be found.

Or maybe someone in Bedford recovered the treasure without mayhem or murder.

24 — Finders Keepers

Paschal Buford was perhaps the most significant citizen in Bufordville.

One candidate is Paschal Buford, the owner of the inn where Beale stayed a month. He may have overheard Beale talking with his men. Or he may have heard things from area people who had heard or seen something. After those thirty days in the area, the bits of information may have come together into a revealing picture.

Not long after Beale made his second trip to Buford's, Paschal showed evidence of significant wealth. He built an entirely new brick home not far from the original Buford's tavern. This is just two years after buying from his father-in-law the elegant brick mansion, "Fancy Farm," and its 1,034 acres of land north of the town of Liberty. Then, two years after that he bought three parcels of land totalling about 600 acres on Goose Creek.

By 1850, Paschal Buford had expanded his holdings in the county to 2,331 acres of land and 48 slaves. He also owned a mill on Goose Creek. All this wealth may have been attained with the treasure.

Paschal was born in 1791, one of the children of Henry Buford whose family had been granted large tracts of land by the king. One of Henry's brothers, Capt. Thomas Buford, died in battle with Indians at Point Pleasant in 1774. Henry's other brothers moved to Kentucky. Henry stayed in Bedford County at "Locust Level," where he operated a tavern and inn generally called "Buford's" tavern. The area there became known as "Buford's." Henry was high sheriff and owned large tracts of land, tracts which had been granted by the king.

When Henry died in 1814, Paschal, 24, inherited much land and took over the tavern. He parlayed his resources and built a reputation as a responsible and distinguished citizen. He was a Justice of the County Court. He donated land to the new railroad for the right-of-way through the area. Paschal arranged for Virginia's contribution of a symbolic rock for the Washington Monument. A boulder from the peak of Bedford's Sharp Top Mountain had been rolled down by youths in the 1820's. Buford had it split. He kept one chunk as a carriage stone at his place. The best block went to Washington, where it became part of the monument and was inscribed "From Virginia's Loftiest Peak." (Even Thomas Jefferson thought Sharp Top was the tallest in the state; later surveys showed that it is one of the tallest, but not the tallest.)

Paschal Buford and his family were respected by neighbors and acquaintances. There is no evidence that Paschal's prosperity came from anywhere other than family resources and business acumen. He was 84 when he died in 1875. His wife, Frances Anne Otey Buford, survived him for seven more years. Neither was alive to comment on *The Beale Papers* pamphlet when it came out in 1885.

Another fascinating native and possible discoverer of the treasure is Harry Wright, who was born in Liberty in 1877. After his father died, Harry and his brothers and sisters left the area and moved to Mexico. The father had left the family with unpaid taxes, but Harry ended up a wealthy man, owning the second largest steel and copper firm in Mexico.

Harry's father, George, had been a founder of the tobacco firm of Bolling Wright, & Co. He owned land north of Liberty, near Fancy Farm. The tobacco plant was destroyed by fire in 1887. George died in 1890. Family properties soon defaulted on taxes, and the court sold land in 1893 to collect those taxes.

The two youngest Wright children were at school, and their mother, Betty, was alive. Why would Harry and his siblings go to Mexico? That country was in ferment: protests, revolution, coups and counter coups. At the start of the twentieth century, the United States was seen as the land of opportunity. Were they running away, or did Mexico look like a place of better opportunity?

At least six of the eight Wright children went to live in Mexico, and in the early 1930's five were still there. Of the eight, only sister Mildred (who studied interior decorating in New York and Paris) and sister Veta (who studied at Hollins) had advanced schooling. But they all had enough money to have the outward appearance of being affluent.

The book, *Our Kin*, tells about those Wright siblings, as of 1930. Veta was an aviatrix, flying around South America. Mildred studied in Paris. Brother Sam was a world traveler. Brother George lived in Latin America and wrote short stories. Brother Max was an amateur golf champion and belonged to a number of clubs. Sister Della traveled and was noted for supporting charities. And Harry himself was known as a philanthropist.

Harry had a warm spot for the Bedford area. He explored the idea of buying one of Bedford's banks in 1927. He donated a silver trophy to the country club to be awarded to the annual golf champion.

He got out of the metal business in the early 1940's, selling his "La Consolidada S.A." to Shields and Company. Then, in 1945, he and a brother-in-law bought a ranch with 2,200 head of cattle in New Mexico. He had earlier bought part interest in another ranch near Silver City. The combined operations had 65,000 acres of grazing land. In addition, they leased 100,000 more acres. In 1948, he donated $25,000 to buy the old Lyle home, so that it could become the "Betty Pannil Wright Home for Old Ladies." He entrusted an old employer, M.T. Harrison, to set up an association to handle the Home. Wright showed much faith: Harrison was 91 at the time.

Harry might have found the Beale treasure and then took off for Mexico to live off its bounty. With so many people in the family, it seems unlikely; surely the story would have leaked out by now. Maybe George Wright did leave his wife and children a nest egg after all. Harry probably was indeed the "business genius" his family said he was. His successes were recognized in *Reader's Digest* and in *Fortune* magazines. He had no children. He apparently shared generously what he had with his brothers and sisters.

Harry Wright was clearly a talented man, who made his way — and a fortune — in a foreign land, but always stayed in touch with friends in Bedford county.

In recent times, others have proudly announced that they have solved the ciphers. One person who has claimed success is Robert E. Hohmann, a communications specialist of New York City. His solution gives some details of the nature of the treasure and also tells with whom Beale wanted to share the treasure.

Hohmann wrote in 1973 that the treasure included chalices and other works that had been looted from Spanish monasteries by an Indian chief. There were also Spanish deoro coins.

He said that cipher No. 3 does not give names and addresses of 29 people of the Beale party. Rather there are just a few names. It mentions a brother, Edward, and a sister, Edith. Others named are Arven and Sarah, who may have been Arven's wife. Arven had died. His share was to go partly to Sarah, partly to a daughter and a son, and partly to a friend — in trust for keeping the children while the company was West. Edward had converted part of his deoros and raw gold into jewels. The Hohmann interpretation is clearly alluding to a Thomas Beale who is not from Fincastle. The Thomas of the Taverner Beale family had neither a brother Edward nor a sister Edith. The kin of Thomas J. Beale of Fauquier county did include an Edward and a Sarah. But this is the Thomas J. Beale who died in 1851 and left an estate valued at $21.92.

Virginia has a "finders keepers" law, but the successful treasure hunter must respect the rights of the landowner. Taxes could be substantial. The federal government would want to tax the find as ordinary income. Virginia would want its share. And if the finder lived outside of Virginia, his home state would also get a share. Even after paying all taxes, the finder would still be substantially enriched by the Beale treasure. Yet some prospectors would try to avoid taxes by keeping their find secret.

Maybe the treasure has been found, and that event has been kept secret. It still seems unlikely that someone found the cache and no news has leaked out. About half of the attendees at the 1986 symposium of the Beale Cypher Association believe that the treasure is still there.

Solving the ciphers would lead to the vault — or reveal that the story is a hoax. The ciphers hold promise of revealing something. Dr. Carl

Rural Montvale.

Hammer, who was Director of Computer Sciences for Sperry Univac at their Washington, D.C., office, said in 1970, "They are not random doodles but do contain intelligence and messages of some sort." Hammer's view is still endorsed by most of the serious analyzers of the Beale ciphers.

A Missouri man tried for years to unravel the ciphers. Then, one night, he woke with a start, having just seen a map in a dream. He sketched that map on paper. Now he has abandoned the codes and is instead looking at Montvale topographic maps to find a match to his vision.

Computers have been of help in examining the ciphers, but finding the key is still most important. The key would unlock the ciphers and reveal the messages.

One way to find the key is to deduce what Beale — or the fiction author — would have used as a key, and then get a copy of that publication. Dr. Stephen Matyas of I.B.M. presumed that each of the three Beale ciphers may well have a different key text, but that those keys would probably have been part of a single printed document or book. The key publication would have to include, of course, the Declaration of Independence that was used to decode Cipher No. 2.

He surveyed the field of printed literature for works that contained the Declaration and that were printed in or before 1822, trying to find a Declaration of Independence version which was identical to the one used to decode Cipher No. 1. By 1986 he personally had collected well over 200 such documents. A 4-volume *View of the American United States* by W. Winterbotham, in print from 1795 to 1819, has a version of the Declaration of Independence that seems to be a close match.

Matyas developed what I will call a grid matrix or box grid method of code construction, which he describes in his 66-page report, *The Beale Ciphers*. In 1997 Matyas summarized this approach on one segment of Arthur Clarke's *Mysterious Universe* about classic examples of unsolved messages.

The sure way to solve the ciphers would be to have in hand the actual document key Beale mentioned in a letter to Morriss. Find that and the solution will surely follow.

That letter from St. Louis to Robert Morriss of May 9, 1822, said that the papers in the box he had given Morriss, "...will be unintelligible without a key to assist you." Beale wrote, "I have left it in the hands of a friend in this place, sealed, addressed to yourself, and not to be delivered until June 1832." The letter was datelined St. Louis.

Apparently it never got to Morriss. If it had, he would have solved the mystery himself, he would have gotten the treasure, and there would never have been *The Beale Papers.*

Some effort has gone into trying to determine where Beale stayed in St. Louis and who he knew there. One searcher even enlisted the St. Louis *Post-Dispatch* to publicize her interest in finding the package or envelope addressed to Morriss. No luck.

The friend in St. Louis may have been Judy Hancock Clark, who was the focus of Beale's duel back in Fincastle long ago, or her husband, the respected General William Clark.

Judy was 31 when she died in 1823. Perhaps the sealed document was then set aside or overlooked. The General took a new wife, the widow Harriet Kennerly Radford. The Clarks may have come across it and became curious. Harriet would have been especially interested for two reasons. The Beale name rang a bell for her. She had heard about the duel over her "sister" involving Beale. And Beale's opponent was Harriet's brother-in-law, James Beverly Risque.

They could have opened it and cashed it in. More likely they decided to honor the ten-year waiting period and then forgot it, with the document getting mixed in with Clark's papers.

Personal papers can travel unlikely journeys. General Clark had five children with Julia, two with Harriet, and two children of Harriet's by adoption. And they in turn had children and grandchildren. Just imagine how many possible places Clark's papers may have end up.

Some sixty-seven William Clark manuscripts turned up in Minnesota more than a century later, in 1953, in a desk which once belonged to Civil War General John H. Hammond. No one knows how they got there.

Searches of some Missouri museums and Mason Lodges have failed to produce that specific key Beale document. The Beale letter is still missing.

If *The Beale Papers* is a hoax, the author could have used a key document published some time after 1822 — perhaps as late as 1883 or 1884. *The Code of Virginia,* a handbook for officials of that state, has gone through many editions, and would have been handy for a hoaxer in creating the Beale ciphers. *The Code* includes not only the Declaration of Independence, but also the U.S. Constitution, the Bill of Rights, and subsequent Amendments.

24 — Finders Keepers

Any book contains peculiar or unique typographical errors. Different editions of *The Code* could be scrutinized to see if any exactly match the Declaration of Indepdence in the Beale pamphlet. If an edition after 1822 does match, and editions before 1822 do not, we would be closer to knowing if *The Beale Papers* is a hoax.

Beale may have used a book of codes, like the old State Department book. It could be a common book of the times — such as Ree's *Encyclopedia* — or one he had seen at Morriss' when he lodged there, a book which he expected Morriss to have or be able to get. It may be a classic book, a dictionary, a book of the Bible. Or the key may be right there for all to see: the very letter Beale wrote to Morriss.

Only if he was the hoaxer would Morriss have had the key or would he have needed a key at all. That possibility prompts research to track down the belongings of Robert Morriss. After he died, any books or documents he had would have passed into the custody of his hosts or heirs, who may in turn have given or thrown them away.

The original cipher sheets and Beale letters would reveal a great deal. The handwriting could be analyzed and the originator might be identified. If only they could be found.

The pamphlet printer worked from the original letters and cipher sheets. If they survived the Virginian fire, we wonder where they are now.

25.
Ready, Set, ...

If Morriss was involved, he gave the cipher sheets to the author in 1862. These were either authentic documents written by Thomas J. Beale or fictional documents prepared by a Beale impostor or by Morriss himself. The author held them, then analyzed them, and then attached them to his manuscript for *The Beale Papers*. The material was given to the printshop, where the printer set metal type, and then the original material (perhaps a bit dog-eared or smudged by then) was returned to the author or his agent, Ward. Unless they were consumed in the fire.

For a fictional story there would be no code sheets nor letters in Beale's handwriting.

The search is on for the manuscript, with or without code sheets and letters by Thomas J. Beale. If the manuscript had the entire story and the cipher sheets and the letters all in the same handwriting, that would virtually confirm the notion that it was fiction. There would have been no good reason to tediously copy the lengthy Beale letters and the ciphers. If they were in different hand, that might absolve the author of fabrication — but not necessarily. The letters and sheets might have been done by a collaborator.

If the author's mood was as he described in the pamphlet, he could have passed off all the documents. Agent Ward could have had them. However, none of the Ward descendants with whom I have spoken had seen or heard of the family having the papers.

The cipher papers, and perhaps the letters and the manuscript, apparently ended up in the hands of Newton Hazlewood. Clayton Hart had been handed some code "sheets." They were well worn. George Hart told Innis that Hazlewood said he had gotten from Ward the original papers so that the pamphlet could not be reprinted.

Hazlewood, a man of integrity, had spoken of his concern for the rights of Beale's associates and their families. But his views changed over time, so that ten years after the pamphlet came out, he showed the cipher sheets to Clayton Hart and let Hart copy them. There is no mention of Hazlewood having any papers other than the cipher sheets.

Of course no one knows if the pamphlet is exactly as "Beale" wrote the ciphers or if the printer made typographical errors. Neither does anyone know if the papers held by Hazlewood were indeed the original cipher sheets written by Beale, or copies of the pamphlet as printed, or a faulty transcription copy of the printed pamphlet. Or perhaps Hart made typographical errors. In any event, the differences of Hart vs. pamphlet complicate matters. Some believe that the ciphers need to be "corrected" or "adjusted" to yield a good solution. That debate raises the issue of which set of ciphers to "adjust" — the Hart version or the printed pamphlet version? The only evidence at hand is the pamphlet, right or wrong.

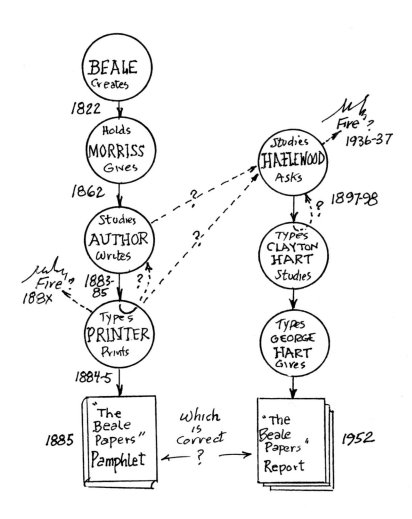

Hart's typed version of the ciphers differs slightly from the printed pamphlet.

Once Hart finished copying, Hazlewood may have saved those sheets. We can only deduce what happened to the Hazlewood sheets.

Years passed. Hazlewood died. The Hart brothers continued to work the problem, still with no success. George moved to Washington and quit the search. Clayton continued. He couldn't solve the ciphers and began to doubt the accuracy of his copies. He sought the original sheets, presuming that they were still in the hands of the Hazlewood family.

Hart developed a friendship with Newton's son, Frank, who was also an employee of N&W. Frank had been living in Roanoke and was planning a new house in Montvale. Hart had a reputation for frugality. Yet he made an extraordinary offer. In 1923, he agreed to lend Frank money to help buy the new house. Did Hart think that Frank Hazlewood had his father's papers — and hope that he could get them from Frank?

The only other time Clayton Hart lent mortgage money was to the owner of a 215-acre tract of land described on court deed records as being "on Goose Creek, 4 miles North of Montvale." (There is that magic "4 miles"!) Obviously, Hart was serious about the treasure hunt. He even wrote a fiction novel, inspired by the Beale pamphlet. In it, Beale was killed by Indians. The book was never published.

Any papers that had stayed with the Hazlewood family may have been in Newton's house when it burned down fifty-some years ago. Clayton Hart died in 1949. Except for his novel, his papers were discarded or burned by his heirs. Brother George Hart wrote the story of their experiences, including the ciphers Clayton used, in a 1952 report, which he gave to the Roanoke Library. It seems unlikely that any papers exist to reveal the origin of the letters and the ciphers.

Clayton Hart tenaciously hunted the treasure for much of his life. Others work on it with great devotion for years — or for decades. They may not admit to themselves why.

What mortal really knows why we do what we do?

Someone starving in Africa, bleeding in a war, or aching in a hospital, cares only about survival or eternity. Behavioral scientist Abraham Maslow noted that we must satisfy our physiological needs before we can get very interested in anything else. Different hunters have different motives or combinations of motives.

Some are driven by avarice or greed and the hope for great riches. Others want to pay bills, buy a new house, or get a new start. Winning a lottery would do that. This is different. This takes work.

And the odds may be even tougher than a lottery. Even if you do find it, you might not get to keep it: the Federal Government might assert a claim to it as a national historical asset, and you could become mired in a prolonged legal battle to establish your right of ownership.

The Beale treasure has already paid off for some folks. The business people of Bedford County don't object to hunters spending money for gas, food and lodging. Authors and publishers of articles and books hope to make money with their printed works about Beale.

Money is not the most common motivation. Some hunters have a strong need to discover. For toy collector Al Marwick, just having custody of an antique toy is not what it's all about. The title of his column in *Antique Toy World* magazine tells the real why: "The Fun Is In The Search." And so it is with the Beale treasure.

Curiosity is a strong motivator. Mankind finally found out what was on the other side of the moon. The U.S. and the U.S.S.R. spend billions to explore the solar system, fathom the atom, and understand nature. It is a rare person who doesn't enjoy a good TV mystery. Beale is a marvelous mystery.

Like gardening or golf, the Beale mystery can take us away from our problems. Howard Woodcock of Chesterfield, England, wrote that it "gave me an interest, a hobby, and a challenge for nearly three years." We can get absorbed in something exotic. We can escape from our routines. We can be in control of what we do and how we do it.

Bedford resident Roger Livesy, who has a deep-sensing metal detector, feels that without the key much more analytic research needs to be done. He commented that he hasn't seen enough good clues yet to warrant "getting up out of my easy chair" and going out into the field with his equipment.

Don Farks, a resident of Bedford County, is an experienced user of portable metal detectors who has found relics of the Revolutionary and Civil Wars, coins, rings, tools, and jewelry. He suggests that the treasure hunter needs to focus the search. Then, he should get sample borings before attacking the earth with big equipment such as backhoes. He speculates that the treasure may yet be located by flying over the area while trailing an airborne proton magnetometer. That type of survey would be costly.

One Beale scholar figures that it is not necessary to search a very large area. If the treasure is "about four miles" from Buford's, the search would have to encompass just a half mile on either side of a circle with a radius of four miles. The net area is about eight square miles. A helicopter flying in concentric circles might do this in half a day. Analysis of the gathered data would, of course, take considerably longer.

If it hasn't already been found, the treasure could turn up accidentally during some construction excavation.

Undoubtedly there will be people who have deduced a treasure site, or who have made some sense of the ciphers. They will be out there digging. And if they do, they will need the landowner's permission.

Secrecy becomes important. To win, you need to know things that your competition doesn't know. So a little bit of paranoia helps protect your competitive position. Sure — tell some of what you know. But don't tell all you know!

One competitive Bedford woman who likes to get things done said, "I'm going to be the one to find that treasure, ... even if it takes a psychic to pinpoint where it is." Airline captain Dick Murray would consult with an avatar.

Frank Aaron enjoys a good challenge. He researched the story and phenomena for many years, uncovering important reference documents and tackling the ciphers with computers. He thoroughly enjoys the search. He told me at breakfast in 1986, "I sort of hope they don't find it soon. It's like hunting for deer. Limit is one. If I get mine early in the morning, it spoils my whole day."

Every crossword puzzle fan knows how nice it feels to fill in all the blanks. The Beale ciphers are more challenging than any crossword puzzle. The reader is dared to figure them out. Some of us are competitive people. We welcome challenge as an opportunity to be better than someone else. An intellectual challenge gives us a chance to show that we are smarter than the next guy. There is the thrill of the chase: who will win?

Here is a puzzle that has defied skilled minds for more than a century. Judge William Sweeney observed that even if there is no treasure out there, it would be quite an accomplishment to solve the ciphers.

To solve the ciphers! Think how you would feel. Solving the puzzle would be the satisfaction. Finding the treasure would be a bonus.

Once you get the Beale treasure into your system, it is hard to get it out. You could get possessed by it. Like drugs or gambling, it can lead a vulnerable person to stake everything on a dream. And Edgar Allen Poe wryly observed, "All that we see or seem is but a dream within a dream."

The Beale mystery can be addictive. The author of *The Beale Papers* offered advice "acquired by bitter experience." It is to "devote only such time as can be spared from your legitimate business ... and if you can

25 — Ready, Set, ...

spare no time, let the matter alone." He later said, "Never, as I have done, sacrifice your own and your family's interests to what may prove to be an illusion; but, as I have already said, when your day's work is done, and you are comfortably seated by your good fire, a short time devoted to the subject can injure no one, and may bring reward."

The late Robert Ripley loved to report anomalies in his newspaper column, "Believe it or Not." With apologies to Ripley:

Beale. Leave it — or not?

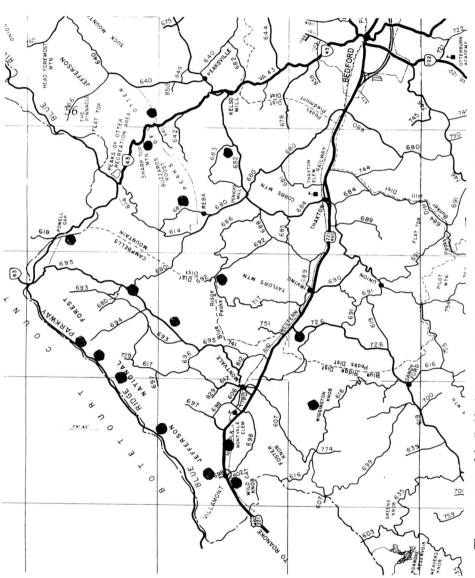

These are some of the Bedford County sites where people have dug looking for the treasure.

Some Dates for Reference

1754	Bedford County begins	1840	James B. Risque dies
1776	Declaration of Independence	1843	*The Gold Bug* published
1782	Campbell County begins	1845	Texas joins Union
1782	Town of Liberty begins	1845	War with Mexico
1783	Britain & U.S. peace treaty	1848	Peace with Mexico
1786	Lynchburg charter	1848	Gold in California
1787	U.S. Constitution	1849	Edgar Allen Poe dies
1787	First brick Bedford courthouse	1851	Railroad through Bufordville
1799	George Washington dies	1855	Gadsden Purchase
1803	Louisiana Purchase	1858	Gold announced in Colorado
1804	Jefferson reelected	1861	Confederacy secedes from Union
1804	Burr kills Hamilton	1861	Mrs. Morriss dies
1804	Lewis & Clark head West	1862	Morriss reveals to author
1806	Beale sells Fincastle lot	1863	Robert Morriss dies age 85
1807	Burr treason trial	1864	Hunter's Raid through Bedford
1808	Clark marries Hancock	1865	Lee surrenders at Appomattox
1810	Poplar Forest ready	1870	Robert E. Lee dies
1812	War with Britain	1875	Paschal Buford dies
1813	Clark territory governor	1883	*Virginian* building fire
1815	Battle of New Orleans	1884	Ward requests copyright
1815	Jackson visits Lynchburg	1885	*The Beale Papers* on sale
1817	Beale heads West	1885	Ferdinand Hutter dies
1818	Beale Jr. in New Orleans	1876	*Tom Sawyer* published
1819	Beale in Bedford & Lynchburg	1890	Liberty becomes Bedford City
1819	Spain cedes Florida to U.S.	1890	Bufordville becomes Montvale
1820	Julia Hancock Clark dies	1898	Spanish American War
1821	Beale second stash	1907	James B. Ward dies
1821	Mexican independence	1909	Newton Hazlewood dies
1822	Beale papers/box to Morriss	1912	Bedford reverts to town status
1825	Wilkinson dies in Mexico	1952	Hart compiles paper
1826	Jefferson dies	1964	Innis "Beale Fortune" in *Argosy*
1828	Jackson defeats Clay	1973	Innis book published
1833	New Bedford Courthouse	1987	*History of a Mystery* published
1835	Texas secedes from Mexico	1989	Mel Fisher digs in Bedford
1836	Aaron Burr dies	1997	*New History of a Mystery*
1840	James B. Ward to Missouri		

Acknowledgements

This book benefits from extensive research done by others. Two publications have been essential: *The Beale Papers* pamphlet, copyright 1885 by James B. Ward, and *Gold In The Blue Ridge* by P.B. and Walter Dean Innis. Historical documents and books that are listed in the bibliography have provided many facts. But the most important sources were the fine people who have been generous with their time and who have shared their knowledge.

Many facts are from organizational archives. Records of deeds, marriages, and wills repose in the courthouses. Mrs. Carol Black and the staff of the Clerk's office of Bedford County were especially helpful. Relevant data also came from the cities of Lynchburg and New Orleans, and the Virginia counties of Amherst, Botetourt, and Campbell. Certain other information came from the George C. Marshall Library, the U.S. Library of Congress and the U.S. National Archives.

Others who graciously supplied information include Bob Caldwell, Beale Cypher Association; Barbara Ring, Bedford Chamber of Commerce; Mrs. Ellen Wandrei, Bedford City/County Museum; David Wiseman and Bernie Brennan, Bedford Public Library; Gene Parker and Dirk Wiley, Blue Ridge Parkway; Phillip Rhodes, Jones Memorial Library; and Ms. Carol Tuckwiller, Roanoke City Public Library.

These are some of the individuals who offered ideas and facts: Kevin Allen, Mrs. Mary Lee Cake, Robert Scott Carr, Jr., Sherrill Coleman, Jay Conley, Sgt. D.E. Cooper, Judge C. Daniel Cornish, Kenneth Crouch, Claude DeGolyer, Lawrence Dick, Kenneth Dooley, Mel Fisher, Art Herman, Elton Hite, Ken Houck, Brent Hughes, Dr. Stanley Hutter, Mrs. Rebecca Jackson-Clause, Capt. Ronnie Laughlin, Linda Markham, Tom Martin, Mrs. Peggy Maupin, James C. McIvor, Dick Murray, Mahlon Nichols, Bill O'Callaghan, Mrs. John B. Oliver, Mr. and Mrs. Carl Overstreet, Don Park, Mrs. Pat Parker, Dan Perkins, Mrs. James Preston, Pat Schrock, Steve Segrave, Ben Shrader, Frank O. Smith, Wilbur Smith, George Stewart, Bruce Thomson, Jr., Elizabeth Walker, and former Sheriff Carl Wells.

I especially thank these Beale scholars who generously provided material, and insight: Albert Atwell, Jacques Boegli, Connie Cordagan, Richard Greaves, Dr. Carl Hammer, Roger Livesy, Robert Murr, Eugene Newsom, and David Workman. Frank Aaron's words have been a delight and his writings have been useful. John C. King and Richard Harman helped my understanding of cryptology. The sustained dedication of Dr. Stephen Matyas was an inspiration. Mrs. Esther McVeigh provided helpful materials, ideas and leads. I give thanks to Mrs. Zuma Salaun, premiere historical researcher of New Orleans. Dr. & Mrs. Robert Gardner offered potential titles for this book, including "For Whom the Beale Tolls" and "Beale: Leave It Or Not."

My wife Cyndi patiently listened as I reported each new discovery or analyzed a new angle. She asked perceptive questions, challenged my logic and proofread the book. Without her support, I could not have written this book.

Any mistakes and errors are unintentional, but my responsibility; I hope you will forgive me. It is my wish that this new edition will spare you from duplicating earlier work. May it accelerate your understanding and help you to find your solution or your own conclusion.

> Peter Viemeister
> Bedford, Virginia
> August 1997

Picture Credits

Maps: Bedford Public Library 170 ; Harpers Weekly 169; Leading Facts Ginn & Co. 56; S.S. Lynn 10; Munn & Co. 103; U.S. Geological Survey 73, 76, 90; VA Dept of Highways 196; and VA State Library Frontespiece.

Drawings: Revelle Hamilton 117; Dana Estes Books 144; *Memoirs of Robert E. Lee* 167; Lossing's 1881*History of the U.S.* 109; C.M. Russell 60, 65; and the *Amer. Revolution Sourcebook* 178.

Photos: Ollie Hamm 153; Bill Moore 72; Mrs. J.B. Oliver 183; C. De Golyer and D. Workman 83, and Anonymous 171.

Other maps, sketches and photos by the author.

Bibliography

ABRIDGED HISTORY of the UNITED STATES, Emma Willard, A.S. Barnes, 1857.

ACROSS THE WIDE MISSOURI, Bernard De Voto, Houghton Mifflin, 1974.

"And the Treasure Hunt Continues," Joe Kennedy, ROANOKE TIMES, August 11, 1982.

AMERICA SPREADS HER SAILS - U.S. Seapower in the 19th Century, Clayton R. Bower, Jr., Naval Institute Press, 1973

ASTORIA, Washington Irving, 1836, G.P. Putnam's Sons, 1868.

BATTLE of NEW ORLEANS, Donald Barr Chidsey, Crown, 1961

BEALE CIPHERS, Stephen M. Matyas, Jr., Private, 1996, 66 pp.

"Beale's Buried Treasure," Douglas Nicklow, RUN Mag.., August 1984.

BEALE CIPHERS in the NEWS, Beale Cypher Assoc., 1983.

"Beale Code No. 3 Deciphered," Robert E. Hohmann, TRUE TREASURE Mag., March-April 1973.

"The Beale Fortune," Pauline B. Innis, ARGOSY Magazine, August 1964

THE BEALE HIDDEN TREASURE, Nora A. Carter, W.P.A. Historical Inventory, 1937.

THE BEALE PAPERS, George L. Hart, Sr., Manuscript to Roanoke Library, 1952, 1964

THE BEALE PAPERS, James B. Ward, Virginian Book and Job Print, 1885.

THE BEALE PAPERS, Clarence R. Williams, Library of Congress, Legislative Reference Service memorandum, April 26, 1934.

"Beale's Treasure Tale Revived," Anon., THE NEWS, April 21, 1972.

"Beale Treasure Termed Hoax," Anon., STAUNTON LEADER, February 5, 1974.

BEDFORD COUNTY, VIRGINIA, 184-1860, W. Harrison Daniel, Virginia Baptist Historical Soc., 1985

"Bedford County's Buried Treasure Lures Hunters," Bill Burleson, LYNCHBURG DAILY ADVANCE, May 19, 1962.

"Bedford Treasure Hunt Goes On and On," Steve Price, LYNCHBURG NEWS, August 20, 1967.

"Believers Still Searching for the Beale Treasure," Anon., BEDFORD BULLETIN-DEMOCRAT August 31, 1967.

BIOGRAPHICAL REGISTER of the OFFICERS and GRADUATES of the U.S. MILITARY ACADEMY, Geogre W. Cullum, Houghton Mifflin, 1891

BOTETOURT BICENTENNIAL, Souvenir Program, 1970.

BRIEF HISTORY of the UNITED STATES, J.B. McMaster, American Book Co., 1907.

BRITISH AT the GATES - The New Orleans Campaign, Robin Reilly, GP Putnam's Soons, 1974

"'Buford County' Still Attracts Buried Treasure Hunters," Anon., BEDFORD BULLETIN-DEMOCRAT, August 1, 1968.

BUCHANAN, VIRGINIA - GATEWAY to the SOUTHWEST, Harry Fulwiler, Jr., Commonwealth Press, 1980.

"Buried Treasure in the Blue Ridge," Dwayne Yancey, COMMONWEALTH, September 1980.

CAMPBELL CHRONICLES and FAMILY SKETCHES, Ruth H. Early, 1927.

"Capt. Hazlewood Dies Suddenly," ROANOKE TIMES, December 2, 1910.

"A Cipher's the Key to the Treasure in Them Thar Hills," Ruth Daniloff, SMITHSONIAN Mag., April 1981.

"Circle Tightens Further on Beale Treasure," Boyd M. Jolley, TREASURE Mag., December 1982.

The CIVIL WAR, Richard M Ketchum & Bruce Catton, American Heritage, 1966

CODE BREAKERS, David Kahn, McMillan, 1976

CODE OF VIRGINIA, William F. Ritchie, Public Printer, Richmond, 1849.

COLONEL CHRISTIAN JACOB HUTTER and DESCENDENTS, Private publication, 1902.

COLONIAL VIRGINIA, J.A.C. Chandler and T.B. Thames, Times-Dispatch Co., 1907

COMPUTER ORIENTED CRYPTANALYTIC SOLUTION for MULTIPLE SUBSTITUTION ENCIPHERING SYSTEMS, Stephen M. Matyas, Doctoral Thesis, University of Iowa, 1974.

Bibliography

CONFEDERATE TREASURE in DANVILLE, J. Frank Carroll, URE Press, 1996, 140 pp.

CONFEDERATE TREASURE TRAIN - (Revised Edit.), Brent Hughes, Conferate History Series, 1989.

"Conspiracy and the Trial of Aarn Burr," John Dos Passos, AMERICAN HERITAGE, Vol.17, No.2. (February 1966).

CYCLOPAEDIA of AMERICAN BIOGRAPHY, Ed. by J.G. Wilson and J. Fiske, D. Appleton & Co., 1888.

"Death of James B. Ward," The LYNCHBURG NEWS, May 17, 1907.

"Death of Major Ferdinand C. Hutter," LYNCHBURG NEWS, February 22, 1885.

The DEVILS BACKBONE, Jonathan Daniel, Pelican Publications, 1987. .

"Died Notice," LOUISIANA GAZETTE, October 23, 1823.

DIRECTORY of LYNCHBURG, Virginian Job Print Co., 1881,1883-84, 1887.

"Discovered, the Secret of Beale's Treasure," Joe Nickell, VIRGINIA Magazine, Vol. 9, No.3 (July 1982).

DREAM of EMPIRE, William Henry Venable, Dod, Mead, 1901.

EARLY TRAILS of the BAPTISTS : A HISTORY 1776-1976 , Strawberry Baptist Association, 1976.

"Duels and Duelists of Bygone Virginia Days," Evan P. Chesterman, From RICHMOND EVENING JOURNAL, 1908-1909.

ECHOES of OLD LIBERTY, Peaks of Otter Chapter of Daughtyers of the American Revolution, 1976.

"Explorations:Cybernauts," PAUL HOFFMAN, OMNI Mag., May 1987

"Famed 1822 Beale Treasure Led Roanoke Brothers to Futile Hunt 66 Years Ago," Raymond Barnes, ROANOKE WORLD NEWS, June 1, 1963.

FATHER MISSISSIPPI, Lyle Saxon, The Century Co., 1927.

FIFTY YEARS in BOTH HEMISPHERES, Vincent Nolte, Redfield, 1854.

FINAL CHALLENGE - the AMERICAN FRONTIER 1804-1845, Dale Van Every, Mentor-New American Library, 1964, 384 pp.

FODOR'S MEXICO 1976, Marjorie Lockett, Area Editor, David McKay Co., 1976

"Following the Trail of Lewis and Clark," Ralph Gray, NATIONAL GEOG. Mag., June 1953

"Follow Guidelines When Treasure Hunting," Anon., LYNCHBURG NEWS, July 14, 1985.

FOOTPRINTS in BEDFORD COUNTY CLAY, Special Section, Bedford Bulletin Democrat, June 29, 1977.

42nd VIRGINIA INFANTRY, John D. Chapla, H.E. Howard, Inc., 1983.

"Funeral Notice," The LYNCHBURG NEWS, June 17, 1923.

GENERAL ASSEMBLY of VIRGINIA - 1619-1978 , Compiled by C.M. Leonard, Va. State Library, 1978.

GEOGRAPHY or a DESCRIPTION of the WORLD, Daniel Adams, Lincoln and Edmonds, 4th Ed., 1819.

GLORIOUS BURDEN, Stefan Lorant, Harper & Row, 1968.

THE GOLD BUG, Edgar Allen Poe, Dana Estes Co., 1899

GOLD in the BLUE RIDGE, the TRUE STORY of the BEALE TREASURE, P.B. Innis & W.D. Innis, Devon Pub., 1973.

THE GREAT WEST, Alvin M. Josephy, Jr. and David Lavender, American Heritage/ Simon & Schuster, 1965.

GUIDE to TREASURE in VIRGINIA and WEST VIRGINIA, Michael Paul Henson, Carson Enterprises, 1982.

HALLS of the MONTEZUMAS, Robert W. Johannson, Oxford Univ. Press, 1985

HANDBOOK of BEDFORD COUNTY, VIRGINIA, R. Kenna Campbell, Bedford Index, 1893.

HARPERS ENCYCLOPEDIA of UNITED STATES HISTORY, Woodrow Wilson, Harper & Bros., 10 Volumes, 1905.

"Harry Wright Industrialist-Sportsman, Purchases Large Ranch in New Mexico," Anon., BEDFORD DEMOCRAT, January 10, 1946.

"Has Beale's Fabulous Treasure Been Found?," Boyd M. Jolley, TREASURE Mag., August 1982.

"Has the Beale Treasure Code Been Solved?," Al Masters, TRUE TREASURE Mag., September-October, 1968.

HISTORICAL & ANALYTICAL STUYDIES in RELATION to the BEALE CYPHERS, Carl W. Nelson, Jr., Proprietary, 1970

HISTORICAL DIARY, BEDFORD, VIRGINIA, U.S.A. : FROM ANCIENT TIMES to U.S. BICENTENNIAL, Peter Viemeister, Hamilton's, 1986.

"Historical Facts Supporting Beale," Frank H. Aaron, PROC. of the FOURTH BEALE CYPHER ASSOC. 1986, BCA, 1987.

HISTORICAL REGISTRY and DICTIONARY of the U.S. ARMY, Francis B. Heitman, Govt. Printng Office, 1903

HISTORICAL SKETCH - BEDFORD COUNTY, VIRGINIA 1753-1907, J.P. Bell & Co., 1907

HISTORY of BEDFORD COUNTY, Lula Jeter Parker, 1954, Reissued, Edited by Peter Viemeister, Hamilton's, 1985

HISTORY of BEDFORD COUNTY with FAMILY HISTORIES AND ROLL OF CIVIL WAR SOLDIERS, Reprinted from 1884 Hardesty, Peter Viemeister, Editor, Hamilton's, 1985.

"History of the Bedford Light Artillery," Rev. Joseph A. Graves, BEDFORD DEMOCRAT, 1903.

"History of Book Ciphers," Albert C. Leighton and Stephen M. Matyas, CRYPTO 84, Ed. by G.R. Blakley and David Chaum, Springer Verlag, 1985.

HISTORY of LYNCHBURG, VIRGINIA 1786-1946, Philip L. Scruggs, J.P. Bell, 1978.

HISTORY of OUR COUNTRY, Cooper, Estill, & Lemmon, Ginn & Co., 1899, 533 pp

"History of Texas," in TEXAS ALMANAC 1958-1959, A.H.Belo Corporation, 1957

HISTORY of the UNITED STATES of AMERICA, Frederick Butler, Deming & Francis, 3rd Ed., 1828.

HISTORY of the UNITED STATES, George Bancroft, C.C. Little & J. Brown, 14th Ed., 1848.

HISTORY of VIRGINIA, Royall B. Smithey, American Book Co., 1915.

HISTORY of VIRGINIA, Vol.5, Virginia Biography, Amer. Hist. Soc., 1924

HISTORY of WILLIAM RADFORD of RICHMOND, VIRGINIA, Robert S. R. Yates, Anundsen Pub., 1986.

HORNBOOK of VIRGINIA HISTORY, Virginia State Library, 1965.

"In the Footsteps of Lewis and Clark," Gerald S. Snyder, NATIONAL GEOGRAPHIC, 1970, 216 pp.

"INTERMENT NOTICE," LOUISIANA GAZETTE, September 11, 1820.

JACKSON, Max Byrd, Bantam Books, 1997, 422 pp

JACKSON and NEW ORLEANS, Alexander Walker, J.C. Derby, 1856.

"Jail Is at the End of Treasure-Hunter's Rainbow," Robert Rubin, ROANOKE TIMES and WORLD NEWS, January 15, 1983.

JAMES MADISON, Irving Brandt, Bobbs-Merrill, 1961.

JEAN LAFITTE, Robert Tallant, Random House, 1951

"Jean Lafitte, The Baratarians, and the Historical Geography of Piracy in the Gulf of Mexico," Robert C. Vogel, GULF COAST HISTORICAL REVIEW, Vol.5 No.2

JOURNAL of JACOB FOWLER, Ed. by Elliot Coues, Univ. Nebraska Press, 1970.

JOURNALS of LEWIS and CLARK, John Bakeless, Ed., Mentor-New American Library, 1964

KEGLEY'S VIRGINIA FRONTIER, F.B. Kegley, Southwest Virginia Historical Society, 1938.

LEE of VIRGINIA, Douglas Southall Freeman, Charles Scribners & Sons, 1958

"Legendary Treasure Quests," Hank Burchard, The WASHINGTON POST, October 5, 1984.

LETTER to L.R. GILLS, Harry Wright, December 14, 1927.

LIFE in AMERICA ONE HUNDRED YEARS AGO, Gailland Hunt, Harper & Brothers, 1914, 298 pp.

LIFE of ANDREW JACKSON, Harquis James, Bobbs Merrill, 1938

LIFE in the FAR WEST, George Frederick Augustus Ruxton, New York, 1859.

LIFE of KIT CARSON, Charles Burdett, Grosset & Dunlop, 1902.

LIFE on the MISSISSIPPI, Mark Twain, Harper & Brothers, 1917.

LONG SURRENDER, Burke Davis, Random House, 1985.

LOUISIANA, a BICENTENNIAL HISTORY, Joe Gray Taylor, W.W. Norton, 1976.

"Lt. Beale and the Camel Caravans Through Arizona," Velma Rudd Hoffman, ARIZONA HIGHWAYS, Oct. 1957

LYNCHBURG - an ARCHITECTURAL HISTORY, S. Allen Chambers, Jr., Virginia University Press, 1981.

LYNCHBURG and ITS NEIGHBORS, Rosa F. Yancey, J.W. Ferguson & Sons, 1935.

LYNCHBURG and ITS PEOPLE, W. Asbury Christian, J.P. Bell, 1900.

LYNCHBURG DAILY ADVANCE, Sesquicentennial Edition, 6 sections, October 12, 1936.

MADISON-BEALE-HITE CONNECTION, Jacques S. Boegli, Presentation at Fourth Beale Cipher Symposium, 1986.

"Many Still Seek Beale Treasure," Anon., LYNCHBURG NEWS, July 14, 1985.

MEMOIRS of ROBERT E. LEE, A.L. Long & Marcus J. Wright, B.F. Johnson & Co., 1886

"Mexico," ENCYCLOPAEDIA BRITANNICA, 11th Edition, 1911, Vol 18, p.340.

MONTVALE - from INDIAN TRAILS to SKYWAYS, Olliemaye Freeman Hamm, private, ca 1992,

MYSTERY THOMAS J. BEALE'S TREASURE CODES BROKEN, Albert Atwell, 1990, 36 pp.

MYSTERY TREASURE, John W. Timm, Tracy Book Co., 1973.

NEW COLORADO and the SANTA FE TRAIL, A.A. Hayes, New York, 1880.

NEW LONDON TODAY AND YESTERDAY, Daisy L. Read, J.P. Bell, 1950.

NEW ORLEANS ARCHITECTURE - JEFFERSON CITY - Friends, of the Cabildo Associates of the Louisiana State Museum, Pelican, 1989

NEW ORLEANS : a PICTORIAL HISTORY, Leonard V. Huber, American Legacy Press, 1971.

NEWS BROADCAST, Kent Jarrell, WUSA-TV (CBS), 6 PM, November 6, 1986.

"Newspaper Reports Cipher of Bedford Treasure Broker," Anon., ROANOKE TIMES, April 20, 1972.

NEW SYSTEM of MODERN GEOGRAPHY, Sidney E. Morse, Geo. Clark, 1828.

NORFOLK & WESTERN - a HISTORY, E.F. Striplin, N&W RR, 1981.

NOTES on the STATE OF VIRGINIA, Thomas Jefferson, 1787, U. of North Carolina Press, 1955.

OFFICIAL LETTER BOOKS of W.C.C. CLAIRBORNE 1801-1816, Ed. by Dunbar Rowland, State Department of Archives & History, 1917.

OLD FREE STATE, Landon C. Bell, 1927, Reprint by Genealogical Co., 1974.

"Old Mines of Bedford," Peter Viemeister, Bedford City/County Museum RETROVIEW, 1986

OLD SANTA FE TODAY, Historical Santa Fe Foundation, Univ. of New Mex., 3rd Ed, 1972.

OLD VIRGINIA HOUSES - THE PIEDMONT , E.F. Ferra & E. Hines, Delmar Pub., 1975.

"100 Millionen! Das Gold in de Hohle," Von Reinhold Ostler, BILD AM SONNTAG, December 1, 1985.

ONE LETTER, ONE ENCLOSURE SUBJECT : the BEALE TREASURE, Richard H. Greaves, Private publication, 1986.

OUR KIN, M. Ackerly and L.E.J. Parker, 1930, C.J. Carrier Co., 1981.

PATRIOT INDEX Daughters of the American Revolution, 1966.

"Peaks of Otter," W.M.E. Rachal, VIRGINIA CAVALCADE, Vol.1, No.2, 1951.

PEAKS of OTTER - LIFE and TIMES, Peter Viemeister, Hamilton's, 1992

PIONEER SPIRIT, R.M. Ketchum, Ed., Amer. Heritage, 1959

POPLAR FOREST , Nora A. Carter, W.P.A. Historical Inventory, 1940.

PROCEEDINGS of the THIRD BEALE CIPHER SYMPOSIUM, Beale Cypher Association, 1981.

PROTOTYPE of a CONFEDERATE HOSPITAL CENTER, Peter W. Houck, Warwick House, 1986

RAILROAD NAMES, William Edson, W. Edson, 1984.

"A Reconstruction of the Keyto Beale Cipher Number Two," John C. King, CRYPTOLOGIA, July 1993, pp 305-318.

RECORD of the FAMILY and DESCENDENTS of COL. CHRISTIAN JACOB HUTTER, Frank Reeder, Eastern Sentinel, 1903

REFLECTIONS of YESTERDAY, 10 part supplement, The News and Daily Advance, 1986.

REGISTER of FORMER CADETS, Virginia Military Institute, 1957.

"Retrial is Ordered for Woman Charged With Disturbing Graves"Anon., RICHMOND TIMES DISPATCH, February 24, 1983.

"Ride That Started the Gold Rush," Paul L. Johnson, GOLD! ANNUAL Mag., Vol. 3 No.1, 1971.

ROMANTIC NEW ORLEANS, Deirdre Stanford and Louis Reens, Viking, 1977.

SANTA FE TRAIL, R.L. Duffus, Univ. New Mex. Press, 1975

ST. STEPHENS EPISCOPAL CHURCH - HISTORICAL RECORDS, 1983.

SEARCH of a GOLDEN VAULT, E.J. Easterling, Avenel, 1995.

"Search for the Key Book to Nicholas Trist's Book Ciphers," Albert C. Leighton and Stephen M. Matyas, CRYPTOLOGIA, Vol. 7 No. 4 (October 1983).

SECRET and URGENT - the STORY of CODES and CIPHERS, Fletcher Pratt, Blue Ribbon Books, 1942

SEEDBED of the REPUBLIC, Robert D. Stoner, Roanoke Historical Society, 1962.

SIGNATURE SIMULATION & CERTAIN CRYPTOGRAPHIC CODES, Carl Hammer, Third Ann. Simulation Seminar, 1971.

"Silent for Years, Famous THer Reveals New Clues to Famous Cache," Richard Ray, TREASURE SEARCH Mag., Jan/Feb 1987.

SKETCHBOOK of LIBERTY 1887 - ITS PEOPLE and ITS TRADE, Edward, Pollock, Hamiltons (reprint), 1993,

SKETCHES and RECOLLECTIONS of LYNCHBURG by the OLDEST INHABITANT (MRS MARGARET CABELL), C.H. Wynne, 1858.

"Solid Gold Mystery," Stefan Bechtel, SOUTHERN WORLD Mag., July/August 1980.

SOUTHWEST VIRGINIA and SHENANDOAH VALLEY, Thomas Bruce, J.L. Hill Pub. Co, 1891

SPANISH WEST, Editors of Life, Time-Life Books, 1976

SPIRIT of NEW LONDON ACADEMY, James Siddons, Heritage Books, 1994

START ALL OVER, Peter Viemeister, Hamilton's, 1995.

"Story of Buried Treasure Has Disappointing Ending," Dorothy S.Brooks, LYNCHBURG DAILY ADVANCE, May 8, 1970.

STORY of NEW LONDON ACADEMY 1795-1945, Ed. by L.L. Barnes, NLA Bd. of Managers, 1945.

"Subject The Beale Treasure," Richard H. Greaves, advertisement in LYNCHBURG NEWS & DAILY ADVANCE, Sept. 21, 1986.

TALES of the HILL CITY, Carter Glass Newspapers, 1985.

THOMAS JEFFERSON's POPLAR FOREST, Barvar McEwan, Warwick House, 1987.

30 MILLION DOLLAR BEALE TREASURE HOAX, Tom Kenny, Private, 1990.

THOMAS JEFFERSON - AN INTIMATE BIOGRAPHY, Fawn M. Brodie, Bantam Books, 1974.

TOM SAWYER, Mark Twain, various

"To Whom it May Concern," Printer's Devil, BEDFORD BULLETIN DEMOCRAT, October 28, 1981.

"Treasure Hunter Freed on Bond," Anon., ROANOKE WORLD NEWS, January 13, 1983.

"Trio Hunts Famed Beale Treasure," Bill Burleson, ROANOKE TIMES & WORLD NEWS, May 8, 1962.

UNDAUNTED COURAGE: MERRIWETHER LEWIS, THOMAS JEFFERSON, and the OPENING of the AMERICAN WEST, Stephen Ambrose, Simon & Schuster, 1996

"Using Computers to Hunt Beale Treasure," Anon., BEDFORD BULLETIN-DEMOCRAT, May 4, 1972.

28th VIRGINIA INFANTRY, Frank Fields, Jr., H.E. Howard, Inc., 1985.

VIRGINIA and the NEW DOMINION, Virginius Dabney, Doubleday, 1971.

THE VIRGINIAN, Owen Wister, McMillan, 1911

"Visit to the Virginian Canaan," Porte Crayon, VIRGINIA ILLUSTRATED, 1871. WILLS AND DEEDS of BOTETOURT COUNTY, Anne Lowry Worrell, 1958.

"When Hutter's Home was Hunter's House," Anon, IRONWORKER Mag., Summer 1947.

"Where is Beale's Treasure?" Hal Ober, SOFT PILLOW for an ARMADILLO, D.C. Heath & Co., 1989

WINNING of the WEST, Theodore Roosevelt, Part IV, G.P. Putnam's Sons, 1896.

Index

Aaron, Frank 194
Adams Bros and Paynes 139, 140
Adams, Daniel 102
Adams, J.H. 158
Adams, John 125
Adams, John Quincy 125
Adams Express 139
Airport 71
Antique Toy World 193
AM&O Railroad 139
Apache Indians 51
Appomattox 172
Arkansas River 58, 63
Arthur, Chester 162
Ashley, Gen. 61
Atocha 9, 18
Audubon Park 111
Aury, Luis 176
Averell, Gen. 160

Baird, James 58, 60, 61
Ballard, Margaret M. 77
Baptist Church 122
Barataria 104
Barite mine 82
Baton Rouge, Louisiana 104, 110
Battle of New Orleans 108
Beale, Celeste 112
    Charles 98
    Edward F. 131
    Eliza 110
    Frances Madison 94
    James Madison H. 98
    James M. 116
    James William 113
    John 97
    Octavine 113
    Richard E. 93
    Sarah 186

    Samuel 93
    Taverner 94, 98
    Thomas 92, 93, 163
    Thomas II 112
Beale Cypher Association 16
Beale Papers 9, 21, 22-44, 140, 190
Beale Street Blues 104
Beall, S.T. 62
Beall, Thomas 62, 94, 95
Bearwallow Gap 72, 87
Beauregard Rifles 160
Becknell, William 60, 61
Bedford, Virginia 14
Bedford, City of 75
Bedford City/County Museum 14
Bedford County 4, 14
Bell's Tavern 121
Benton, Thomas Hart 128
Berry, James 45
Big Lick, Virginia 4, 70, 132, 137, 150
Bird, James 6
Blackhawk, Chief 128
Blackhawk War 128
Black Horse Gap 72
Black Horse Tavern 72
Blue Ridge Mountains 13
Blue Ridge Parkway 69
Bobblet's Gap 72, 182
Boegli, Jacques 98
Bolling Wright & Co. 184
Boogher, Archer 155
Botetourt County, Virginia 63, 96, 119
Bowyer, Thomas M. 150
Box grid 187
Britain 55, 58, 105, 108, 121
Brocke, Fawn 178
Buchanan, Virginia 67
Buffalo 58

Buford, Henry 70, 72, 183
    James 70, 71
    Lucy 80
    Paschal 19, 70, 87, 124, 132, 148, 183
    Rowland 148
    Simeon 133
    Thomas 70, 183
    William 61, 70
Buford's Gap 69, 81
Buford's Tavern 65, 80
Bufordville, Virginia 71, 150, 170
Bull Run 135, 151
Bunch, James 84
Burchard, Hank 17
Burial 66, 69, 171
Burkeville 169
Burr, Aaron 50, 102, 120, 126
Burton, Charles T. 46, 86, 115
Button, Charles and Joseph 141
Byron, Lord 177

Cabell, Mrs. 123
Campbell County, Virginia 141, 150
Campeachy 176
Canal Street 113
Carr, Robert Scott, Jr. 82
Carroll, Frank 168
Catawba Creek 121
Caves 82, 83, 144
Chandler, A.B. 45
Charleston 177
Chartre Street 105
Cherokee Indians 99
Chesterfield County, Virginia 122
Cheyenne 63
Chickamauga Indians 99
Christ Episcopal Church 155
Civil Conservation Corps (CCC) 74
Claiborne, William 106
Clarke, Arthur 15
Clark, E. & Co. 152
Clark, William 57, 96, 120, 124, 159, 188

Clay, Henry 125
Claytor, A.B. 17
Clinton, George 102
Cobbs, Emma 161
Coca-Cola 154
Code Books 50
Code of Virginia 188
College of Washington in Virginia 119
Colorado 57
Colston, Rev. 142
Comanche Indians 57
Confederate States / Confederacy 134, 157, 166, 167
Conrad, Glen 75
Cool Spring Church 78, 182
Cooper, D.E. 11
Copyright Office 140
Coronado 55
Cotton 106, 110
Coves, Elliot 60
Cover story 164, 166
Craighill, Ed 136
Creole 102, 129
Crook, Gen. 160
Crowes 61
Cryptograms 50
Cryptography 51, 179

Daniel's Hill 158
Daniloff, Ruth 47, 85, 118
Danville 160, 167
Davis, Jefferson 134, 137, 167
Declaration of Independence 49, 187
"Deep Blue" 52
DeGolyer, Cluade 82
Delancy / Delaney, Chloe 115
de Grandpre, Celeste 110
de Mun, Jules 59
de Niza 55
Detamore, Joe and Joe, Jr. 19
Dick, Lawrence 46
Dickenson, Charley 17

Index 207

Dickey, Wanda Lee 175
Donald, Andrew 87
Dooley, Lee 85
Dooley, Otis 85
Dooley, Kenneth 85, 86
Dooley, Sharon 78
Dos Passos, John 126
Dowsing 17
Duel 120
Durand, Joseph 63, 77, 182
Dzilan Bravo 177

Early, Jubal 136
Easterling, E.J. 81
Entick's Dictionary 50

Fabyan, George 48
Falwell, Dr. Jerry 162
Fancy Farm 87, 136, 183
Faribault, G.H. 11
Fiction 164
Fincastle, Virginia 4, 67, 72, 95
Finn, Huckelberry 144
Fisher, Mel 9, 18, 181
Flat Top 89
Fodor 177
Fort Early 91
Fort Sumter 134
Fowler, Jacob 60, 61
France 55, 105, 129, 178
Franklin, Benjamin & Lucy 132
Franklin Hotel 47, 125
Freemasons 135
Friedman, William F. 52

Galveston Island 175
Garfield, James A. 161
George (slave) 127
George III 70
Ghent, Treaty of 109
Giles, M.M. 77
Glasscock, Esau 174
Glenn, Col. 61

Goggin, Belle 160
Gold in California 131
Gold in Colorado 145
Gold Bug, The 144
Gold Sphinx 164
Goose Creek 20, 132, 183
Goose Creek Valley 16, 69
Government 193
Graham's Mill 19
Grand Terre Island 104, 107, 175
Grant, U.S. 136
Greaves, Richard 45, 96, 118, 148
Greenville, S.C. 99
Grubbs, Cyndi 78
Gulf of Mexico 58, 176

Hamilton, Alexander 102
Hamilton, Jean 66, 85, 92
Hammer, Dr. Carl 51, 187
Hammond, John 188
Hancock, George 96, 121
    John 119
    Julia (Judy) 95, 118, 124
Harman, Richard 172
Harrison, M.T. 185
Harrison, William H. 130
Harvey, Nat 81
Hart, Clayton 15, 141, 148, 190-192
Hart, George 15, 142, 148, 190-192
Hazlewood, Alice 153
    Charlotte 154
    Ella 154
    Frank 153, 192
    James 154
    Lottie 153
    Mary 153
    Newton H. 149, 155, 161, 163, 190
    Newton H., Jr. 154
    Walter 154
    William 152
Hayes, A.A. 145
Hayes, Rutherford B. 139, 160

Heist 167
Hemings, Sally 178
Hemings, Tom 178
Henry, Patrick 119
Herbert, Hiram Jr. 15
Hidalgo, Father 58, 176
Higgins, Mary 98
Hill City Lodge 134
Hite, Elton 47
Hite, Anne 99
    Eleanor 99
    Elizabeth 99
    Frances M.B. 99
    George 99
    Jacob 99
Hodges, William L. 13
Hohmann, Robert E. 51, 185
Holland, J.J. 47, 81, 91
Houston, Sam 131
Hughes, Brent 168
Hunter, Gen. David 136, 168
Hunter's Hill 130, 142, 160
Hutter, Adeline 157
    Charlotte 139, 158
    Christian S. 142, 161
    Edward S. 135, 136, 157, 158, 169
    Ferdinand C. 126, 135, 138, 157
    George Christian 125, 126, 128, 135, 136, 157
    Harriet Risque 125
    James L. 161
    James Risque 135, 139, 157, 158
    Johann Ludwig 161
    Mary L. 160

Igloe 161
Illegitimate son 92, 178
Impostor 124, 174, 179, 190
Indentureds 153
Indians 55, 61, 99, 116, 192
Innis, P.B. 15, 117, 145, 149, 154, 178
Ironville, Virginia 81
Iturbide 60

Jackson, Andrew 58, 108, 121, 125, 128
Jackson, Stonewall 135
James River 63, 139
Jancik, Joseph 11
Jefferson City, Missouri 128.
Jefferson, Thomas 55, 57, 103, 116, 120, 121, 125, 136, 173, 178
Jefferson Barracks, Missouri 125, 159
Jenkins, M.E. 59
Johnson, Andrew 172
Johnson, Richard 151
Johnston, General J.E. 137, 172
Jolley, Boyd 182
Jordan, Catherine 98

Kahn, David 45
Kasparov 52
Kearny, Gen. Stephen 131, 166
Kelso Mill 87
Kennerly, Eliza 119
    Harriet 119, 141
Kentucky 96, 120
Kidd, Captain 144
Klemme, Gordon 18
Kokette, Jean 78

Laffite/Lafitte, Pierre 107, 175
Lafitte, Jean 63, 104, 114, 173
Lafitte National Park 177
Lafflin 177
LaLande, Baptiste 57
Langhorn, Lt. Col. 150
Langhorn, Nannie 158
Latham's Battery 151
Leighton, Dr. Albert 52
Lee, Robert E. 131, 134, 138, 160, 166, 171
Lewis, Joshua 108
Lewis, Meriwther 57, 96, 120
Lexington, Virginia 119
Liberty, Virginia 4, 72, 136, 183
Liberty Hall Academy 119
Lincoln, Abraham 134, 172

Index

Lisa, Manuel 58
Litz, Manfred A. 14
Livesy, Roger 193
Long, A.L. 166
Louisiana Purchase 55
Louisiana Territory 59, 107
Luck, G.P. 84
Luck, Jimmy 77
Lynch, John, Jr. 135
Lynch Station 150
Lynchburg, Virginia 14, 120, 147, 150
Lynchburg City Cemetery 91
Lynchburg Female Seminary 122
Lynchburg-Salem Turnpike 70, 124
Lynn, S.S. 47
Lynx 176
Lyons, James 160
Lyons, James, Jr. 162
Lyons, Mary 160

Madison, James 109
Mahone, Gen. 152
Manassas, Virginia 135
Marriott, Mary 150
Marshall, John 104
Marshall Lodge 134
Martin, Thomas M. 64
Marwick, Al 193
Maslow, Abraham 192
Matyas, Stephen 54, 182, 187
Maupin, Peggy 77
    Harry 77
McCaleb, Thos. 115
McFall's Mountain 66
McIvor, James C. 12, 14
McKinley, William 160
McKnight, Robert 58, 60
Memphis, Tennessee 104
Mexican War 160, 166, 184
Mexico 60, 103
Mexico City 58, 125, 131, 166
Mining 82

Minnix, Ray 14, 47
Mississippi 55, 59, 104, 107
Missouri River 59, 107
Mobile, Alabama 125
Monticello 178
Montrose Hotel 70
Montvale, Virginia 13, 20
Morrison, William 57
Morriss, Robert 22, 45, 92, 113, 123, 125, 135, 141, 145
Morriss, Sarah 123, 132, 135, 141
Mountain Gate Toll Gate 74
Mountain View Church 11, 12, 77
Murder 182
Murr, Robert 82
Murray, Dick 194
Museum, Bedford City/County 2
Murrill's Gap 85
Mysterious Universe 8, 187

Napoleon 58
Nelson, Carl, Jr. 51, 62, 93
New London, Virginia 136
New London Academy 153
New Mexico 54
New Orleans, Louisiana 101, 108, 174
New Spain 55
Nickell, J. 49, 92
Nolte, Vincent 108, 110
Norfolk & Western Railway 82, 149, 152
Northside Supply 87

Otey, Angeline 130
    Frances 184
    George 136, 138, 158
    Harriet 130
    John 138
    John 126, 130, 132, 139
    Kirkwood 138, 158
    Peter 138, 58
    Samuel 136
    Van Rensselaer 136

Overseer of the Poor 153
Overstreet, Carl 16

Parker, Lula Jeter 78
Parks, Don 193
Parsons, Marilyn 11, 77
Patterson, Commodore 107
Pawnee 60, 179
Pawnee Rock 61
Payne, J.G. and E.O. 140
Peaks of Otter 4, 87, 88, 136
Peaks of Otter — Life & Times 87
Permission 13, 19, 75, 79, 89, 193
Peter (slave) 126
Petersburg 170
Petroleum depot 71, 72
Pickett's Charge 158
Pierce St. 162
Pike, Zebulan 57
Pirate (see Lafitte)
Planters & Merchants Hotel 113
Platte River 57, 61
Poe, Edgar Allen 144, 194
Point Pleasant 70
Polk, James 131
Poplar Forest 117, 136, 139, 161, 178
Porter's Mountain 11, 77
Privateers 104 (also see Lafitte)
Psychic 59, 62, 92, 194
Pueblo, Colorado 62
Purcell, James 57
Pursley, James 57

Radford, Harriet Kennerly 124, 188
    John 124
Ree's Encyclopedia 51, 189
Reilly, Robin 177
Richmond, Virginia 159, 167
Rio Grande River 57
Risque, Adeline E. 120, 124, 126, 130
    Eliza 121
    Ferdinand 120, 126
    Harriet 120, 125, 131, 159
    James B. 95, 104, 118, 142, 159
    John Pickerel 162
Rivermont Bridge 158
Rives, J.H. 161
Roanoke, Virginia 14, 70, 139
Rodenburg, W. 82
Roosevelt, Theodore 104
Roslin/Roslyn 162
Ross, Col. 107
Ruxton, George F.A. 145

St. Charles, Missouri 130
St. Louis, Missouri 57, 118, 125, 129, 158, 187
St. Paul's Episcopal Church 138, 141
St. Phillip Street 105
Salem, Virginia 124, 137
Sandusky 126, 137, 158
Sangre de Christo 62
Santa Anna, General 131
Santa Fe 47, 54, 145
Santa Fe Trail 61
Saul, Joseph 110
Saunders, David 135, 157
Sawyer, Tom 144
Scott, John W. 87
Scott, Winfield 131, 166
Sensing probe 89
Sharp Top Mountain 68, 72, 88, 184
Silver City, New Mexico 185
Simmons, R. Gordon 155
Sites, treasure 196
Slaves 111, 122, 126, 172, 174
Smith, Frank 47, 82
Smyrna 84
Snowlins and Morrill 133
Southside Railroad 150
Spain 54, 103
Spanish Louisiana 55
Steenbergen, Elizabeth 98
Stoner, Robert 96
Stratford Hotel 155

Index

Sweeney, William 13, 194
Sweet Springs 74

Taylor's Mountain 46, 72, 78
Tennessee 121
Texas 131
Thaxton, David 74
Thayer, Vic 61
Thespian Society 124, 138
Thorpe, Roy 12
Traders 60
Train 167
Transportation 64
Treason 125
Treaty of Hidalgo 166
Truth 165
Truxtun, Commodore 104, 131
Twain, Mark 144
Tyler, John 130

U.S. Forest Service 74
U.S. Military Academy 94, 126
U.S. Park Service 74
U.S. Territory 36
Unsolved Mysteries 8, 91

Vera Cruz 131
Villamont, Virginia 19, 81
Virginia & Tennessee RR 70, 132, 150, 171
Virginia Military Institute (V.M.I.) 158
Virginian, The 139, 143
Virginian Job Printing House 141
Voda Family Trust 19

Walden, Daniel 115
Walker, Alexander 108
Walnut Grove Church 84
War of 1812 58, 108, 121
Ward, Adeline 124, 127, 138
    Annie 132
    Charles 133, 139
    David C. 131

    Ella R. 138
    Giles 124, 127, 132, 142
    Harriet 130, 135, 142
    James A. 139
    James B. 18, 22, 92, 126, 128-142, 156
    James B., Jr. 124, 131, 133
    Mary B. 138
    Otey B. 137
Washington, George 119
Washington & Lee University 119
Washington Hotel 28
Washington Inn 124
Washington Monument 183
Watt, John 52
Watts, William 151
Wells, Carl 181
White House 106
Wiggington Knob 11, 69, 72
Wilkerson Mill 86
Wilkinson, James 50, 57, 103, 125
Williams, Clarence 45
Williams, Ezekial 58
Woodcock, Howard 193
Workman, David 82
Wright, Betty 184, 185
    Della 184
    George 184
    Harry 184
    Max 184
    Mildred 184
    Sam 184
    Veta 184

Yancey, Rosa 95, 100, 104
Yellow Fever 110, 112
You, Dominique 107
Yucatan 177

Other Good Books

Historical Diary of Bedford, Virginia, U.S.A. — From Ancient Times by Peter **Viemeister**. Chronicle of life here; in peace and war. People and events. Revolution. List of militia men. Jefferson's Poplar Forest. Civil War. The Depression. D-Day. War times. The 50's and 60's. Smith Mountain dam. Valuable reference: 2500 item index. A graphic treasure: 2nd printing   256 pictures. 132 big pages. ISBN 0-9608508-209   Cloth hardcover. $ 32.00

History of Aviation - They Were There - by Peter **Viemeister**. Virtually every phase of aviation, from the first balloons to outer space. First person reports by famous and not famous. Many of the folks were from Virginia. Wide coverage of World War II and Vietnam. With rare photos. 12-page index   A great gift for any aviation buff.   Detailed index.   348 pages.   298 photos.
ISBN 0-9608598-5-3   Flexible cover. $ 19.95

Parker's History of Bedford County - Lula Jeter **Parker**. Details of early villages, churches, schools, turnpikes, taverns, homes, social life, and wars. First published in 1954. This new edition includes 15 pages of index. Essential for genealogists.152 pages.
ISBN 0-9608598-4-5   Flexible cover. $16.95

Peaks of Otter - Life and Times by Peter **Viemeister**. A history of Virginia and America, with the Blue Ridge Mountains as the stage. Indians, frontier days, Civil War, the full story about Union General Hunter's Raid, ghosts and murders, herd of elks, the missing Town, C.C.C.boys, building the Blue Ridge Parkway,   wildlife and plane crashes. 200 illustrations. 278 pages.   3rd printing.
ISBN 0-9608598-9-6   Cloth hardbound. $24.50

1887 Sketchbook of Liberty Va - Its People and its Trade - By Edward **Pollock**, author and illustrator. Last published before Bedford County's center town changed its name from Liberty to Bedford. Filled with facts, drawings, and old timey ads. Reissued now by Hamilton's, on bright heavy stock. 1993. 5 1/2 x 7 3/4. 144 pp.
ISBN 0-9608598-7-X   Flexible cover. $14.95

Start All Over - An American's Experience - Peter **Viemeister**'s 7th book, the best yet. Exciting people, places, and lessons learned in the historical, cultural, and emotional settings of the 30's, 40's. The war homefront. The 50's and the turbulent Vietnam War years. People overcoming handicaps.

Here is what they never told you about how big companies are really run and how deals are made. Listed in *Who's Who in the World* and chosen as Bedford Citizen of the Year, Viemeister takes you inside closed doors of the Grumman corporation that built the craft which landed men on the moon, and behind the scenes in a small community. The true story of the Bedford Health Foundation. The facts about the proposed nuclear dump. 241 illustrations. 451 pages.
ISBN 0-883912-01-6   Cloth hardbound. $32.00

History of Bedford - With Family Histories and Roster of Civil War Soldiers - From 1884 **Hardesty**'s Encyclopedia for Virginia. Great for genealogists: includes 217 family histories. Service info for more than 800 soldiers.   40 pages.   3rd printing
ISBN 0-9608598-1-0   Flexible cover. $13.50

Available through your local bookstore, or by mail.
Virginia residents must add 4.5% for sales tax. If ordering one book, please add $2 for surface mail or $3 for Priority Mail. For overseas delivery, inquire first. If ordering more than one book, shipping is 10% of total order.

Prices subject to change without notice.

Hamilton's

155 W. Main Street,   P.O. Box 932,   Bedford, VA 24523
540-586-5592   FAX 540-586-6235